The NATURALISTIC NOVEL of the NEW WORLD

A Comparative Study of Stephen Crane, Aluísio Azevedo, and Federico Gamboa

João Sedycias
California State University, Sacramento

UNIVERSITY
PRESS OF
AMERICA

Lanham • New York • London

University Press of America® Inc.
4720 Boston Way
Lanham, Maryland 20706

3 Henrietta Street
London WC2E 8LU England

Library of Congress Cataloging-in-Publication Data
Sedycias, João.
The naturalistic novel of the New World : a comparative
study of Stephen Crane, Aluísio Azevedo, and Federico Gamboa /
João Sedycias.
p.   cm.
1. Latin American fiction—19th century—History and criticism.
2. American fiction—19th century—History and criticism.
3. Naturalism in literature.   4. Crane, Stephen, 1871–1900. Maggie,
a girl of the streets.   5. Gamboa, Federico, 1864–1939. Santa.
6. Literature, Comparative—Latin American and American.
7. Literature, Comparative, American and Latin America.
I. Azevedo, Aluísio, 1857–1913. Cortiço.
PQ7082.N7S4   1993   809.3'0097—dc20   92–35432 CIP

ISBN 0–8191–8941–3 (cloth : alk. paper)

 The paper used in this publication meets the minimum requirements of
American National Standard for Information Sciences—Permanence
of Paper for Printed Library Materials, ANSI Z39.48–1984.

To my parents

Acknowledgments

Several people contributed in various ways to this study. I would like to thank my teachers at the State University of New York at Buffalo for their largesse of spirit, caring, and for imparting to me their love of learning and passion for literature. The model of reading, scholarship, and dialogue which they set before me during my years at SUNY-Buffalo has helped to make this a better book. I owe a special debt to my doctoral thesis advisor, Jorge Guitart, for his perceptive comments, support, and patience. I am also indebted to Cesáreo Bandera and Henry Sussman, whose elegant insights and cogent teachings inspired many of my ideas. Peter Boyd-Bowman, Arthur Efron, Wilma Newberry, Kenneth Rasmussen, and George Schanzer provided helpful criticism and encouragement during the early stages of this project.

I also wish to express my gratitude to the following colleagues and friends who read the manuscript and provided invaluable feedback: Arnold Highfield, Marilyn Jones, and Joseph Klucas. They all gave generously of their time and care, and I benefited immensely from their comments.

Finally, it is a pleasure to acknowledge the lifelong inspiration and support of my parents, Juraci and Dinamérico, to whom this book is dedicated.

With regard to the quotations in this study that go beyond my publisher's 250-word fair use limit, grateful acknowledgment is made to the following authors and publishers for permission to reprint excerpts from copyrighted material:

Contents

Preface

Despite the fact that the naturalistic novel of most countries in the New World has been studied individually at considerable length, little attention has been given to a comprehensive examination of the genre in this hemisphere. The studies that have been produced on the subject to date generally concentrate on a specific country, author, or work. Because of this narrow focus, the naturalistic movement is seldom viewed as the worldwide or hemisphere-wide intellectual phenomenon that it was.

My aim in this book is to examine three leading New World naturalists in a comparative context. Their works are central to the movement in three major national literatures: American (Stephen Crane's *Maggie: A Girl of the Streets*), Brazilian (Aluísio Azevedo's *O cortiço*), and Mexican (Federico Gamboa's *Santa*). I propose to investigate certain aspects of the discontinuity between European naturalistic ideology and literary practices in the New World and to explore the ways in which these writers differ among themselves as naturalists. Analyses of character and plot, along with questions that probe the authors' cultural and religious backgrounds, provide the setting for a discussion of their works. Foremost among these considerations are the authors' attitudes toward the fallen woman, desire, prostitution, and religious salvation.

New World naturalistic writers of the latter half of the nineteenth century for the most part are believed to have uniformly adopted the theoretical precepts of European Naturalism. However, an examination of the literature of that period reveals that these precepts were violated to varying degrees in different countries. My study demonstrates that although they wrote their respective novels according to a Zolaesque model of the *roman expérimental*, Crane, Azevedo, and Gamboa differ significantly from Zola as well as among themselves. Specifically, I argue that there is as much naturalistic literary ideology in *Maggie*, *O cortiço*, and *Santa* as there is puritanical aversion to prostitution (Crane), irreligious enjoyment and celebration of sensuality (Azevedo), and Catholic condemnation of carnal sin (Gamboa).

Of the works examined, *O cortiço* comes the closest to an orthodox model of the *roman expérimental*. *Maggie* and *Santa* stand at the opposite ends of this prototype. In Crane's case, this distancing results from his novel's puritanical tone and harsh denouement, whereas Gamboa sets himself apart from other naturalistic writers because of the sense of clemency and redemption that permeates his work. Azevedo at times goes beyond his French mentor in his depiction of the sordid and the crude, while Gamboa skillfully indicts the traditional view of Naturalism as little more than an outgrowth of Realism infused with a pessimistic determinism.

My readings of *Maggie*, *O cortiço*, and *Santa* are based on a combination of two approaches. The first part of the study relies on a traditional analysis of the language, theme, and structure of the texts, while the second half is couched in René Girard's theory of mimetic desire. In addition to questions pertaining to character and plot development, some of the theoretical principles set forth in Girard's *Deceit, Desire, and the Novel*, specifically those that deal with the notion of mimetic desire, serve as the critical backdrop against which these works are analyzed.

In addition to having been written according to a prescriptive model of the *roman expérimental*, the three novels in question share another important common denominator. All three present a prostitute as a major character: the protagonist in *Maggie* and *Santa*, and a central figure in

O cortiço. I pay special attention, particularly in the first part of my study (Chapters 1 through 3), to the ways in which Crane, Azevedo, and Gamboa conceive and develop the prostitutes in their novels. Some of these characters are also examined in Part Two (Chapters 5 through 7), but to a lesser extent than in Part One. *Maggie*, *O cortiço*, and *Santa* were selected for the present study because they are works of relevance, historically as well as textually, and are prime examples of the naturalistic movement in general in their respective countries.

A note on the translations: unless otherwise indicated, all English translations of passages from *O cortiço*, *Santa*, and any other material quoted in the original foreign language (French, Spanish, or Portuguese) in this book are my own.

An earlier and abridged version of Chapter 6 appeared in *Studies in Modern and Classical Languages and Literatures I*, ed. Fidel López Criado (Madrid: Orígenes, 1987): 83-90.

João Sedycias

California State University, Sacramento

Part One

The Prostitute in New World Naturalistic Fiction

Chapter 1

Stephen Crane's *Maggie*:

The Fallen Woman as Religious Allegory

Stephen Crane's first novel, *Maggie: A Girl of the Streets* (1893), is the story of a young woman's coming of age and her struggle for survival in the Bowery district of New York City during the second half of the 19th century. Maggie Johnson and her brother Jimmie have the misfortune to be born into a family environment in which abuse and neglect are the norm. Their father routinely resorts to physical violence in his dealings with his children, and their mother is constantly drunk. Despite these wretched conditions, Maggie somehow manages to rise above the squalor and brutality that thrive around her, and throughout the novel she remains an attractive and caring young woman. As members of the lower working class, both children are expected to provide for themselves at a very young age. Jimmie finds work as a truck driver, and Maggie is hired as a collar maker in a local sweatshop. The older she gets, the more disillusioned she becomes with her life at home and at work. She yearns for a gentler and more refined ambience, and dreams of escaping her real world. Through her brother Jimmie, Maggie meets Pete, a bartender a few years older than she. He shows a modicum of kindness toward her, and she takes a liking to him. Pete is quick to take advantage of the situation by seducing Maggie and having her move in with him for a few weeks. This prompts her alcoholic mother, in a fit of self-righteous indignation, to disown Maggie. Subsequently, Pete leaves Maggie for another woman, and, heartbroken and confused, the girl turns to prostitution. Later, alone and disgusted with the life that she has been forced to lead, Maggie commits suicide.

Crane's own commentary best sums up the theme of *Maggie*: "environment is a tremendous thing in the world and frequently shapes lives regardless."[1] This naturalistic formula must have appealed to Crane, since he used it several times as the dedicatory inscription in copies presented to friends, often repeating it verbatim.[2]

When it came out in 1893, *Maggie* was viewed primarily as a grim document that appeared to follow closely the precepts of French Naturalism. "Its sordid materials and impersonal style," David Fitelson observes, "led most reviewers to see it as little more than a fictionalized sociological study of the slums."[3] In his 1893 critique of *Maggie* in the *Arena*, Hamlin Garland remarks that "[this] book is the view of the slums . . . the most truthful unhackneyed study I have yet read, fragmented though it is."[4] William Dean Howells comments in his review for the *New York Press* the following year that "there is so much realism of a certain kind in it that unfits it for general reading, but once in a while it will do to tell the truth as completely as *Maggie* does."[5]

For the most part, the early reaction to *Maggie* was, as Fitelson remarks, one of "discomfort verging on shock."[6] The commentaries by John Barry, editor of the *Forum*, and those of an English critic writing for the *Boston Globe* exemplify this response. In his letter of March 22, 1893 to the author, Barry reacts with typical aversion to the violent language and morbid subject matter of Crane's novel:

> Your book [*Maggie*] is pitilessly real and it produced its effect upon me — the effect, I presume, that you wished to produce, a kind of

horror. To be frank with you, I doubt if such literature is good: it closely approaches the morbid and the morbid is always dangerous. Such a theme as yours, in my judgment, ought not to be treated so brutally . . . as you have treated it: you have printed too black a picture, with no lights whatever to your shade. I know one might say that the truth was black and that you tried to describe it just as it was; but, one ought to bear in mind that literature is an art, that effect, the effect upon the reader, must always be kept in view by the artist and as soon as that effect approaches the morbid, the unhealthful, the art becomes diseased. . . . The lesson of your story is good, but . . . you have driven that lesson too hard. There must be moderation in well-doing; excess enthusiasm in reform is apt to be dangerous. The mere brooding upon evil conditions, especially those concerned with the relation of the sexes, is the most dangerous.[7]

The *Globe* critic goes further than Barry in his harsh criticism of *Maggie*. He concentrates on the effect of the vulgar language in Crane's work, and denounces the relentless violence and gloom that permeate the novel:

Mr. Crane always shouts in his writings; in fact he positively blares, with never a pause. To read his latest book, "Maggie," is to put one's ears into the bell of a cornet blown by giant lungs. It leaves one limp, exhausted, mistreated. The book is like a lump of red, raw beef. It is food for tigers, not for men and women.[8]

In varying degrees and for different reasons, other literary critics and historians have come to regard *Maggie* as a grisly naturalistic work. The August 15, 1898 issue of the Nashville *Banner* carried a review of *Maggie* in which Crane is censured for not living up to the ideals of good art. According to the reviewer, these ideals were to "inspire, please, and enlighten by tender and uplifting sentiments."[9]   While conceding that *Maggie* is not an immoral book, the critic severely criticizes the author for infusing his work with too much filth and squalor:

> [*Maggie*] is a strong sermon urging the need of greater charity of sentiment, as well as of gold for the poverty-hardened people of the slums. But in spite of its strength, it is a failure. Why? Because it is too hopeless, too full of misery, degradation and dirt. The reader flounders in a mire of pessimism, never once receiving from the author the offer of a helping hand or a word of encouragement, and the memory of the book is a nightmare, and the thought of it inexpressibly hopeless and depressing.[10]

An unidentified English critic takes a slightly different view of Crane's work and goes so far as to praise it for the manner in which it achieves its overall effect. Yet, the critic cannot come to terms with the violence in *Maggie* nor reconcile the novel's sordid conception of life with the author's literary craftsmanship:

> It is surely a fine tribute to the art in a book that the reviewer should be compelled to praise it against his will. And this tribute must certainly be given to Mr. Stephen Crane's latest story. "Maggie" is a study of life in the slums of New York, and of the hopeless struggle of a girl against the horrible conditions of her environment; and so bitter is the struggle, so black the environment, so inevitable is the end, that the reader feels a chill at his heart, and he dislikes the book even while he admires it.[11]

By and large, one can confidently take the views presented above to be characteristic of the early response to *Maggie*. As Fitelson points out, if later Crane came to be seen as an impressionist,[12] at the time he was working on *Maggie* and other Bowery tales, the author was regarded primarily as a naturalist.[13] And rightly so, because, as John Berryman, Charles Walcutt, Lars Ahnebrink, Robert Stallman, and Robert Spiller point out, many of Crane's early works bear the distinctive traits of European Naturalism.[14]

In its language, theme, and form, *Maggie* follows the literary precepts of European Naturalism. In his first *roman expérimental*, Crane indicts the subjectivism and imaginative escapism that seemed to characterize the romantic school.[15] There is very little in *Maggie* that could be called romantic, sentimental, or melodramatic. In place of a gentle language that was supposed to soothe, inspire, and enlighten, one finds a type of discourse so fiercely violent as to have been considered by Crane's early critics to be unfit for general reading. The first half of the novel contains some of the most brutal language in any nineteenth-century literary genre. For example, of the fight between the young urchins from Rum Alley and those from Devil's Row, Crane writes:

> Howls of renewed wrath went up from Devil's Row throats. Tattered gamins on the right made a furious assault on the gravel-heap. On their small convulsed faces shone the grins of true assassins. As they charged, they threw stones and cursed in shrill chorus.[16]

Later in the novel, the author provides a meticulous description of Maggie's brother after the scuffle. Here, as in other passages, Crane spares no detail of a character's sorry condition: "[Jimmie] had bruises on twenty parts of his body, and blood was dripping from a cut in his head. His wan features looked like those of a tiny insane demon" (42). A few pages later, the author continues with his brutal description:

> A stone had smashed in Jimmie's mouth. Blood was bubbling over his chin and down upon his ragged shirt. . . . His roaring curses

of the first part of the fight had changed to a blasphemous chatter. In the yells of the whirling mob of Devil's Row children there were notes of joy like songs of triumphant savagery. The little boys seemed to leer gloatingly at the blood upon the other child's face (44).

In many respects, the descriptions of the characters in *Maggie*, as we follow the antecedents and circumstances of their struggle against nature and each other, bear a close resemblance to medical case histories.[17] To Crane, these men and women appear more important as specimens than individual characters. As a result, one detects a certain lack of sympathy for them on the part of the author.[18] Crane's fiction becomes more detached and brutal as it concentrates on the lowest and darkest side of human nature.[19] Indeed, the young novelist describes his characters the way one might write about animals. Consider, for instance, the scene in which Jimmie observes in terror one of the many fights between his parents:

There was a crash against the door, and something broke into clattering fragments. Jimmie partially suppressed a yell and darted down the stairway. Below he paused and listened. He heard howls and curses, groans and shrieks — a confused chorus as if a battle were raging. With it all there was the crash of splintering furniture. The eyes of the urchin glared in his fear that one of them would discover him (52).

Terms such as "howls," "groans," and "shrieks" seem more appropriate to wild animals than to human beings, however violent they may be.[20] In this type of characterization, Zola's influence is apparent. Here, Crane resorts to the experimental method advocated by the French writer in which characters are used to typify a specific idea.[21] In the case of *Maggie*, the pervasive idea is that the violence that ensures survival is the only absolute value.[22] In the context of literary history, *Maggie* serves as a prime example of Naturalism. The apparent influence of Zola and other French naturalists in Crane's work has prompted critics to point out that *Maggie* has a European antecedent in Zola's *L'Assommoir*. Berryman is representative of the many students of Crane who have argued that the author "probably read *L'Assommoir*, and was influenced by it."[23] On the whole, Crane was perceived by his European contemporaries, especially the British, as a writer who borrowed heavily from the French and who owed the continental naturalists a considerable debt.[24] This attitude no doubt must have annoyed Crane. In a letter to James Huneker in 1897, he vents his displeasure at being typed as an imitator of French naturalistic writers:

> [The British] let fall my hand and begin to quickly ask me how much money I make and from which French realist I shall steal my next book. For it has been proven to me fully and carefully by authority that all my books are stolen from the French. They stand me against walls with a teacup in my hand and tell me how I have stolen all my things from De Maupassant, Zola, [and] Loti.[25]

In his article on the American background of *Maggie*, Marcus Cunliffe notes that, despite Crane's protest, the author was regarded as a devoted follower of French Naturalism.[26] The comment by Spiller on this matter is particularly instructive:

> There is no doubt that [Crane] took direct inspiration from these French realists [De Maupassant and Flaubert], and even more certainly from Zola, for *L'Assommoir* probably provided the plot for *Maggie*, and *La Débâcle* bears a close resemblance to *The Red Badge of Courage*, though [Crane] denied ever having read it. His work shows the stamp of European Naturalism. . . .[27]

Other critics such as Ahnebrink and Stallman have also observed that *Maggie* bears some resemblance in theme and method to *L'Assommoir*. In his study of nineteenth-century American Naturalism, Ahnebrink presents a detailed analysis of relevant passages from both novels, and argues that

> *Maggie* comes close to the theme and method of *L'Assommoir*. Both authors described a good woman's way toward ultimate destruction, and both told their stories with frankness and objectivity. . . . The slum environment together with a weak temperament was in part responsible for the inevitable catastrophe; both novels gave evidence of the curse of alcohol not only for the individual but for society at large.[28]
>
> Some of the parallels recorded here may have been accidental, but taken together they confirm the assumption that Crane was indebted to *L'Assommoir* in his first novel as to plot, characterization, techniques, episodes, and particulars. . . .
>
> Since it is obvious that *Maggie* owes considerable debt to *L'Assommoir*, one may suspect that Zola also exerted an influence on Crane's next novel, *The Red Badge of Courage*, a war novel like *La Débâcle*.[29]

Stallman does not go as far as Ahnebrink in linking *Maggie* to *L'Assommoir*, and points out that "it is impossible to say where Crane got the stuff and craft of *Maggie*."[30] Nevertheless, Stallman acknowledges the possibility that the author either "invented the plot or he took it from Zola's *L'Assommoir*."[31] While not entirely agreeing with the above statement on Crane, Cunliffe concedes that Stallman points out one important fact about *Maggie*, namely, that the author wrote a first draft of the book in 1891, when he was a college student in Syracuse, New York, and "knew very little about the Bowery, slum life, and prostitutes."[32] In conception, therefore, the novel precedes Crane's personal knowledge of the subject. Thus, it would not be unreasonable to say that Crane either invented it or else borrowed something from other writers.[33] According to Cunliffe, however, we do not have sufficient evidence to assert that Crane did indeed borrow the stuff of *Maggie* from Zola. On the one hand, Cunliffe observes that

> Certainly Crane *could have* read *L'Assommoir*. Two translations of it were available in America within two or three years of its publication in 1877. . . . We must admit, too, that Crane's novel does have something in common with Zola's. Both demonstrate the overpowering effect of environment. Both deal frankly, and gloomily with human experience. Both take for their characters the city poor, and in both, the daughter of the family — Maggie, Nana — becomes a prostitute. Both books end in death, though in Zola's novel it is Nana's mother, Gervaise, on whose death the story closes.[34]

However, Cunliffe also argues that

> None of these resemblances seems to me strikingly close, nor do the particular instances cited by Mr. Ahnebrink. On the contrary, they seem less convincing than the dissimilarities. . . . Let us assume, for the sake of argument, that a) Crane had never read *L'Assommoir* when he wrote *Maggie* [and] b) *Maggie* was, however, not a complete invention of Crane's. If we put aside *L'Assommoir* for a while, we can start to look for other possible "influences."
>
> The most obvious place to search is not Europe but America, not Zola's Paris but Crane's New York.[35]

According to Cunliffe, Crane is a good example of a writer who has been classified with a "fallacious neatness."[36] Cunliffe acknowledges that to a certain extent the author of *Maggie* structured some of his early novels according to the literary precepts espoused by writers such as Zola and De Maupassant. Still, he views with skepticism the manner in which Crane has come to be regarded as an orthodox naturalist:

> Largely on the strength of his first novel, *Maggie*, Crane has been labeled as a naturalist. As such, he is supposed to have borrowed from other naturalists. Whatever he did not borrow from them, Crane is thought to have gotten from his own direct experience, or to have absorbed at second-hand from the experiences of others. Naturalistic *influences* and personal experiences would seem to fill out the picture completely. Certainly these do count for something, but not for everything. They leave out a great deal of knowledge and atmosphere that Crane must have absorbed merely through living in America at a certain time, under certain circumstances.[37]

These other influences may have played as important a role in shaping Crane's writing as did Darwins's theories, Spencer's teachings, Zola's novels, or the literary tenets of the naturalistic movement. The critics who call our attention to the parallels between *Maggie* and *L'Assommoir* overlook the differences that set the main characters in the two novels apart. The contrast between Maggie and Nana is evidenced in the way the two women try to cope with an increasingly pernicious environment. Crane seems to have grasped this fundamental distinction between his heroine and Zola's. A few years after the publication of *Maggie*, commenting on *Nana* and the main character in each novel, Crane remarks that

> This girl [Nana] is a real streetwalker. I mean, she does not fool around making excuses for her career. You must pardon me if I cannot agree that every painted woman in the streets of New York was brought there by some evil man.[38]

To Crane, however, Maggie is not at all like Nana. Cunliffe holds, and I concur, that Crane's point here is that "some evil man" is directly responsible for Maggie's fall. Maggie is "seduced from the paths of virtue by the wiles of some heartless seducer." If Crane later came to think otherwise, at this time he imagined Maggie as essentially the victim of circumstances. Nana, on the other hand, is "dans le vice comme un poisson dans l'eau"[39] [as comfortable with vice as a fish is comfortable in the water]. Crane portrays Maggie as pure and innocent: "None of the dirt of Rum Alley seemed to be in her veins." In part, Crane's treatment of her is naturalistic, but in other respects it is not. Cunliffe correctly observes that altogether Maggie is a somewhat unreal creature. Her life as a prostitute is handled by Crane with an apparent lack of certainty. Of Maggie and her newly acquired profession, Crane writes:

> A girl of the painted cohorts of the city. She threw changing glances at men who passed her, giving smiling invitations to those of rural or untaught pattern and usually seeming sedately unconscious of the men with a metropolitan seal upon their faces (101).

The above passage presents a woman who appears to have succeeded in her struggle for survival. She is well dressed, and in all likelihood can afford to lead a life of relative comfort as a prostitute. Why, then, does she commit suicide? This question has been posed by many students of Crane, but the answers given thus far have been problematic at best.[40] While it may appear to be a fitting conclusion for a naturalistic novel, the denouement in *Maggie* reflects either a marked degree of inexperience on the part of the author or some other motive to close the novel with the young prostitute's terse and unexplained suicide.

Crane has been criticized for guessing at his subject matter and for portraying a protagonist who is no more spared by his stinging irony than the rest of his characters.[41] Joseph Brennan notes that however sympathetic in other respects Maggie may be portrayed, her tastes and mental perceptions, especially at the point in the novel when she is about to be seduced by Pete, at times are absurd to the point of exasperation.[42] Other critics contend that this is the writing of an unseasoned author who probably knows about his subject only from hearsay or from his reading.[43] Cunliffe argues that the tone of Crane's work is definitely naturalistic, but it is not the naturalism of Zola, although he concedes that something of the French writer is present.[44] We see an element in *Maggie* that sets it apart from other naturalistic novels and which may be as central to Crane's work as other influencing factors. Cunliffe describes this element as

> . . . a moral, didactic motive, a slight preachiness. Thus, in the dedicatory inscriptions which state that "environment . . . frequently shapes lives regardless," Crane continues: "If one proves that theory, one makes room in Heaven for all sorts of souls, notably an occasional street girl, who are not confidently expected to be there by many excellent people." These words could nearly be the words of a clergyman; and there were several clergymen of the period who might nearly have uttered them.[45]

Cunliffe buttresses the connection between Crane's narrative and the religious writing of the time by identifying some remarkable similarities between *Maggie* and the prose of the Reverend Thomas DeWitt Talmage. The latter was a New York minister who gained notoriety around the turn of the century with his vivid and racy sermons.[46] Cunliffe further argues that Crane could easily have drawn material for *Maggie* from popular American writing of the day. But Cunliffe is cautious as to how far one can go in asserting that the American religious writing of Crane's time served as a source for *Maggie*:

I am not suggesting that we should substitute the name of DeWitt
Talmage for that of Émile Zola as a certain or even probable
influence upon Crane.   We have no proof that Crane had read
either author, though it is hard to believe that he could *avoid* having
heard of the publicity-conscious Mr. Talmage.[47]

Cunliffe's argument loses strength when one remembers that Crane
was profoundly anti-clerical, as his correspondence and several passages
in *Maggie* make clear.[48]   Still, Crane seems to be affected by the
American religious ethos.   To some extent, despite himself, he belongs
to it just as Talmage does.   Maggie commits suicide against the novel's
own logic.   It could be said that this is a naturalistic convention.   But is
it not also a moralist's solution?   To most preachers of Crane's time, the
wages of sin was death, and that seems to hold true for the author as
well.[49]

In various other small ways, *Maggie* reflects the effect of the
general American moral-religious ethos.[50]   This should not come as a
surprise when one remembers that both of Crane's parents were closely
associated with the Methodist church, and must have transmitted to their
son some of the moral teachings of Protestantism.   His father, the
Reverend John Townley Crane, was a devout Christian whom George
Genzmer describes as

a strict Methodist of the old stamp . . . deeply concerned about
such sins as dancing, breaking the Sabbath, reading trashy novels,
playing cards, billiards, and chess, and enjoying tobacco and wine,
and too innocent of the world to do more than suspect of the
existence of greater viciousness.[51]

Furthermore, Mrs. Crane is described by her son as "more of a
Christian than a Methodist."[52]   The connection between the religious-
moralistic climate of the time and Crane's own fiction is further

supported by Cunliffe:

> There is, in America, no cleavage between religion and rationalism
> comparable to that in, say, France. So, when young Crane writes
> with would-be savage candor of the slums, the preachers have been
> there before him. He cannot help borrowing some of their
> material. In later writing he pushes further and further away from
> subjects that can be encompassed by well-meaning pastors. He
> does so because he wants to write fiction; and fiction, in America,
> is still too close to didacticism — to the religious tract and the
> philanthropic survey. "Preaching," Crane observes, "is fatal to
> literature." Like other Americans before him, Crane aims at direct
> experience, simply rendered; the comment, if any, often takes the
> form of irony (as if to say, *this is the way the preachers would put
> it — and it's just possible they may be right*).[53]

In his study of New Testament inversions in Crane's fiction,
William Stein contends that the rigid naturalistic interpretations of *Maggie*
are inadequate because they tend to obscure the broader implications of
the author's recreation of Bowery existence. Stein argues that

> It is not enough, for instance, to say that the novel is the sum of
> "innocence thwarted and betrayed by environment." Such a
> categorical statement implies that Crane's view of reality is
> unalterably objective, concerned only with the transcription of
> calculable sociological data. Actually his creative imagination is
> deeply stirred by the religious aspects of the setting.[54]

Here, Crane's background is the point at issue. Reared in a
confining religious atmosphere, he was trained to think in the ideological
framework of Christianity and, more specifically, within the puritanical
parameters of American ethical and religious thought. Even in rebellion

against institutionalized religion, Stein points out, Crane could not completely subdue the incontrovertible affirmations of the Puritan ethic. This dilemma is exemplified, for instance, in the way the author deals with mission evangelism in *Maggie*. On the one hand, he abhors the self-righteousness that he associates with the preachers of his day. On the other hand, however, he introduces scenes and incidents that are clear manifestations of an intuitive loyalty to the ethical teachings of Protestantism and to a tradition that is essentially puritanical and moralistic in character.[55]

The same influence seems to be at work in Crane's poetry as well. In his article on the theme of bohemianism in Crane's early poems, John Blair argues convincingly that while "Crane's conception of the Christian God [may appear to have been] divided between an affirmation of faith and a total denial of Christianity," the author of *Maggie* "never truly rejected the God either of his father or of his maternal relatives." According to Blair, at the time Crane was writing *Maggie*, *George's Mother*, and other Bowery tales, he came across as a "very young, very impressionable, [and] very insecure man." As a result, he "adopted the appearance of rebellion while still adhering to a core of beliefs which were entirely conventional." He set out to cultivate a tough, rebellious façade most likely as a way to win recognition and to be accepted by his peers.[56]

We see in *Maggie* something of the young author's ambiguous position. With his first novel, Crane ostensibly seeks to denounce social injustice, and writes with would-be candor and moral outrage about the plight of an innocent Bowery prostitute, perhaps in an attempt to "make room in Heaven for all sorts of souls, notably an occasional street girl." Still, *Maggie* can hardly be considered the bold statement of a rebel, as the author would have us believe. On the contrary, Crane's view of prostitution — a subject about which he had little or no direct knowledge — actually has a great deal in common with the mission evangelists whom he criticizes in *Maggie*. Their attitudes toward the fallen woman, and the zeal with which they deal with her "problem," are patronizing at best, and betray a deeply rooted sense of right and wrong that is essentially puritanical in nature. Thus, Crane's effort to provide a candid portrait of the lower class generates only a "naive and overwritten"[57] novel that more often than not offends the sensibility of the modern reader by indulging some of the darkest beliefs and prejudices from the young author's religious background and strict, moralistic upbringing.

Notes

[1] Stephen Crane, *Stephen Crane: An Omnibus*, ed. Robert Stallman (New York: Alfred Knopf, 1966) 594.

See also Lee Clark Mitchell, "Face, Race, and Disfiguration in Stephen Crane's The Monster," *Critical Inquiry* 17 (1990): 174-192. In this article, Mitchell touches on an important aspect of Crane's fiction, namely, the question of disfigurement and eventual annihilation of the self as the result of destructive forces in nature and in society. Henry Johnson, the main character in *The Monster*, and Maggie have their "lives shaped regardless" by forces which they can neither control nor fully understand. They are both mangled — one psychologically, the other physically — by a society that takes a grotesque pleasure in gawking at freaks but is only too eager to turn its back on them if they should ask for help. "Disfigurement," Mitchell writes, "tends to deny the identity it also boldly reasserts by compelling us to imagine a perfectly unmarred former configuration, reminding us of a family resemblance at 'all but' the moment we mark the defect" (175). In Maggie's case, the emotional and psychological disfigurement that she suffers at the hands of her family and lover alters her identity by turning her into something which she is not (a prostitute) but which she has to become in order to survive. "To be confronted by disfiguration," Mitchell argues, "is to desire precisely what is now gone, to want nothing more than the deformed object restored to its original state" (175). Unable to realize this goal, and confronted with a version of herself that she can neither accept nor renounce, Maggie turns to suicide as the only way out of her predicament.

[2] Crane, *Omnibus* 594.

[3] David Fitelson, "Stephen Crane's *Maggie* and Darwinism," *American Quarterly* 16 (1964): 183.

[4] Hamlin Garland, "Book Review: An Ambitious French Novel and a Modest American Story," *Arena* 8 June 1893: xi.

[5] William Dean Howells, "Book Review," *New York Press* 15 April 1984: xxxviii.

[6] Fitelson, "Darwinism" 183.

[7] Stanley Wertheim, ed. *The Merrill Studies in Maggie and George's Mother* (Columbus, Ohio: Charles Merrill, 1970) 2-3.

[8] Wertheim, *Studies* 19.

[9] Wertheim, *Studies* 16.

[10] Wertheim, *Studies* 16-17.

[11] Wertheim, *Studies* 17.

[12] Fitelson, "Darwinism" 183.

[13] A number of scholars disagree with the assessment of *Maggie* as a naturalistic work. These include Sergio Perosa, Donald Pizer, James Nagel, and Tamara Minks. While conceding that the novel exhibits naturalistic traits, especially in setting, they contend that Crane is more of an impressionistic rather than a naturalistic writer.

See Sergio Perosa, "Naturalism and Impressionism in Stephen Crane's Fiction," in *Stephen Crane: A Collection of Critical Essays*, ed. Maurice Bassan (Englewood Cliffs, New Jersey: Prentice-Hall, 1967): 80-94.

Donald Pizer, "Stephen Crane's *Maggie* and American Naturalism," in

Stephen Crane's Career: Perspectives and Evaluations, ed. Thomas Gullason (New York: New York University Press, 1972): 335-343.

James Nagel, *Stephen Crane and Literary Impressionism* (University Park: The Pennsylvania State University Press, 1980).

Tamara Minks, "Maggie Johnson: An American Eve in a Fallen Eden," *Recovering Literature* 16 (1988): 23-35.

[14] John Berryman, *Stephen Crane* (New York: William Sloane, 1950) 63.

See also Charles Walcutt, *American Literary Naturalism: A Divided Stream* (Minneapolis: University of Minnesota Press, 1956) 69.

Lars Ahnebrink, *The Beginnings of Naturalism in American Fiction: A Study of the Works of Hamlin Garland, Stephen Crane, and Frank Norris with Special Reference to Some European Influences* (New York: Russell and Russell, 1961) 249-276. Ahnebrink sees a close connection between Zola's *roman expérimental* and Crane's early works, and writes: "Like *Maggie*, Crane's second novel [*George's Mother*] of the New York slums bears the stamp of Zola" (271). Other works by Crane that are also Zolaesque in nature, particularly in the choice of milieu and sordid detail, include "An Experiment in Misery," "The Men in the Storm," "A Desertion," "A Dark Brown Dog," and "The Scotch Express" (276).

Robert Stallman, foreword to *Maggie: A Girl of the Streets*, in *Stephen Crane: An Omnibus*, by Stephen Crane (New York: Alfred Knopf, 1966) 6.

Robert Spiller, *Literary History of the United States*, ed. Robert Spiller et al. (New York: Macmillan, 1974) 1: 1022.

[15] "Naturalism," *The Reader's Encyclopedia*, 1965 ed.

See also "Naturalism," *The Oxford Companion to American Literature*, 1965 ed.

"Naturalisme," *The Oxford Companion to French Literature*, 1969 ed.

"Naturalism," *A Handbook to Literature*, 1980 ed. According to Zola, the "ideal of the naturalist is . . . the selection of truthful instances subjected to laboratory conditions in a novel, where the hypotheses of the author about the nature and operation of the forces that work upon human beings can be put to the test."   The *roman expérimental* applies the principles of scientific determinism to literary fiction, having as its basic premise the belief that "everything that is real exists in nature, nature being conceived as the world of objects, actions, and forces which yield the secrets of their causation and their being to objective scientific inquiry." In a naturalistic universe, human beings are viewed merely as "animals . . . responding to environmental forces and internal stresses and drives" which they can neither control nor understand ("Naturalism").

[16] Stephen Crane, *Maggie: A Girl of the Streets*, in *Stephen Crane: An Omnibus*, ed. Robert Stallman (New York: Alfred Knopf, 1966) 43.   All subsequent quotations from *Maggie* are from this edition. Citations by page number appear in parentheses in the text.

[17] "Naturalisme," *Companion*.

[18] This is also the conclusion that Frank Norris reaches in his review of *Maggie* published in the *San Francisco Wave* of July 4, 1896. Wertheim, *Studies* 22.

[19] "Naturalisme," *Companion*.

[20] Arthur Edelstein, introduction, *Three Great Novels by Stephen Crane: Maggie, George's Mother, and the Red Badge of Courage*, by Stephen Crane (New York: Fawcett Publications, 1970) 11-28. Crane's propensity to infuse his descriptions with more energy than perhaps is needed has prompted critics to note that stylistically *Maggie* is not at the same level as some of his later works, such as *The Red Badge of Courage*. In one of the more lucid and even-handed reviews of the novel, Edelstein writes that "despite their virtues, both *Maggie* and *George's Mother* are somewhat clumsy novels." The critic correctly points out that, like Joseph Conrad, Crane tends to overuse adjectives, a habit that "muddies the waters of his texts." This "adjectival insistence" is apparent in Crane's constant and at times annoying editorializing as well as in

his choice of "editorial modifiers" — *gloomy, gruesome, barbaric, insane* — a practice that in Edelstein's view serves only to "deprive the facts of their own voice by announcing to the reader his obligatory responses" (18).

While recognizing the literary merits of *Maggie* as the first and arguably the most important naturalistic work in American letters, Edelstein nevertheless contends that "in all this straining after emphasis, the thing that gets most firmly emphasized is the author's anxiety to strike an effect. The result is a strange aura of sentimentality. Though the fiction is full of toughness, it is laced with extraneous sentiment, an air of self-conscious bedazzlement in its own daring. Too often that famous irony, which Crane was to wield with such sure precision in *Red Badge*, loses its way amid all this buffeting. The Crane of *Maggie* is a writer who uses an avalanche to drive a nail. . . . Though the nail, to be sure, gets driven, it splinters the credibility of the announced perceptions. One sees in the passage not only Maggie's distorting innocence but the fervent presence of an author arranging as total a contrast as possible between event and perception. The irony, in brief, visits itself on Crane as well as upon his characters, by exposing his interference. Howells had said that Crane was a writer who sprang into life fully armed, but the fact is that he was overarmed" (18-19).

[21] Dorothy Loos, *The Naturalistic Novel of Brazil* (New York: Hispanic Institute, 1963) 48.

[22] Fitelson, "Darwinism" 188.

[23] Berryman, *Crane* 63.

[24] Marcus Cunliffe, "Stephen Crane and the American Background of *Maggie*," *American Quarterly* 7 (1955): 33.

[25] Crane, *Omnibus* 674-675.

[26] Cunliffe, "Background" 33.

[27] Spiller, *History* 1: 1022.

[28] Ahnebrink, *Beginnings* 251.

[29] Ahnebrink, *Beginnings* 264.

[30] Stallman, *Omnibus* 6.

[31] Stallman, *Omnibus* 6.

[32] Stallman, *Omnibus* 5.

[33] Cunliffe, "Background" 34.

[34] Cunliffe, "Background" 34.

[35] Cunliffe, "Background" 35.

[36] Cunliffe, "Background" 32.

[37] Cunliffe, "Background" 33.

[38] Crane, *Omnibus* 675.

[39] Cunliffe, "Background" 36. Unless otherwise indicated, all English translations throughout this book are my own.

[40] Cunliffe, "Background" 37.
See also James Colvert, "Structure and Theme in Stephen Crane's Fiction," *Modern Fiction Studies* 5 (1959): 203-204.
Robert Stallman, "Crane's *Maggie*: A Reassessment," *Modern Fiction Studies* 5 (1959): 257-258.
William Stein, "Stephen Crane's Homo Absurdus," *Bucknell Review* 8

(1959): 175-176.

Ahnebrink, *Beginnings* 251.

Thomas Gullason, "Thematic Patterns in Stephen Crane's Early Novels," *Nineteenth-Century Fiction* 16 (1961): 61.

Joseph Brennan, "Ironic and Symbolic Structure in Crane's *Maggie*," *Nineteenth-Century Fiction* 16 (1962): 313-314.

Florence Leaver, "Isolation in the Work of Stephen Crane," *The South Atlantic Quarterly* 61 (1962): 527-528.

Fitelson, "Darwinism" 191-193.

[41] Brennan, "Structure" 313-315.
See also Fitelson, "Darwinism."

[42] Brennan, "Structure" 314.

[43] Cunliffe, "Background" 37.

[44] Cunliffe, "Background" 44.

[45] Cunliffe, "Background" 37.

[46] Cunliffe, "Background" 37-38.

[47] Cunliffe, "Background" 40.

[48] Cunliffe, "Background" 49.

[49] Cunliffe, "Background" 41.

[50] Cunliffe, "Background" 42.

[51] "Jonathan Townley Crane," *Dictionary of American Biography*, 1964 ed.

[52] Berryman, *Crane* 9.

[53] Cunliffe, "Background" 43.

[54] William Stein, "New Testament Inversions in Crane's *Maggie*," *Modern Language Notes* 73 (1958): 268.

[55] These are essentially the same findings of Daniel Hoffman, William Stein, Lawrence Hussman, Jr., and Carol Green. See Daniel Hoffman, *The Poetry of Stephen Crane* (New York: Columbia University Press, 1957).
Stein, "Inversions" 268-272.
Lawrence Hussman, Jr., "The Fate of the Fallen Woman in *Maggie* and *Sister Carrie*," in *The Image of the Prostitute in Modern Literature*, ed. Pierre Horn and Mary Beth Pringle (New York: Frederick Ungar, 1984): 91-100. Like many students of Crane before him, Hussman sees a connection between Crane's Methodist upbringing and the denouement that the author chooses for the protagonist in *Maggie*. The critic argues that "when Crane sent Maggie to her self-imposed doom, it was not only because of the logic of such a denouement given the characterization of his heroine as a girl of exceptional sensitivity but also because he was indulging his moral prejudices instead of breaking new ground with a realistic presentation of the prostitute's plight. *Maggie: A Girl of the Streets* is far from a revolutionary naturalistic document in its treatment of the woman's code of sexual conduct. Indeed, it moves only a quarter step forward, replacing death before dishonor with death immediately after dishonor" (97).
Carol Green, "Stephen Crane and the Fallen Women," in *Stephen Crane*, ed. Harold Bloom (New York: Chelsea House, 1987): 99-115. Green provides a useful synopsis of the studies dealing with Crane's attitude toward women as reflected in his fiction and personal life. Among the more insightful readers and biographers of Crane reviewed in Green's article are John Berryman and Daniel Hoffman. In his 1950 biographical study of Crane, Berryman calls attention to "the writer's attraction to older, often unattainable, and sometimes morally dubious women and his continuous fascination with prostitutes,

culminating in his common-law marriage to Cora Stewart, proprietor of . . . a brothel in Jacksonville, Florida" (100). Berryman offers a Freudian explanation to this penchant on the part of the young author, seeing him as a prime example of the male described in Freud's "A Special Type of Choice of Objects Made by Men." The patient and central character in this psychoanalytical case study "seeks a woman in whom another man has some 'right of possession,' and/or one who is to some extent 'sexually discredited' and whose 'fidelity and loyalty' are open to doubt. The lover, intense and sincere, will manifest, in his compulsion to repeat such relationships, a desire to rescue the woman" (100). However cogent the above interpretation may be, other students of Crane such as Daniel Hoffman have disagreed with Berryman's strict Freudian assessment. Hoffman does not believe that "the explanation of Crane's behavior is to be found solely in psychology, but also in religion." To him, "Crane's 'mode of interpreting experience' can be seen as deeply influenced by his Methodist heritage" (100).

[56] John Blair, "The Posture of a Bohemian in the Poetry of Stephen Crane," *American Literature* 61 (1989): 215-218.

[57] Robert Spiller, "The Significance of *Maggie*," in *Stephen Crane's Maggie: Text and Context*, ed. Maurice Bassan (Belmont, California: Wadsworth, 1966): 122. In addition to the scholars mentioned in this chapter, other recent critics of Crane include:

Edwin Cady, *Stephen Crane* (Boston: Twayne, 1962).

Charles Walcutt, ed., *Seven Novelists in the American Naturalist Tradition* (Minneapolis: University of Minnesota Press, 1963).

Warner Berthoff, *The Ferment of Realism: American Literature, 1884-1919* (New York: Free Press, 1965).

Donald B. Gibson, *The Fiction of Stephen Crane* (Carbondale: Southern Illinois University Press, 1968).

Robert Stallman, *Stephen Crane: A Biography* (New York: George Braziller, 1968).

Jean Cazemajou, *Stephen Crane* (Minneapolis: University of Minnesota

Press, 1969).

Edwin Cady, "Howells and Crane: Violence, Decorum, and Reality," in *The Light of Common Day* (Bloomington: Indiana University Press, 1971): 161-181.

Lilian Furst and Peter Skrine, *Naturalism* (London: Methuen, 1971).

Marston LaFrance, *A Reading of Stephen Crane* (Oxford: Clarendon Press, 1971).

Milne Holton, *Cylinder of Vision: The Fiction and Journalistic Writing of Stephen Crane* (Baton Rouge: Louisiana State University Press, 1972).

Joseph Katz, ed., *Stephen Crane in Transition: Centenary Essays* (DeKalb: Northern Illinois University Press, 1972).

Richard M. Weatherford, ed., *Stephen Crane: The Critical Heritage* (London: Routledge and Kegan Paul, 1973).

Allen North Smith, "Stephen Crane and the Darwinian Revolution," Ph.D. dissertation, Michigan State University, 1974.

Frank Bergon, *Stephen Crane's Artistry* (New York: Columbia University Press, 1975).

Yoshinobu Hakutani and Lewis Fried, *eds.*, *American Literary Naturalism: A Reassessment* (Heidelberg, Germany: Carl Winter Universitätsverlag, 1975).

Mark Scott Piper, "A Sublime Egotism: Irony and Meaning in the Fiction of Stephen Crane," Ph.D. dissertation, University of Oregon, 1975.

Jean Carroll Wyrick, "Decorum and Structure in the Short Fiction of Stephen Crane," Ph.D. dissertation, University of Texas at Austin, 1975.

Laurence Frederic Gross, "Stephen Crane: Social Critic," Ph.D. dissertation, Brown University, 1976.

Arno Heller, *Experiments With the Novel of Maturation: Henry James and Stephen Crane* (Innsbruck: Institut für Sprachwissenschaft, University of Innsbruck, 1976).

Toni Oliviero, "People as They Seem to Me: Determinism and Morality as Literary Devices in Three Novels of Stephen Crane," *Seminaires* (1976): 167-181.

Mark J. Freiman, "The World View of American Literary Naturalism in the Fiction of Stephen Crane," Ph.D. dissertation, Stanford University, 1978.

V. John Vacca, "Ethical Perspective in the Fiction of Stephen Crane," Ph.D. dissertation, University of Wisconsin, Madison, 1979.

Paul F. Boller, Jr., *American Thought in Transition: The Impact of Evolutionary Naturalism* (Lanham, Maryland: University Press of America, 1981).

Lee Clark Mitchell, *Witness to a Vanishing America: The Nineteenth-Century Response* (Princeton, New Jersey: Princeton University Press, 1981).

Brenda Murphy, "A Woman With Weapons: The Victor in Stephen Crane's *George's Mother*," *Modern Language Studies* 11 (1981): 88-93.

Erminio G. Neglia, "Fictional Death in Stephen Crane's *The Blue Hotel* and Jorge Luis Borges's *El Sur*," *Chasqui* 10 (1981): 20-25.

Ben Shatterfield, "From Romance to Reality: The Accomplishments of Private Fleming," *College Language Association Journal* 24 (1981): 451-464.

Aida Farrag Graff, "Metaphor and Metonymy: The Two Worlds of Crane's *Maggie*," *English Studies in Canada* 8 (1982): 422-436.

Clarence Oliver Johnson, "A Methodist Clergyman — of the Old, Ambling-Nag, Saddle-Bag, Exhorting Kind: Stephen Crane and His Methodist Heritage," Ph.D. dissertation, Oklahoma State University, 1982.

Donald Pizer, *Twentieth-Century American Literary Naturalism: An Interpretation* (Carbondale: Southern Illinois University Press, 1982).

Geraldine L. Smith, "Melville, Twain, and Crane: Narrative Environments and Individual Victims," Ph.D. dissertation, Rutgers University, 1982.

Laura Hapke, "The Alternate Fallen Woman in *Maggie: A Girl of the Streets*," *Markham Review* 12 (1983): 41-43.

Sydney Krause, "The Surrealism of Crane's Naturalism in *Maggie*," *American Literary Realism* 16 (1983): 253-261.

Ellen Carol Samsell, "American Realists Challenge Conventions, Clichés, and Critics," Ph.D. dissertation, Indiana University, 1983.

Allen Gardner Smith, "Stephen Crane, Impressionism, and William James," *Revue Français d'Études Américaines* 8 (1983): 237-248.

Chester L. Wolford, *The Anger of Stephen Crane* (Lincoln: University of Nebraska Press, 1983).

James Colvert, *Stephen Crane* (San Diego, California: Harcourt Brace Jovanovich, 1984).

John J. Conder, *Naturalism in American Fiction: The Classic Phase* (Lexington: University Press of Kentucky, 1984).

Alice Hall Petry, "Gin Lane in the Bowery: Crane's *Maggie* and William Hogarth," *American Literature* 56 (1984): 417-426.

Donald Pizer, *Realism and Naturalism in Nineteenth-Century American Literature* (Carbondale: Southern Illinois University Press, 1984).

Philip Fisher, *Hard Facts: Setting and Form in the American Novel* (New York: Oxford University Press, 1985).

June Howard, *Form and History in American Literary Naturalism* (Chapel Hill: University of North Carolina Press, 1985).

Faye Mertine Lenarcic, "The Emergence of the Passionate Woman in American Fiction, 1850-1920," Ph.D. dissertation, Syracuse University, 1985.

Michael Robertson, "The First 'New Journalism' and American Fiction, 1880-1925: Studies in Howells, James, Crane, Dreiser, and Hemingway," Ph.D. dissertation, Princeton University, 1985.

João Sedycias, "Crane, Azevedo, and Gamboa: A Comparative Study," Ph.D. dissertation, State University of New York at Buffalo, 1985.

Joyce Caldwell Smith, "The Comic Image in the Fiction of Stephen Crane," Ph.D. dissertation, Georgia State University, 1985.

Rosalie Murphy Baum, "Alcoholism and Family Abuse in *Maggie* and the *Bluest Eye*," *Mosaic* 19 (1986): 91-105.

Joseph Edward Church, "Images of Authority in Stephen Crane," Ph.D. dissertation, University of California, Irvine, 1986.

John Rocco Maitino, "Literary Impressionism in Stephen Crane, Joseph Conrad, and Henry James," Ph.D. dissertation, University of California, Riverside, 1986.

Lee Clark Mitchell, *New Essays on the Red Badge of Courage* (New York: Cambridge University Press, 1986).

Harold Bloom, ed., *Stephen Crane* (New York: Chelsea House, 1987).

Michael Fried, *Realism, Writing, Disfiguration: On Thomas Eakins and Stephen Crane* (Chicago: University of Chicago Press, 1987).

Patricia Kluss Heilman, "The Journalism-Fiction Connection in American Literature as Seen in Selected Works of Stephen Crane, Ernest Hemingway, and Tom Wolfe," Ph.D. dissertation, Indiana University of Pennsylvania, 1987.

David F. Hillsman, "Crane's *Maggie* and Huysman's *Marthe*: Two Naturalist Prostitute Novels," Ph.D. dissertation, Florida State University, 1987.

Bettina L. Knapp, *Stephen Crane* (New York: Ungar, 1987).

Brita Lindberg-Seyersted, *Ford Madox Ford and His Relationship to Stephen Crane and Henry James* (Atlantic Highlands, New Jersey: Humanities, 1987).

Walter B. Michaels, *The Gold Standard and the Logic of Naturalism: American Literature at the Turn of the Century* (Berkeley: University of California Press, 1987).

H. S. Bais, *Stephen Crane: Pioneer in Technique* (New Delhi: Crown Publications, 1988).

Paul Alan Broer, "Stephen Crane: Man Adrift," Ph.D. dissertation, City University of New York, 1988.

Donald B. Gibson, *The Red Badge of Courage: Redefining the Hero* (Boston: Twayne, 1988).

Lee Clark Mitchell, "Naturalism and the Languages of Determinism," in *Columbia Literary History of the United States*, ed. Emory Elliott (New York: Columbia University Press, 1988): 525-545.

William Leslie Brown, "Recreation and Representation in America, 1880-1900: The Economy of Play in the Work of Stephen Crane," Ph.D. dissertation, Stanford University, 1989.

David Halliburton, *The Color of the Sky: A Study of Stephen Crane* (New York: Cambridge University Press, 1989).

Lee Clark Mitchell, *Determined Fictions: American Literary Naturalism* (New York: Columbia University Press, 1989).

Chester L. Wolford, *Stephen Crane: A Study of the Short Fiction* (Boston: Twayne, 1989).

Christopher Benfey, *The Double Life of Stephen Crane* (New York: Alfred Knopf, 1992).

Chapter 2

Aluísio Azevedo's Representation of

the Prostitute in *O cortiço*

O cortiço [the tenement, "beehive"] (1890) chronicles the development of a tenement in Rio de Janeiro during the second half of the nineteenth century. The first chapters deal with the financial rise of João Romão, a Portuguese merchant who emigrates to Brazil "para fazer fortuna" [to get rich]. Through avarice and shrewd profiteering, he amasses enough money to acquire a tenement house that he plans to control and exploit. His tenants are mostly laborers, maids, laundresses, bricklayers, garbage collectors, street peddlers, and an occasional prostitute. In this small though thriving microcosm, adults live in squalor, and the children cannot expect much but to grow up to be like their parents.

The first half of the novel is taken up by a detailed account of how João Romão's *cortiço* [tenement] grows and how its relationship with a neighboring *sobrado* [mansion] develops. By the second half, the reader has become acquainted with those characters around whom much of the action is developed. João Romão is the landlord and ruler of the tenement. His neighbor Miranda is a wealthy immigrant. Like the owner of the tenement, Miranda also hails from Portugal, and has come to Brazil in search of fame and fortune. Jerônimo and his wife, Piedade, two ill-fated tenement dwellers, are Portuguese immigrants of humble origins seeking a better life for themselves and their young daughter. They are the quintessential strangers in a strange land. The exotic life of the New World fascinates and at the same time corrupts the parents and child alike. Jerônimo, Piedade, and their daughter are eventually overwhelmed by the moral laxity of their new home, and become as degenerate as their neighbors in the tenement. Firmo is a Carioca *malandro* [rogue, con artist] and the voluptuous Rita Baiana, his girlfriend. The two lovers form a lethal love triangle with the Portuguese immigrant, Jerônimo. Léonie is a prostitute who serves as a godmother of sorts to several girls in the tenement, especially to Pombinha [little dove], her favorite protegée. Pombinha is the attractive daughter of a former socialite whose wealthy husband had committed suicide after going bankrupt. Pombinha was still young when this happened. Later, she was forced, along with her widowed mother, to move to João Romão's tenement. The girl eventually opts for a life of relative comfort as a prostitute over an existence of deprivation in the slums.

Following closely the literary precepts associated with the Zolaesque *roman expérimental*, *O cortiço* aims to address certain problem areas in human society in general and in the Brazilian social milieu of the second half of the nineteenth century in particular. Azevedo is especially interested in those aspects of Brazilian life at the turn of the century that have to do with the lower class and which to him appear either dysfunctional or pathological. The critic Massaud Moisés describes *O cortiço* as a novel that

> Toca numa das chagas da sociedade fluminense do século XIX: a habitação coletiva, o "cortiço," onde impera a promiscuidade . . . O cortiço, com os seus moradores animalizados pela exaltação dos sentidos e cinicamente explorados, é o pano de fundo, incaracterístico e vil, da ascenção social e econômica do português João

Romão, acompanhada da inicial concorrência do seu vizinho Miranda, também português, ambicioso e desfibrado. O contraponto do sobrado e da venda com o cortiço é a espinha dorsal da obra.[1]

Touches on one of the ulcers of 19th-century society in Rio de Janeiro: the tenement house, the ghetto, where promiscuity reigns. . . . The tenement, with its inhabitants animalized by the exaltation of the senses and cynically exploited, is the backdrop, mundane and corrupt, of the social and financial rise of the Portuguese João Romão, followed by the initial competition of his neighbor Miranda, also Portuguese, greedy and spineless. The counterpoint between [Miranda's] mansion and [João Romão's] grocery store vis-à-vis the tenement is the backbone of the novel.

Throughout the novel, Azevedo's message is reiterated time and again: the debilitating seduction of the tenement will eventually engulf those who come in contact with it. Jerônimo and Pombinha are only two among many victims who exemplify the effects of the destructive influence of their milieu. Jerônimo's physical strength and moral fiber slowly dissipate as the story unfolds, eventually leading to the breakup of his family. Pombinha is a naive girl whose conception of her world stands in stark contrast with the depraved environment in which she must fight for survival.

As a conscious follower of Zola, Azevedo favors an objective or scientific approach to his subject.[2] In *O cortiço*, he focuses on Brazilian society at the turn of the century. This was a society whose bourgeois value system was undergoing profound changes. New concepts were emerging. Older ideas were rapidly becoming obsolete. There was then both a sense of renewal and of dissolution. Many of the social conventions of the time were shown to be dated and on that basis were challenged on a public and personal level. From this sense of disintegration, Brazilian naturalistic writers derive the pessimism and bitterness that permeate their works. As a result, most characters in Brazilian novels from the turn of the century are portrayed as sick or sickened individuals at the mercy of environmental forces and inner drives which they can neither understand nor control.

Azevedo is careful to depict the universe of the lower class in all its wretched aspects, the "social cloaca" which Victor Hugo describes in *Notre Dame de Paris*. From this world of destitution and deprivation, some particularly loathsome types emerge. This is the microcosm that the author uses as the substance and medium of his novel. Although some of these types are developed considerably in *O cortiço*, they are different from the highly individualized characters associated with other genres, such as the romantic novel. To be sure, a number of men and women in *O cortiço* have special qualities that set them apart from the other characters in the novel. Still, the role of these individuals is not to express some personal truth but rather to delineate and characterize their environment. In Azevedo's work, the detailed analysis of a character usually gives way to a wider view of large segments of the population. In a naturalistic novel such as *O cortiço*, the social group and their physical world are more important than any one person. Conversely, the author depicts the masses and the environment as if he were describing individual characters. The social group, whose importance was perceived but never fully explored during the romantic period in Brazil, becomes a central topic in naturalistic fiction, and figures prominently in the novels of the time.

The concept of environment as a shaping force in an individual's life is prevalent in *O cortiço*. In his description of the tenement's development, Azevedo draws a parallel between the genesis of João Romão's slum and the birth of a living organism. His characterization bears close resemblance to the scientific concept commonly known as spontaneous generation. In the nineteenth century, this theory, also known as abiogenesis, gained favor in many scientific circles in Europe as well as in North and South America. Abiogenists maintained that plant and animal life originated from nonliving matter.[3] The appearance of bacteria and other microorganisms, which could be observed growing from rotting food, was thought to be the result of the decaying process itself. That is to say, the rotting organic matter was believed to have given rise to these organisms. The latter were said to have come into being "spontaneously." Azevedo characterizes the emergence of the tenement in similar terms:

> E naquela terra encharcada e fumegante, naquela umidade quente e lodosa, começou a minhocar, a esfervilhar, a crescer, um mundo, uma coisa viva, uma geração, que parecia brotar espontânea, ali mesmo, daquele lameiro, e multiplicar-se como larvas no esterco.[4]

> And in that wet and steamy soil, in that warm and humid mire, there began to stir, to teem, to grow forth, a world, something alive, a generation that seemed to sprout spontaneously, right then and there, from that swamp, and to multiply like maggots in manure.

As the above excerpt shows, Azevedo depicts João Romão's *cortiço* as a living creature. Sometimes the author describes it as a vermin and at other times as a formidable tree that grows lustily, pushing aside everything in its way:

> Durante dois anos o cortiço prosperou de dia para dia, ganhando forças, socando-se de gente. E ao lado o Miranda assustava-se, inquieto com aquela exuberância brutal de vida, aterrado defronte daquela floresta implacável que lhe crescia junto da casa, por debaixo das janelas, e cujas raízes piores e mais grossas do que serpentes, minavam por toda a parte, ameaçando rebentar o chão

em torno dela, rachando o solo e abalando tudo (21).

In the space of two years, the tenement prospered from day to day, gaining strength, stuffing itself with people. And beside [João Romão's grocery store], Miranda grew frightened. That brutal exuberance of life troubled him. He was terrified by the forest that now thrived and expanded inexorably right next to his mansion, under the windows, and whose roots, more loathsome and thicker than serpents, spread everywhere, threatening to crack open the ground all around him, shattering the floor and disturbing everything.

The notion of environment as an autonomous organism capable of causing serious harm remained in vogue among many Brazilian men and women of letters throughout the nineteenth-century. This concept is apparent in Azevedo's treatment of what Massaud Moisés calls "uma chaga da sociedade fluminense do século XIX" [an ulcer of nineteenth-century society in Rio de Janeiro]. Also, allusions to mud, vermin, and putrescence are pervasive throughout *O cortiço*. Obviously, the author's view of the lower class and their mores is not a positive one, as his final reflection on João Romão's tenement makes clear:

> Viveiro de larvas sensuais em que irmãos dormem misturados com as irmãs na mesma lama; paraíso de vermes, brejo de lodo quente e fumegante, donde brota a vida brutalmente, como de uma podridão (156).

> Birthplace of lustful larvae in which brothers sleep with their sisters in the same muck; paradise of vermin, marsh of hot and steamy mire, where life gushes forth brutally, as if from putrescence.

In *Maggie*, the main struggle is between a highly individualized protagonist and the forces of the environment in which she finds herself trapped. The same could be said of *Santa*. *O cortiço* is different from both novels in this respect because anything resembling a central character seems to be missing altogether. However, this difference between the three works is perhaps merely one of focus. Azevedo could, for instance, zero in on a specific character, and portray him or her as being representative of the lower class as a whole. In essence, he would not be dealing with individuals per se but rather with the social group to which they belong. Crane or Gamboa, on the other hand, could move to an unfocused position with respect to the main character in their stories and fade the protagonist into the more prevailing milieu. In either case, the result would be a novel with a structure similar to that of *O cortiço*. Such a novel would follow closely the form and method of the *roman expérimental*, in which individual characters are used to typify a specific idea.[5] This is not to say that Maggie or Santa are typical of all Bowery girls or Mexican prostitutes. In the case of Maggie, however, the tragic outcome of her misapprehension of reality can be taken to be an accurate illustration of what may happen to those individuals unable or unwilling to observe the inexorable laws of a violent microcosm. Her predicament illustrates how the world of the lower class operates. She was destroyed because she was unable or unwilling to conduct her life in accordance with the precepts of that specific environment.

Among the many accounts of moral ruin in *O cortiço*, one is noteworthy because certain parallels can be drawn between it and the stories of Maggie and Santa. The corruption of Pombinha in Azevedo's novel bears a close resemblance to Maggie's own fall from grace. Like her counterpart in Crane's work, Pombinha also grows up in a "mud puddle." However, by some twist of fate she develops into an attractive and considerate young woman:

> Era a flor do cortiço. Chamavam-lhe Pombinha. Bonita, . . .

loura, muito pálida, com modos de menina de boa família (31).

She was the flower of the tenement. They called her Pombinha
[little dove]. Pretty, . . . blond, very pale, with manners befitting
a girl from a good family.

Azevedo describes Pombinha as a young woman whose manners
reflect her good upbringing. Her behavior and conception of the world
set her apart from the other residents of the tenement. Of the way she
carries herself in public, he writes:

Andava sempre de botinas ou sapatinhos com meias de cor, seu
vestido de chita engomado; tinha as suas joiazinhas para sair à rua,
e, aos domingos, quem a encontrasse à missa na igreja de São João
Batista, não seria capaz de desconfiar que ela morava em cortiço
(32).

She always went around in fine leather boots or slippers with
colorful stockings, her calico dress [neatly] starched and pressed;
she had some jewelry, which she wore when she went out, and on
Sundays, whoever saw her in church at Saint John the Baptist's
would not be able to suspect that she lived in a tenement.

Even though they both grow up in the worst of conditions,
Pombinha and Maggie seem to belong to a more refined segment of the
population. Crane is fairly explicit in his portrayal of Maggie as a
genteel and virtuous woman. He declares at the outset of *Maggie* that
"none of the dirt of Rum Alley seemed to be in her veins," and describes
the protagonist in his novel as a pretty girl who "blossomed in a mud
puddle." Azevedo, on the other hand, is less forthright than Crane in
praising his character's qualities. Nevertheless, he refers to Pombinha as
"a flor do cortiço" [the flower of the tenement], but does not elaborate

further. While these descriptions appear promising for the two characters, their situation is actually analogous to that of a beautiful though
fragile plant perched precariously on the edge of a desert. Their survival
is problematic at best.[6] Because of their world view and the way they
conduct themselves, Pombinha and Maggie start out as severely
handicapped individuals. Their chances of survival in their environment
are very slim. They leave home hoping somehow to find happiness and
peace of mind, neither of which they have at home. They also want to
be loved and respected. Abruptly, they are jolted by real-life situations,
and are forced to come face to face with the violence and corruption
which they had previously chosen to ignore.[7] Like Maggie, Pombinha
is one of the few characters in *O cortiço* to elicit genuine concern and
sympathy from the reader. Forced to live with her widowed mother in
João Romão's slum, Pombinha is placed in a situation with limited
alternatives. The only hope she and her mother have of escaping is
through Pombinha's fiancé:

> Seu noivo, João Costa, moço de comércio, estimado do patrão e
> dos colegas, [tinha] muito futuro. . . . Daquele casamento
> dependia a felicidade de ambas, porque o Costa, bem empregado
> como se achava em casa de um tio seu, de quem mais tarde havia
> de ser sócio, tencionava, logo que mudasse de estado, restituí-las
> ao seu primitivo círculo social (31).

> Her fiancé, João Costa, a young businessman, well liked by his
> employer and colleagues, [had] a promising future. . . . The
> happiness of both mother and daughter depended on that marriage
> because Costa, who had a good position in the business
> establishment of an uncle, where he would become a partner later
> on, intended to restore the two women to their previous social
> circle as soon as his promotion came through.

Azevedo portrays Pombinha as a kind and refined young woman. Despite the squalor and promiscuity that thrive around her, she manages to preserve an inner core of kindness and dignity. Being one of the few people in the tenement who can read and write, she helps the other tenants with their correspondence. Every Sunday afternoon, she sets up a table with paper, pen, and an inkwell, and patiently puts down on paper the many messages of her neighbors. The licentiousness that predominates in the slum, however, eventually catches up with her despite her noble intentions. Like countless individuals before her, Pombinha eventually succumbs to the demands of her corrupt milieu.

In Crane's novel, the catalyst of Maggie's ruin is her seducer, Pete. In *O cortiço*, the individual who aids in Pombinha's moral downfall is her "godmother," the prostitute Léonie. The latter preys upon the girls of the tenement the same way Pete and Jimmie prey upon the young women of the Bowery. From their introduction in each novel up to the point when they are both seduced, Pombinha and Maggie think alike. One is as naive as the other. However, the common path shared by the two girls thus far diverges markedly after each has her first sexual encounter. Pombinha is more keenly aware of "right and wrong," at least as far as her survival is concerned, and tries to resist the advances of the prostitute in a display of instinctive self-protection. Unlike Maggie, Pombinha turns out to be more articulate whenever she feels that something of value to her is at stake. The scene in which she is seduced by Léonie illustrates her assertiveness:

> Vem cá, minha flor . . . e a [prostituta] devorava-a com beijos violentos, repetidos, quentes, que sufocavam a menina, enchendo-a de espanto e de um instintivo temor, cuja origem a pobrezinha, na sua simplicidade, não podia saber qual era. . . . Pombinha assentou-se, constrangida, no rebordo da cama, [Léonie] nada mais fazia do que afagar-lhe a cintura, as coxas e o colo. Depois . . .

começou a desabotoar-lhe o corpinho do vestido. Não! . . . não quero despir-me. . . . Estou bem assim. Não quero. E, apesar dos protestos, das súplicas e até das lágrimas da infeliz, [Léonie] arrancou-lhe a última vestimenta, e precipitou-se contra ela, a beijar-lhe todo o corpo, a empolgar-lhe com os lábios o róseo bico do peito. . . . Não! Não! balbuciou a vítima, repelindo [a prostituta] (92-93).

Come here, my little flower . . . and the [prostitute] devoured [Pombinha] with violent, repeated, and impassioned kisses, which choked the young woman, filling her with surprise and an instinctive fear whose origin the poor girl, in all her simplicity, could not fathom. . . . Pombinha sat down, ill at ease, at the edge of the bed, [Léonie] was busy caressing her waist, thighs, and lap. Then . . . she began to unbutton her corset. No! . . . I don't want to get undressed. . . . I'm fine the way I am. I don't want it. However, despite the objections, the pleading, and even the tears of the unfortunate girl, [Léonie] tore away [Pombinha's] last piece of clothing, and threw herself on top of her, kissing her all over her body, grabbing and arousing her rosy nipples with her lips. . . . No! No! stuttered the victim, pushing [the prostitute] away.

However, this is the last time Pombinha resists. The passage that follows the above account is indicative of the extent to which she is susceptible to the debilitating influence of environmental forces and internal drives which she can neither control nor understand:

Pombinha arfava, relutando; mas o atrito daquelas duas grossas pomas irrequietas sobre o seu mesquinho peito de donzela impúbere e o roçar vertiginoso daqueles cabelos ásperos e crespos nas estações mais sensitivas da sua feminilidade, acabaram por foguear-lhe a pólvora do sangue, desertando-lhe a razão ao rebate dos sentidos. Agora espolinhava-se toda, cerrando os dentes, fermindolhe a carne em crispações de espasmo; ao passo que a outra, por cima, doida de luxúria, irracional, feroz, revoluteava, em corcovos de égua, bufando e relinchando. E metia-lhe a língua tesa pela boca e pelas orelhas, e esmagava-lhe os olhos debaixo dos seus beijos lubrificados de espuma, e mordia-lhe o lóbulo dos ombros, e agarrava-lhe convulsivamente o cabelo, como se quisesse arrancá-lo aos punhados. Até que, com um assomo mais forte, devorou-a num abraço de todo o corpo, ganindo ligeiros gritos, secos, curtos, muito agudos, e afinal desabou para o lado, exânime, inerte, os membros atirados num abandono de bêbedo soltando de instante a instante um soluço estrangulado (93).

Pombinha gasped for air and resisted, but the friction of those two thick and restless breasts over her small chest and the dizzying rubbing of Léonie's coarse pubic hairs on the more sensitive parts of her body, succeeded in setting her blood on fire, her reason deserting her as her senses were being assaulted. Now she squirmed with pleasure, grinding her teeth while her body trembled and quivered in spasmodic frenzy, whereas Léonie, all over [Pombinha], mad with lust, irrational, wild, twisted and writhed like a bucking mare. And she thrust her stiff tongue into [the girl's] mouth and into her ears, smothering her eyes with froth-lubricated kisses, biting her shoulders, and seizing her hair convulsively, as though she wanted to tear it out by the handful. Then, in a more forceful move, [Léonie] embraced [Pombinha's] whole body as though she were going to devour it, howling sharp, dry, short screams, and at the end she rolled to the side, motionless, inert, her arms thrown about as if she were drunk, letting out every so often a choked yelp.

After her first sexual experience, Pombinha is engulfed by the promiscuity that thrives around her. She becomes an active part of her milieu. Her musing on the nature and role of her male acquaintances marks the beginning of an important process in her life. For the first time, she sees her world for what it is. At last she comes to understand her position in it. She realizes that she can opt to play the role of predator instead of victim, and thus finds a place for herself in her sex-hungry environment:

> Compreendeu como era que certos velhos respeitáveis . . . deixavam-se vilmente cavalgar pela loureira [Léonie], cativos e submissos, pagando a escravidão com a honra, os bens, e até com a própria vida, se a prostituta, depois de os ter esgotado, fechava-lhes o corpo. E continuou a sorrir, desvanecida na sua superioridade sobre esse outro sexo, vaidoso e fanfarrão que se julgava senhor e que no entanto fora posto no mundo simplesmente para servir ao feminino; escravo ridículo que, para gozar um pouco, precisava tirar da sua mesma ilusão a substância do seu gozo; ao passo que a mulher, a senhora, a dona dela, ia tranqüilamente desfrutando o seu império, endeusada e querida, prodigalizando martírios que os miseráveis aceitavam contritos, a beijar os pés que os oprimiam e as implacáveis mãos que os estrangulavam (100-101).

> She understood how it was that certain respectable older gentlemen . . . disgracefully allowed themselves to be mounted and ridiculed by the fair [Léonie], captive and submissive, paying for that bondage with their honor, their wealth, and even their own life, if the prostitute, after having run them dry, would deny them her body. And [Pombinha] continued to smile, filled with pride and vanity at her superiority over this proud and boisterous sex, who saw himself as master, yet who was placed on this Earth only to serve its female counterpart; this foolish slave who, in order to enjoy a little pleasure, needs to take from his very illusion the substance of his enjoyment; whereas the woman, his lover and ruler, calmly enjoys her domain, deified and lusted after, lavishing pain and suffering that the wretches accept sheepishly, kissing the

feet that oppress them and the implacable hands that choke them to death.

This new awareness is significant because it represents perhaps the most important factor behind Pombinha's decision to fight and adapt. In order to survive, she uses any available means. In this respect, she differs markedly from Maggie. From this point on in Azevedo's novel, any concern or pity that we may have felt for Pombinha gradually vanishes. She is no longer the defenseless girl introduced at the beginning. Rather, she has become keenly aware of the conditions around her and is bent on being successful in her struggle for survival:

> Mediu com as antenas da sua perspicácia mulheril toda aquela ester-queira. . . . E sentiu diante dos olhos aquela massa informe de machos e fêmeas, a comichar, a fremir concupiscente, sufocando-se uns aos outros . . . ferreiros e hortelões, e cavoqueiros, e trabalha-dores de toda a espécie, um exército de bestas sensuais. . . . E na sua alma enfermiça e aleijada, no seu espírito rebelde de flor mimosa e peregrina criada num monturo, violeta infeliz, que um estrume forte demais para ela atrofiara, a moça pressentiu bem claro que nunca daria de si ao marido (101).

> She carefully measured with the antennas of her feminine perspi-cacity the pigsty in which she had grown up. . . . And she saw before her eyes a shapeless mass of males and females, itching, quivering with lust, choking each other . . . blacksmiths, farm hands, construction workers, and laborers of all kinds, an army of prurient beasts. . . . And in her sickly and crippled soul, in her rebellious spirit of delicate flower raised in a dung heap, unfor-tunate violet, atrophied by a manure that proved much too strong for her, the young woman clearly foresaw that she would never give of herself to her husband.

Maggie and Pombinha inherit the indifference, hopelessness, and cynicism of their respective slum worlds. However, Pombinha now elicits admiration and even praise, from reader and tenement dweller alike, as she strives to rise above the tenement and to have some control over her own life. Maggie, on the other hand, merely evokes pity. As Joseph Brennan observes, the protagonist in Crane's novel will pay an awful price for trying to improve her lot in a world of cruelty and indifference. She is a victim whose punishment does not fit her crime, because she has committed none. She is the innocent, seduced, trampled upon, and abandoned by her lover and family alike.[8] Although both women are among the most vulnerable members of their respective communities and grow up in similar slum environments, only Maggie remains a "flower." Pombinha adapts:

> Agora as duas cocotas [Pombinha e Léonie], amigas inseparáveis, terríveis naquela inquebrantável solidariedade, que fazia delas uma só cobra de duas cabeças, dominavam o alto e o baixo Rio de Janeiro. Eram vistas por toda parte onde houvesse prazer . . . Por cima delas duas passara uma geração inteira de devassos. Pombinha, só com tres meses de cama franca, fizera-se tão perita no ofício como a outra (155).

> Now, the two coquettes [Pombinha and Léonie], inseparable companions, terrible in their steadfast solidarity, which transformed them into a kind of two-headed serpent, ruled all parts of Rio de Janeiro. They were seen wherever there was pleasure. . . . Over their bodies a whole generation of depraved men had passed. With only three months working as a prostitute, Pombinha proved to be the acknowledged equal of [her mentor, Léonie].

The lives of Maggie and Pombinha are circumscribed by what appear to be inexorable laws. Their existence is anything but enchanted.

Their fundamental condition is amorality and violence. David Fitelson notes that a world structured within these parameters provides certain guidelines for the way of life that is to be lived in it. Thus, a character will be successful in his struggle for survival to the extent that he conducts his life in accordance with these guidelines. This character will be free from violence and frustration to the degree that he understands the nature of the environment where he must fight for survival. The world of *Maggie* or *O cortiço* provides little distinction between right and wrong action, except insofar as right action is whatever ensures survival. And survival is, in effect, the overriding concern and basis of morality in both novels.[9] Pombinha adapts remarkably well to the demands of her environment. Having undergone and survived, physically as well as psychologically, a brutal initiation into the world of rampant promiscuity in which she is condemned to live, she learns her painful lesson well. As a result, she adapts, and undergoes an extraordinary change, becoming a formidable predator, preying both on her clients and on the girls of the tenement:

> Fez maravilhas na arte; parecia adivinhar todos os segredos daquela vida; seus lábios não tocavam em ninguém sem tirar sangue; sabia beber, gota a gota, pela boca do homem mais avarento, todo o dinheiro que a vítima pudesse dar de si . . . Pombinha abria muito a bolsa, principalmente com a mulher de Jerônimo, a cuja filha, sua protegida predileta, votava agora, por sua vez, uma simpatia toda especial, idêntica a que noutro tempo inspirava ela própria a Léonie. A cadeia continuava e continuaria interminavelmente; o cortiço estava preparando uma nova prostituta naquela pobre menina desamparada, que se fazia mulher ao lado de uma infeliz mãe ébria (155).

She worked wonders in the art of prostitution; she seemed to decipher all the secrets of that life; her lips never touched anyone without drawing blood; she knew how to extract systematically from the stingiest man all the money the victim could give. . . . Pombinha was very generous with her money, especially with Jerônimo's wife, whose daughter, her favorite protegée, now received special attention from her, much like she did herself from Léonie when she was a young girl. The chain continued and would continue endlessly; the tenement was preparing yet another prostitute in that poor and unprotected girl who was coming into womanhood beside her unhappy and drunken mother.

Azevedo provides graphic illustration of the unbroken chain of vice that exists between Pombinha's slum and the fashionable flats of downtown Rio, where Pombinha eventually ends up as a courtesan to the rich and powerful in Carioca society. Just as Léonie brought Pombinha into prostitution, so would Pombinha bring other deprived girls from the *cortiço*. And the chain would go unbroken as long as there were tenements like João Romão's.

In terms of social Darwinism, Pombinha's actions are justified, to the extent that she has pursued a course of action that has ensured her survival. Maggie, on the other hand, must be regarded as a failure. She is noticeably less aggressive than the other characters in the novel, and turns out to be unable to compete successfully for survival.[10]

As we have seen, Pombinha quickly adapts to the demands that her environment makes on her, whereas Maggie is unable to do the same. The girl in *O cortiço* becomes an experienced prostitute. She no longer clings to the unrealistic aspirations of her recent past nor does she make any excuse for her occupation. She survives. On the other hand, Maggie's inability to adapt contrasts poignantly with the successful struggle for survival on the part of her mother, brother, and lover. In his reading of *Maggie*, Fitelson uses the Darwinian concept of survival of the fittest to focus on those aspects of the novel that conform to a pattern of violence that upholds survival as the only absolute value.[11]

According to Fitelson, in another context Maggie's actions might signify something different. They could represent the symbolic triumph of her vision of a dream world or evidence of the possibility of escape from her oppressive milieu. It appears to her that escape to such a dream world can be accomplished only by means of a forcible exit from her real environment. Consequently, on a rainy night she jumps in the river and drowns. It looks as though she has achieved her goal. But the final irony, Fitelson contends, is that Maggie's illusion in the end proves to be unprofitable. It substitutes for the absolute value of survival. The most incredible self-deception is perfectly acceptable as long as it helps the individual in his struggle for existence. In Maggie's case, however, illusion is the underlying cause of her downfall and eventual death. As such, it must be regarded as an undesirable alternative because it removes the protagonist from the struggle for survival.[12]

Fitelson presents a compelling argument, but his interpretation of the denouement in *Maggie* strictly as a naturalistic convention is unsatisfactory. To be sure, conclusions in which individuals are destroyed by forces beyond their control are stock finales in naturalistic novels. Still, an ending in which a young prostitute commits suicide, clearly against the logical development of the novel, belongs more in the value system of a moralist than in a naturalistic universe. It is this moralistic tendency, the "added ingredient" referred to in the previous chapter, that seems to be absent from Azevedo's novel. We find no indication of any moral or didactic motive in *O cortiço*. Also missing is the religious influence that permeates *Maggie*.

Crane makes clear that he was not very friendly to Christianity as it was practiced in his time, voicing his disapproval in his fiction and in his private life. He was particularly hostile to the repressiveness that has largely characterized the American religious experience. Several passages in *Maggie* reflect the extent to which the author repudiated the strict mores prevalent in the religion and society of his time. This puritanical moral severity was unpalatable to Crane as it must have been unpalatable to the prostitutes whom he counted among his close friends.[13] However, friendly or not toward this moral tradition, he was nevertheless influenced by the American religious ethos despite his overt rejection of its more restrictive tenets.

The influences exerted on Azevedo are of a different nature from those that Crane experienced. Azevedo was a conscious disciple of Zola. What the French writer was doing with his natural and social history of a family in France, Azevedo had visions of duplicating in Brazil.[14] Like Zola, he tried to divorce himself from the constraints of any religious or ethical tradition as he moved in for a close-up view of his world. Azevedo's dissociation from moral concerns is evident in his propensity to use material that in his time would have been considered sensational or crude. By comparison, Crane significantly restricts the sensationalism and the choice of coarse material in his novel. When viewed from this angle, Crane does not appear to be as orthodox a naturalist as Azevedo. This becomes even more apparent when we realize that although *Maggie* is a novel about seduction and prostitution, it has no passages dealing explicitly with sex.[15]

Azevedo portrays his characters as sick individuals at the mercy of forces beyond their control. The major characters in *O cortiço* are driven either by sex or by a desire for money and power. In this novel, it is the forces in the physical environment that are held directly responsible for the characters' actions.[16] Azevedo makes ample use of erotic material, and we never see any moralistic condemnation of sex in his work. The Brazilian novelist differs from his American counterpart most of all in his attitude toward the subject matter in his novel. Crane is a moralistic writer, despite his anti-clerical feelings. This is exemplified by the denouement in *Maggie*. Although writing as a naturalist, Crane maintains an inherently moralistic attitude as he selects his material and brings the novel to a close. Azevedo, on the other hand, is amoral by comparison. Not only does he not have any qualms about using unseemly material in his work, he also appears indifferent to the fate of his characters.

Like Zola, Azevedo makes frequent use of sexual, sensational, and obscene material. But he goes further than his French mentor to cover what his nineteenth-century audience would doubtless have regarded as the seamier aspects of sex: satyriasis, nymphomania, incest, rape, and abortion. He also treats sensationally the by-products of such activities: prostitution, homosexuality, and children born out of wedlock, who are often abandoned to die or, if they survive at all, to live as criminals or streetwalkers. In all his principled grimness, Zola would have serious reservations about writing in great detail on lesbianism among prostitutes the way his Brazilian counterpart does. As we have seen, Azevedo does not hesitate to confront the subject squarely and dispassionately. At times he actually seems to derive pleasure from this exercise. His insistence on the ugly, the brutal, and the vulgar, and his nonchalant description of his characters as individuals caught in the grip of their own destructive instincts have led some critics to observe that, above all, the author's objective is to shock his audience. Dorothy Loos characterizes this particular aspect of Azevedo's work as an attempt on the part of the Brazilian author to "out-Zola Zola himself."[17]

Brazilian literature in general has little to do with the ugly or the obscene in human behavior. For the most part, these topics constitute the domain of Brazil's naturalistic novel. Although unquestionably influenced in its inception by foreign sources, this genre is distinctly Brazilian in character. And it could not be otherwise, given the unique cultural traits of its birthplace and the social milieu in which it developed. Azevedo illustrates better than any other writer of his time the complex process of adaptation and transformation of European literary ideology to the realities of the New World. To be sure, the Zolaesque *roman expérimental* serves as the model for his own experimental novel. However,

Azevedo's fiction, while reflecting something of Zola, differs markedly from that of his French mentor. In addition to his views on class and race examined in Chapter 8, Azevedo's blunt and often sensational treatment of lesbian sex is one among many topics that set the two writers apart. Thus, we do Brazilian naturalists a disservice when we insist upon our outdated definition of their art as simplistic and derivative. To approach the naturalistic movement in Brazil as little more than an attempt at copying French or other European literary models denigrates the importance of the genre because, as Dorothy Loos observes:

> [This prejudice] disregards the obvious fact that Brazil had a novelistic tradition of its own and that the naturalistic novel, though produced under the technical aegis of a foreign literary fashion, could not . . . turn its back completely on its own tradition or fail to concern itself with those themes, problems and ideas which were central to the period and locale in which it was written.[18]

More than any other genre, the naturalistic novel of Brazil addressed social questions unique to Brazilian society. Many of these themes — which novelists such as Azevedo, Júlio Ribeiro and Adolfo Caminha treated either sensationally or with little concern for the sensibilities of the time — had been taboo to the romantic and realist writers who had preceded them. To be sure, the naturalists caused a great deal of controversy as they aimed to paint an accurate and lively picture of Brazilian society at the turn of the century. But in the process they helped to lay the foundation for other important literary forms that were to follow, especially the *romance regionalista* [regionalist novel], a genre indigenous to Latin America, which was to occupy an important position in Brazilian letters in the 1920s.

Notes

[1] "O cortiço," *Dicionário de literatura*, ed. 1969.

[2] In its language, setting, and theme, there is little question that Azevedo follows closely the French model of the *roman expérimental*. In his private correspondence and in the preface to some of his novels, the Brazilian author acknowledges his debt to French naturalists such as Émile Zola, Alphonse Daudet, Guy de Maupassant, Joris-Karl Huysmans, Henry Céard, and Edmond and Jules Goncourt. My point here, therefore, is not to demonstrate that *O cortiço* is indeed a naturalistic novel. This fact, I think, is apparent. However, the connection between Azevedo and Zola runs the risk of being taken too far if one chooses to view the naturalistic novel of Brazil merely as a straightforward and simplistic New World adaptation of European aesthetic and literary precepts. On the question of adoption and transformation of European literary patterns to the physical and social reality of New World, see:

Juan Armando Epple, "Aluísio Azevedo y el naturalismo en Brasil," *Revista de crítica literaria latinoamericana* 6 (1980): 29-46. Writing on the critical and historical assessment of the Brazilian naturalistic novel, Epple notes that "hay algunos críticos que, haciéndose eco de las opiniones de Sílvio Romero y de las observaciones críticas que hizo en su tiempo Machado de Assis, han valorado el naturalismo brasileño como un movimiento imitativo y superficial. Para Nélson Sodré, constituye un episodio aislado de la evolución literaria del país, una concesión a la moda literaria llegada de Francia y Portugal, que es incapaz de reflejar artísticamente las situaciones esenciales del período. Para Lúcia Miguel Pereira, es el resultado de una receta estética mal asimilada, que dio muy pobres resultados literarios" (34). [There are some critics who, echoing the opinions of Sílvio Romero and the critical observations made by Machado de Assis during his time, have regarded Brazilian Naturalism as an imitative and superficial movement. To Nélson Sodré, it is an isolated episode in the country's literary evolution, a concession to literary trends imported from France and Portugal, which is unable to reflect artistically the essential conditions of the period. To Lúcia Miguel Pereira, it is the product of a poorly assimilated aesthetic recipe that produced very meager literary results].

While conceding that Brazilian Naturalism was not "un proyecto estético enteramente original" [an entirely original aesthetic project], Epple correctly points out that neither was it merely "una mala imitación" [a poor imitation] of its European counterpart. In his view, "los autores naturalistas brasileños establecen, respecto al naturalismo europeo, la misma relación que encontramos en la literatura hispanoamericana del período: asumen el naturalismo exclusivamente como un modelo literario al servicio de la representación detallada de la realidad local, pero desde perspectivas de valoración del mundo distintas en cada caso" (35). [The Brazilian naturalistic authors establish, with respect to European Naturalism, the same relationship that we find in the Spanish-American literature of the time: they accept European Naturalism strictly as a literary model at the service of a detailed representation of the local reality, but in each case with very different frames of reference and value judgments about the world].

See also Enrique Laguerre, "De Rita Baiana a Teresa Batista: personajes de la novel brasileña," *Sin nombre* 12 (1982): 25-37. Laguerre is another student of the naturalistic novel of Brazil who contends that Brazilian naturalistic writers such as Aluísio Azevedo, Júlio Ribeiro, and Raul Pompéia were eminently successful in their attempt to adapt the *roman expérimental* to the different social and intellectual conditions of the Americas, thus creating something new and characteristically Brazilian in the process. He views the product of this experiment in a positive light and considers the Brazilian naturalistic novel to be "la mejor de Iberoamérica" (25) [the best in Iberian America].

Antônio Cândido, "Literature and the Rise of Brazilian National Self-

Identity," *Luso-Brazilian Review* 5 (1968): 27-43.

[3] "Bacteriology," *McGraw-Hill Encyclopedia of Science and Technology*, 1982 ed.

[4] Aluísio Azevedo, *O cortiço* (São Paulo: Editora Ática, 1981) 21. All subsequent quotations from *O cortiço* are from this edition. Citations by page number appear in parentheses in the text.

[5] Dorothy Loos, *The Naturalistic Novel of Brazil* (New York: Hispanic Institute, 1963) 48.

[6] David Fitelson, "Stephen Crane's *Maggie* and Darwinism," *American Quarterly* 16 (1964): 188.
See also Charles Darwin, *The Origin of the Species* (New York: Philosophical Library, 1958) 75.

[7] Thomas Gullason, "Thematic Patterns in Stephen Crane's Early Novels," *Nineteenth-Century Fiction* 16 (1961): 61.

[8] Joseph Brennan, "Ironic and Symbolic Structure in Crane's *Maggie*," *Nineteenth-Century Fiction* 16 (1962): 313-315.
See also Robert Stallman, "Crane's 'Maggie': A Reassessment," *Modern Fiction Studies* 5 (1959): 258-259.

[9] Fitelson, "Darwinism" 184. The point that Fitelson makes about Maggie's oppressive environment and her predicament in it applies equally well to Pombinha.

[10] Fitelson, "Darwinism" 184.

[11] Fitelson, "Darwinism" 188.

12 Fitelson, "Darwinism" 188-189.

13 Edwin Cady, *Stephen Crane* (Boston: Twayne, 1980) 55-56. According to Cady, Crane had "some kind of 'involvement' with four disturbed, if not disreputable, women in 1896." One of these women, Dora Clark, was a New York prostitute with an active police record. The fourth was Cora Stewart, a luxury-loving Boston socialite who moved to Florida to work as a brothel madam in Jacksonville, and who eventually became "Mrs. Stephen Crane" (56). On the question of Crane and his notoriety, especially vis-à-vis prostitutes and women about town, Cady observes that "the century-long tradition of romantic reputation founded luridly on Byron, DeQuincey, Poe, seemed to apply perfectly to Stephen Crane. And there was no dearth of volunteers to plaster it on him. . . . Wholly false gossip about Crane's drunkenness and opium addiction were assiduously spread; and then, of course, since he had neither home nor wife and was a notorious Bowery haunter, women. Obviously, to the Victorian mind, the author of *Maggie* must have been addicted to whores. . . . Semiprofessional Crane-baiters had New York ringing with such tales in 1896. And at least on the question of women, Crane handed them devastating ammunition. It is, in fact, impossible to know how much fire there was beneath the smoke, [and] the question remains complicated by the lifelong preacher's kid's defiance of moralism. . . . Not only did he refuse to protect his reputation, he deliberately, publicly courted as a celebrity about New York the disapprobation he had been trained to avoid at all costs in childhood and had rebelliously sought since early adolescence" (55).

See also James Colvert, *Stephen Crane* (New York: Harcourt Brace Jovanovich, 1984) 102.

Robert Stallman, *Stephen Crane: A Biography* (New York: George Braziller, 1968) 239-240.

Eric Solomon, *Stephen Crane: From Parody to Realism* (Cambridge, Massachusetts: Harvard University Press, 1966) 142. Solomon suggests that the love story between "the dark, passionate Nora and the casual, tough-minded Coleman" in *Active Service* in many ways is analogous to the relationship between Stephen and Cora Crane. He believes that this aspect of Crane's life and literary career may be of special interest to the Freudian psychoanalytical critic because in his opinion "in Crane's life the Nora Black figure was Cora Crane, who did catch the correspondent. The fantasy life revealed in this novel parallels that of *The Third Violet*: Crane dreams of the American girl, pristine in purity, and rejects the scarlet woman — the reverse of his real-life relationships" (142).

Lillian Gilkes, *Cora Crane: A Biography* (Bloomington: Indiana University Press, 1960).

Thomas Beer, *Stephen Crane: A Study in American Letters* (New York: Knopf, 1923) 108-138.

[14] Loos, *Novel* 42.

[15] Leslie Fiedler, "The Fatal Consequences of Seduction," in *Stephen Crane's Maggie: Text and Context*, ed. Maurice Bassan (Belmont, California: Wadsworth, 1966): 146-148. Fiedler also notes the conspicuous absence in *Maggie* of any passages dealing with sex or sensuality, even though the novel is purportedly a work about seduction and prostitution. Fiedler observes that "the book [*Maggie*] provided no titillation at all — the physical seduction going undescribed — only a great, gray brutality of language (no 'dirty' words, to be sure, though much profanity) and a constant play of irony" (148).

This prudish willingness to sanitize or omit altogether descriptions that might prove too risqué to the general public can be seen at work not only in American naturalistic novels such as *Maggie* but also in the English translation of naturalistic fiction from other countries. Aluísio Azevedo's *O cortiço* is a case in point. When it was first translated from Portuguese into English and made available to American readers in 1926, certain key passages in the original text dealing openly with sex were purposely left out. We can only surmise that the translator, Harry W. Brown, either felt that these passages might prove offensive to an American audience and should not appear in his English version, or he was merely following instructions from his editor regarding what should be included or bowdlerized from the original text. Whatever the case may be, the fact remains that the gaps in this sole English translation of *O cortiço* published in the United States proved too numerous and relevant for me to be able to use it in the present study. For this reason, I took it upon myself to translate into English all the quotations from Azevedo's work that appear in this book. See Aluísio Azevedo, *A Brazilian Tenement*, trans. Harry W. Brown (New York: R. M. McBride, 1926).

[16] Loos, *Novel* 45.

[17] Loos, *Novel* 44-45.

[18] Loos, *Novel* 11-12. Even though Loos does not deal with the *roman expérimental* of Mexico or the United States in this book, her cogent observations about the genesis, development, and character of the naturalistic novel of Brazil also apply to the movement in other countries of the New World.

Chapter 3

Beyond Naturalism: Federico Gamboa and

the Mexican Background of *Santa*

Santa (1903) is the story of a young *campesina* [farm girl] from Chimalistac, a small village in the Mexican countryside. The protagonist, Santa, falls in love with Marcelino, a second lieutenant in the Mexican Army, who seduces and later abandons her. She becomes pregnant by him and is thrown out of her home when her mother and two brothers learn of her miscarriage. Dishonored and rejected, Santa decides to go to Mexico City, where she finds employment in Elvira's brothel, one of the more exclusive houses of prostitution in the Mexican capital. Her career as a courtesan to the rich and powerful in Mexican society is interrupted twice, first when she moves in with an Andalusian bullfighter, and again when she becomes the mistress of one of her wealthy married customers. After these two short interludes, both of which come abruptly to an end because of Santa's alcoholism and promiscuity, her life disintegrates. She descends from the most luxurious to the most squalid of brothels in Mexico City and ends up totally devastated, physically as well as psychologically. In the end, she is rescued from the gutter by Hipólito, the blind piano player from Elvira's brothel who has steadfastly loved and stood by her from the very beginning of her plight in the

Mexican capital. But she is near death when he comes to her aid. She has contracted cancer and dies during surgery. Subsequently, she is buried by Hipólito and his *lazarillo* [blind man's guide] in her native Chimalistac.

In their respective studies of the Latin-American novel, Manuel Pedro González and Kessel Schwartz observe that Naturalism has earned a place among the major literary movements in Latin-American letters.[1] According to González, of all Mexican writers in the late 19th century, Federico Gamboa is perhaps the most loyal and enthusiastic follower of the Brothers Goncourt and Émile Zola.[2] Other critics go further in seeing the work of Gamboa almost entirely as the result of Zolaesque influences. One such critic is Francisco Mena. He argues that Gamboa's work as a whole bears all the unmistakable traits of Naturalism. In his article "Federico Gamboa y el naturalismo, como expresión ideológica y social," Mena reads *Santa* in the light of the literary themes and formulas of the Zolaesque *roman expérimental*.[3] To be sure, he points out characteristics in Gamboa's novel that are indeed naturalistic, but at the same time he overlooks others that call into question the orthodox Naturalism that he seeks to expose.

Mena contends that Santa is brought into prostitution because of hereditary factors. What the critic appears to be saying is that even if Santa were helped (which she is), sooner or later she would still turn to prostitution. He views Santa as a woman without alternatives. According to Mena, the protagonist cannot help giving in to her instincts. Santa acknowledges that she is unable to control the forces that push her toward prostitution, and tries to deal with her plight as best she can. She is, in short, a "víctima de sus propios instintos"[4] [victim of her own instincts]. Here, the view of the protagonist as a helpless individual controlled by heredity and environment conforms neatly, perhaps too neatly, to naturalistic literary ideology. Indeed, one wonders if the concept of naturalistic determinism as used by Gamboa is not being forced onto the work so as to make it conform to pre-established literary precepts rather than the other way around, as Mena suggests.

The language, theme, and form of *Santa* clearly characterize it as a naturalistic novel. Descriptions that emphasize the crude, the obscene and the grotesque prevail throughout the work. On the surface, Gamboa appears to be moving in the same direction as Crane and Azevedo. The Mexican author presents descriptions that bear clear naturalistic traits. He strives to give as accurate and detailed a description of Santa's world as possible, without any softening or exaggeration. However, sometimes he makes use of this type of discourse not so much to shock his readers by exposing the ugly, the crude, or the obscene, but rather, oddly enough, to preach *against* prostitution.[5] Passages structured along these lines are nowhere to be found in *O Cortiço*. Azevedo does not sermonize against the evils of prostitution or the vices of the lower class, nor does he present the sordid milieu of his characters in any didactic or moralistic light.

Although influenced by his Catholic upbringing and the mores of his cultural heritage, Gamboa nonetheless manages to write effectively as a naturalist. To the casual reader, his novels seem to embody most of the literary precepts advocated by the French naturalists. In *Santa*, Gamboa succeeds in rendering a scrupulous reproduction of the life of the Mexican lower class in all its aspects. The detailed and objective depiction of reality advocated by Zola is exemplified, for instance, in Gamboa's account of Santa's miscarriage:

> Destacábase, sin embargo, con admirable y doliente precisión, el aborto repentino y homicida a los cuatro meses más o menos de la clandestina y pecaminosa preñez, a punto que Santa, un pie sobre el brocal del pozo, tiraba de la cuerda del cántaro, que lleno de agua, desparramándose, ascendía a ciegas. Fue un rayo. Un copioso sudar; un dolor horrible en las caderas, cerca de las ingles,

y en la cintura atrás; un dolor de tal manera lacerante que Santa
soltó la cuerda, lanzó un grito y se abatió en el suelo. Luego, la
hemorragia, casí tan abundosa y sonora cual la del cántaro, roto al
chocar con las húmedas paredes del pozo. Agustina, inclinada
junto a ella, aclarando el secreto, titubeante entre golpearla y
maldecirla o curarla y perdonarla . . . el [perro] "Coyote" lamiendo
la sangre que se enterraba, y uno de los gallos de lidia, cantando
inmotivamente.[6]

The sudden and murderous miscarriage in the fourth month of
[Santa's] clandestine and sinful pregnancy stood out with
remarkable and painful clarity [in her mind]. . . . Santa, with her
foot on the curbstone of the water well, was pulling out the bucket,
which spilled all of its water as she grew blind [with pain]. It was
like lightning. She was sweating profusely; a terrible pain in her
hip, near her groin, and in her lower back; such a raging pain that
Santa let go of the rope, let out a cry, and threw herself on the
ground. Then, the hemorrhage set in, almost as abundant and
sonorous as that of the shattered bucket. Leaning over her
daughter, Agustina discovered [Santa's] secret, and could not decide
whether she should beat and curse her or care for her and forgive
her. . . . [Their dog] Coyote was meanwhile licking the blood that
was fast vanishing into the ground, and a fighting cock crowed
dispassionately.

Later in the novel, Gamboa presents another among many passages
that characterize his work as distinctly naturalistic. Again, the author
concentrates on the lowest and darkest side of human nature. He reveals
Hipólito, arguably the most endearing character in the entire novel, to be
subject to the same drives that control Santa and her customers.
Although he has waited patiently for Santa's affection, and has gone so
far as to entertain the idea of paying for her services, he has received

nothing from her in terms of sexual favors, and he feels cheated. Thus, in a fit of rage, the blind man gives in to his instincts and momentarily forsakes his role as Santa's friend and protector. Realizing that, as he puts it, "si más aguardo, no me tocará nada" (299) [if I wait any longer, I will not get anything], he rapes his protegée:

> La lucha se tornó implacable, con encarnizamiento de enemigos. Ya no había ídolo ni idólatra, sino el eterno combate primitivo de la hembra que se rehusa al macho que persigue. . . . Un descuido de Santa que se resbaló en el suelo; luego dos gritos, el de pavor de ella y el de victoria de él; luego . . . un jadear meramente animal, de personas enlazadas que forcejan, el ciego encima, magullando la carne idolatrada que al mundo entero pertenecía, abriéndose brecha con crueldades de gorila (299).

> The struggle became relentless, with the fury of enemies. No longer was there idol or worshipper, only the primitive battle between the female who refuses and the male who pursues his goal relentlessly. . . . [Because of] a false move on her part, Santa slipped and fell to the floor . . . then, two cries were heard: one of terror from her and another of triumph from him; shortly thereafter . . . the animalistic panting of individuals bound together in a fierce struggle, the blind man on top, pounding the idolized flesh that had been enjoyed by everyone else, making his way [through her body] with the ferociousness of a wild beast.

Descriptions like the one above are in keeping with the general tone of the naturalistic novel. Here, and in many other passages in *Santa*, Gamboa appears as a faithful disciple of Zola. Like his French mentor, Gamboa makes terrible things happen in his novel. Without fully realizing what is happening to her, the protagonist in *Santa* is wrenched from her tranquil life in the countryside, only to be placed at the center of a horrifying drama that works itself out in dishonor, humiliation, and ultimately in death. In some respects, Santa's story bears a resemblance to classical Greek tragedy. Hers is a life that evokes pity. In order to inspire this emotion, Gamboa has his protagonist undergo a drastic and traumatic change of fortune. Just as Aristotle prescribes, this is not the story of an entirely virtuous person thrust from a high and enviable position to a low one. Neither is *Santa* the story of an evil person's promotion from a low position to a prosperous state. Santa elicits pity, and her environment inspires fear because the ordeal at the heart of the novel involves someone who is not entirely virtuous nor thoroughly corrupt but, like most people, somewhere between these two extremes. Hers is the story of an unfortunate soul who experiences great misfortune as a result of what Aristotle calls *hamartia*, a mistake, an error in judgment or conduct.[7]

Santa arouses pity because the suffering of the protagonist is in part undeserved. Her misfortune evokes compassion just as her environment provokes fear. These responses are central to our understanding of Gamboa's work because it is by a reasonably skillful manipulation of them that the author manages to purge the feelings of pity and fear that his novel elicits in the reader. The environment in which Gamboa chooses to present his grim story is as wretched and frightful as Santa's ordeal itself: "nido de víboras, trono del hampa, albergue de delincuentes, fábrica de dolencias y alcázar de la patulea" (302) [nest of vipers, throne of the underworld, den of criminals, source of disease and suffering, and fortress of the rabble]. Here, as throughout the novel, the author aims to merge realistic elements with his particular style — which at times can be romantic, sentimental, or even melodramatic — and the world of the novel in order to make his fiction appear verisimilar, a chief objective and a hallmark of naturalistic writing.

The passages presented thus far place *Santa* in the general corpus of naturalistic novels. They establish clearly that Gamboa subscribes to

Zola's literary agenda and that he is indebted to the French naturalists as far as the language, theme, and form of *Santa* are concerned. Mena's reading of *Santa* addresses these points, and seeks to find in the novel its salient naturalistic characteristics. Mena points out that Gamboa observes his surroundings carefully and aims to describe human society as objectively and truthfully as the subject matter of science is studied and presented. However, there are other aspects of Gamboa's work that Mena either misses or chooses to ignore. The most obvious of these are the lyrical passages that crop up unexpectedly in many places throughout the novel. Although Gamboa still presents himself as a deterministic writer, he is not necessarily as punitive as Crane nor as disdainful of humanity and its works as Azevedo. We can see that, despite his cynicism, Gamboa retains certain attitudes that are at odds with traditional naturalistic literary ideology.[8] Alongside Zolaesque descriptions of the crude, the ugly, and the immoral (by the accepted standards of the time), one can also find in *Santa* idealized characterizations, interventions of nature, pathos, sentimentality, and melodrama. The passage in which the author extols the wholesomeness of the idyllic environment in which poor country girls grow up exemplifies this juxtaposition and apparent discontinuity:

> La historia vulgar de las muchachas pobres que nacen en el campo y en el campo se crían al aire libre, entre brisas y flores; ignorantes, castas y fuertes; al cuidado de la tierra, nuestra eterna madre cariñosa; con amistades aladas, de pájaros libres de verdad, y con ilusiones tan puras, dentro de sus duros pechos de zagalas, como las violetas que escondidas crecen a orillas del río que meció su cuna blandamente, amorosamente, y después se ha deslizado, a espaldas de la rústica casuca paterna, embravecido todos los otoños, revuelto, espumante; pensativo y azul todas las primaveras preocupado de llevar en su seno los secretos de las fábricas que nutre, de

los molinos que mueve, de los prados que fecundiza, y no poder
revelarlos sino tener que seguir con ellos a donde él va y muere,
lejos, allá . . . ¡dicen que al mar! (39)

The simple story of impoverished girls who are born and grow up
in the countryside, in the open air, with the [gentle] breeze and
flowers; naive, chaste and strong; looked after by mother Earth,
our eternal and loving mother; with the winged friendship of birds
that are truly free, and with such pure illusions inside their firm
young girl's breasts, like the violets that grow hidden on the banks
of the river that gently, lovingly rocks their cradle to and fro, and
afterwards swiftly slides towards the sea . . . pensive and blue . . .
intent on taking in its bosom the secrets of the factories that it
nourishes, of the water mills that it turns, of the meadows that it
fertilizes, and not being able to disclose them but rather having to
take them along to its deathbed, far, far away in the sea.

Another passage that illustrates this mawkish type of discourse appears at
the beginning of the novel. Here, the author describes Santa's home in
the countryside as a pastoral haven:

Por todas partes aire puro, fragancia de las rosas que asoman por
encima de las tapias, rumor de árboles y del agua que se despeña
en las dos presas.   En el día, zumbar de insectos, al sol; en la
noche, luciérnagas que el amor enciende y que se persiguen y
apagan cuando se encuentran. Detrás de la casita, una magueyera
inmensa, de un verde monótono y sin matices; a los dos lados,
huertas y jardines; al frente, la propiedad del padre Guerra . . .
más allá el cementerio, abierto y silencioso, sin mármoles ni
inscripciones, pero brindando un cómodo asilo para el eterno sueño,
con sus heliotropos y claveles que al echarse encima de los
sepulcros, tapan codiciosamente los nombres de los desaparecidos
y las fechas de su desaparecimiento. . . . En ese cuadro, Santa de

niña, y de joven más tarde; dueña de la blanca casita; hija mimada de la anciana Agustina, a cuyo calor duerme noche a noche; ídolo de sus hermanos Estéban y Fabián, que la celan y vigilan; gala del pueblo; ambición de mozos y envidia de mozas; sana, feliz, pura . . . ¡cuánta inocencia en su espíritu! (42-43)

Fresh air everywhere, the fragrance of roses that peek above the walls, the murmur of trees and of the water that hurls itself down the dam. During the day, the buzzing of insects in the sun; at night, fireflies kindled by love chase one another, their lights going out as they run into each other. Behind [Santa's] house, an enormous maguey tree, with monotonous hues of green; on both sides, orchards and gardens; in front, Father Guerra's property . . . and further down, the cemetery, open and silent, without marble or inscriptions, but offering its comfortable shelter for one's final rest, with its heliotropes and carnations that cover covetously the names of the deceased and the dates of their demise as they throw themselves on the graves. In this environment, Santa [lived] as a little girl, and as a young woman later on; lady of the little white house; the pampered daughter of old Agustina, who kept her warm night after night; worshipped by her two brothers Estéban and Fabián, who watched over her and protected her; the pride and joy of her little village; the dream of the town's young men and source of jealousy to the other girls; wholesome, happy, pure . . . so much innocence in her soul!

The first type of discourse that I have examined — the language of violence and crudeness of the vulgar scenes — shows Gamboa's work as naturalistic, whereas the second does not conform neatly to a Zolaesque conception of the world. Indeed, there are episodes in *Santa* in which the language used by Gamboa rivals that of the romantic school in its "sentimentality and melodramatic traits."[9] In isolation, these different types of discourse have little significance. What is of relevance here is the contrapuntal interplay between the two, which Gamboa uses as a key structural device in the novel. We can see this counterpoint at work in the passage following Santa's expulsion from home. Having decided to seek refuge in Elvira's brothel, Santa is greeted by the doorkeeper, who calls attention to the grim future that awaits the protagonist:

> Condolida . . . de verla allí, dentro del antro que a ella le daba de comer; antro que en cortísimo tiempo devoraría aquella hermosura y aquella carne joven que ignoraba seguramente todos los horrores que la esperaban (14).

> Sorry . . . to see [Santa] there, in the den of iniquity that provided her own livelihood; the lair that in very little time would ravage the beauty and young body of this girl who most certainly ignored all the horrors that awaited her.

However, Gamboa lessens the crudeness of this description by following it immediately with a passage that stands in stark contrast to the first. This line lacks any trace of naturalistic coarseness, and is very positive in tone: "La portera, humanizada ante la belleza de Santa . . . sonrió con [amable] sonrisa" (13). [The porter, touched by Santa's gracefulness . . . put forth a friendly smile]. In many other parts of the novel, the author employs the same contrapuntal movement. For example, note the passage in which Pepa, one of the older prostitutes at Elvira's brothel, displays her decrepit and hideous body to Santa:

> E impúdicamente, se levantó el camisón, con trágico ademán triste, y Santa miró, en efecto, unas pantorrillas nervudas, casi rectas; unos muslos deformes, ajados, y un vientre colgante, descolorido, con hondas arrugas que lo partían en toda su anchura, cual esas tierras exhaustas que han rendido cosechas y cosechas enrique-

ciendo ciegamente al propietario, y que al cabo pierden su secreta
e irremplazable savia, para solo conservar la huella del arado, a
modo de marca infame y perpetua (19).

And [the prostitute] lewdly raised her nightgown with a tragic and
sad gesture, and Santa gazed at her sinewy, almost upright calves;
her crumpled, deformed thighs, and her droopy, colorless belly,
with deep wrinkles . . . like the exhausted earth which has yielded
one harvest after another, blindly enriching its proprietor, and
which in the end loses its secret and irreplaceable sap, only to
retain the scars made by the plough, like an infamous and eternal
mark.

The grotesque display on the part of the old prostitute is attenuated
at once by her own remarks on the detrimental effects of prostitution on
one's body. If the author were to interject moralistic considerations on
the evils of prostitution here, that would not be in keeping with the setting
and atmosphere that he has created thus far. As a general rule, readers
do not expect streetwalkers to go on puritanical tirades attacking
prostitution on ethical or religious grounds, especially in a naturalistic
novel. Faced with this restriction, Gamboa settles for the next best thing.
Through a character with many years of experience as a courtesan, the
author provides a ghastly description of the physical toll that prostitution
takes on a woman's body. Although this account contains all the literary
accouterments of naturalistic discourse, it fails to gloss over or do away
with its inherently moralistic tone:

Tú misma, que ahora me ves y oyes espantada, tampoco has de
apreciar esto. Te sientes sana, con pocos años, con una herida allá
en tu alma, y no te conformas; quieres también que tu cuerpo la
pague . . . pues menudo que es el desengaño, hija; el cuerpo se nos
cansa y se nos enferma . . . huirán de ti y te pondrás como yo,

hecha una lástima (18-19).

> You yourself, who look on and listen to me in amazement now,
> won't fully understand this either. You feel wholesome, young,
> your heart has been broken, and you can't accept it; you also want
> your body to pay for it. . . . Well, girl, insignificant though your
> disappointment may be, your body will become diseased . . .
> people will avoid you, and you will end up like me, like a wretch.

The author makes a clear attempt to lessen the harshness of his
naturalistic descriptions with positive remarks or interjections. This is
accomplished in a pattern in which the former are invariably followed and
abated by the latter. Mena's study seems incomplete because he
concentrates almost exclusively on those aspects of *Santa* that place the
novel in the general corpus of naturalistic works while ignoring others
that are just as relevant. *Santa* is done a disservice when one disregards
a juxtaposition that is so recurrent, and hence compels the reader to see
the novel from a more complex perspective.

We detect in Gamboa a sense of propriety that is missing from
Azevedo and, to a certain extent, from Crane. To be sure, *Maggie* and
Santa have more in common with each other than they do with *O cortiço*.
Both novels bear signs of an ethical or religious heritage. They differ,
however, as far as the nature of these heritages is concerned. Crane is
moralistic, but in a puritanical and punitive way, whereas Gamboa shows
more compassion toward his characters, and as a result offers them the
possibility of redemption. The difference between Gamboa and other
naturalistic writers such as Crane stems primarily from their backgrounds
and from the way they react to the religious and ethical influences of their
respective cultures. In his book *La novela de Federico Gamboa*,
Alexander Hooker observes that a certain Catholic sense of propriety
pervades Gamboa's fiction, and draws a parallel between the Mexican

writer and a major exponent of naturalism in Spain, Emilia Pardo Bazán:

> A pesar de lo que dice Gamboa . . . hay una gran incompatibilidad entre sus creencias religiosas y la concepción naturalista de la vida. La teoría del naturalismo supone que el individuo está sometido a unas leyes de herencia y de medio ambiente que determinan de un modo fatal el curso de su vida. De esa manera el hombre que tiene padre alcohólico o vicioso o que vive en los bajos fondos sociales tendrá que ser inmoral y desgraciado. Pero esa premisa es falsa según la religión. El cristianismo tiene el concepto del libre albedrío por el cual el hombre puede salvarse a pesar de su herencia y de su medio ambiente. Es más, el pobre tiene más probabilidad de llegar al cielo que el rico. A causa del conflicto entre el optimismo católico y el pesimismo ateo, el naturalismo no tuvo muchos discípulos en España ni en Hispanoamérica. El caso de Gamboa es semejante al de la Pardo Bazán: a pesar de los asuntos que presentan, el tono de sus novelas es casto y moral. . . . En las novelas de Gamboa es la ciudad . . . que ejerce una mala influencia sobre las personas, pero éstas tienen que pagar sus pecados. . . . La vida de Santa es determinada por su medio ambiente, y su muerte trágica después del descenso por los bajos fondos sociales realza la moralidad de la novela. . . . Aquí la fuerza de la voluntad religiosa puede más que las influencias desmoralizadoras que iban destruyendo la vida de [Santa]. . . . En todas las novelas de Federico Gamboa . . . el fin casto y moral justifica los medios que utiliza el novelista.[10]

Despite what Gamboa says . . . there is a great incompatibility between his religious beliefs and the naturalistic conception of life. The theory of Naturalism supposes that the individual is subject to the laws of heredity and nature that determine in an irrevocable way the course of his life. Thus, the man who has an alcoholic or dissolute father, or who is a member of the lower class, will have to be immoral or ill-fated. According to religion, however, this premise is false. Christianity has the concept of free will by which man can be saved despite his heredity or environment. Moreover, the poor have a better chance of going to heaven than the rich. Due to the conflict between Catholic optimism and atheist pessimism, Naturalism did not have many followers in Spain or Spanish America. Gamboa's case is similar to that of [Emilia] Pardo Bazán: despite the topics that they present, the tone of their novels is chaste and moral. . . . In Gamboa's novels, it is the city . . . that exerts an evil influence on the characters, but the latter have to pay for their sins. . . . Santa's life is determined by her environment, and her tragic death after she has sunk to the lowest levels of the underclass highlights the morality of the novel. . . . Here, the forces of religious desire are more powerful than the demoralizing influences that were destroying [Santa's] life. . . . In all of Gamboa's novels . . . the chaste and moral ending justifies the means used by the author.

Even in those passages that are not central to the story line, Gamboa counterbalances the crudeness of his naturalistic descriptions. He does this with elements that diminish the harshness of such passages and purge the reader's feelings of repulsion and fear. For example, in the first part of the novel, the author presents a grim description of Hipólito:

¡Que horroroso era! . . . Picado de viruelas, la barba sin afeitar, lacio el bigote gris y poblado, la frente ancha, grueso el cuello y la quijada fuerte. Su camisa, puerca y sin zurcir en las orillas; . . . las manos huesosas, de uñas largas y amarillentas por el cigarro (31).

How disgusting he looked! . . . Pockmarked, unshaven, with his withered and grey moustache, a broad forehead, a thick neck, and a strong chin. His shirt, filthy and with the edges of the collar and the cuffs yet to be mended; . . . his bony hands, with long fingernails yellowish from smoking.

However, immediately following the above passage, the author lessens the negative impact of this grotesque account by bringing to notice the blind man's artistic abilities. Now, Hipólito is described as a skilled pianist, and the tone of the characterization changes markedly:

> ¡Qué lindamente tocaba! . . . [las manos] expresivas y ágiles, ora saltando de las teclas blancas a las teclas negras con tal rapidez, que a Santa le parecía que se multiplicaban, ora posándose en una sola nota, tan amorosamente, que la nota aislada adquiría vigor y sonaba por su cuenta, quizás más que las otras (31).

> How beautifully he played! . . . his expressive and agile [hands] leaping from the white to the black keys with such swiftness that to Santa they seemed to multiply, sometimes hovering over a single note, so lovingly, that the winged note seemed to acquire energy and sounded on its own, perhaps longer than all the others.

This sense of propriety is pervasive throughout the novel. Whether one calls it Hispanic, Mexican, or Catholic, one can safely assume that among New World naturalistic writers it is unique to Gamboa. It is certainly absent from either Crane's or Azevedo's works. The Brazilian novelist seems to indulge in his depiction of what, to the aesthetic and social sensibility of his time, would no doubt have been considered ugly, sordid, and obscene. He has no reservations about depicting in minute detail sexual acts between lesbians, something that even Zola himself would have hesitated to do. Gamboa touches on the topic of lesbianism, only to dismiss it altogether from his novel. His propriety is apparent in his condemnation of this sexual practice:

Vaya, la propia "Gaditana," apasionada igualmente de Santa
por efecto no de una perversión, sino de una perversidad sexual,
luengos años cultivada poníalo [a Hipólito] en menos atrenzos que
el "diestro": primero porque Santa abominaba de la práctica
maldita . . . y segundo, porque . . . a Hipólito no le producía la tal
celos propiamente dichos, producíale más bien indulgencia y
risa. . . .

Esta pasión de la "Gaditana" hacia Santa, no era un misterio
para ninguna de las de la casa. . . . Santa le despepitó la
ocurrencia desde que ella apuntó:

— ¡Hipo! ya no aguanto a la "Gaditana." Figúrese usted que
está empeñada en que yo la quiera más que a qualquier hombre.
¿Se habrá vuelto loca? . . . Se lo dije, le dije: "Anda y acuéstate,
mujer, para que se te pase la cruda y te vengan otros pensamientos,
no seas tonta . . ." mira, "Gaditana," me alegro por la noticia y
márchate a tu cuarto, que me voy a levantar (149-150).

Gaditana herself, also in love with Santa due not to some
perversion but rather to a sexual fixation, which she developed over
the years, posed less of a threat [to Hipólito] than did the bullfighter: first, because Santa loathed that wicked practice . . . and
second, because . . . [Gaditana] didn't necessarily make Hipólito
feel jealous. He was actually tolerant of [Gaditana's amorous
overtures toward Santa], and would have a laugh or two at Gaditana's expense. . . .

Gaditana's passion for Santa was no secret to the women of
the brothel. . . . Santa strongly repudiated [Gaditana's advances],
and made things quite clear from the very beginning:

Hipo, I can't stand Gaditana anymore! Can you believe she
actually wants me to love her more than any other man? Has she
gone mad? I told her [in no uncertain terms]: "Go on, woman, go
to sleep, so that you may get over your hangover, and have better
thoughts, don't be silly" . . . look, Gaditana, I'm happy for the

news, now go to your room because I'm going to get up.

Santa's disapproval of lesbianism exemplifies the divergence that exists between Gamboa and the more radical factions of Naturalism. This difference becomes apparent when one compares Santa to Pombinha. Viewed from this perspective, Azevedo appears to follow the precepts of Naturalism more closely than Gamboa. Of the two, the former is the more orthodox naturalist.

Besides those passages in which the crudeness of naturalistic language is attenuated by positive remarks, Gamboa also makes use of a discourse that stands on its own as a clearly moralistic stance against the very subject matter of his novel (i.e., prostitution). Reflecting on the fate that befalls a virgin who chooses to stray from the path of righteousness, Gamboa writes:

> Cuando una virgen se aparta de lo honesto y consciente, que la desgarren su vestidura de inocencia; cuando una mala hija mancilla las canas de su madre, de una madre que ya se asoma a las negruras del sepulcro; cuando una doncella enloda a los hermanos que por sostenerla trabajan, entonces, la que ha cesado de ser virgen, la mala hija y la doncella olvidadiza, apesta cuanto la rodea y hay que rechazarla, que suponerla muerta y que rezar por ella (69).

When a virgin strays from the path of honesty and responsibility, she should be stripped of her cloak of innocence; when a disobedient daughter blemishes her mother's grey hair, a mother who is about to leave this world; when a young woman disgraces her brothers who work hard to support and protect her, then, she who is no longer a virgin, the bad daughter and the forgetful maiden infects and corrupts all those around her, and she must therefore be shunned, she must be considered dead, and prayers ought to be said for her.

None of the patterns analyzed earlier is as revealing as the one in which there is a clear intention on the part of Gamboa to exonerate his protagonist from any blame or responsibility for her predicament. At first, the pattern seems to conform to naturalistic tenets. In a *roman expérimental*, man is merely an animal responding to environmental forces and drives over which he has no control and which he cannot understand. In Gamboa, however, there is more than just the faithful observance of the literary directives put forth by European naturalists. As in *Maggie*, there is in *Santa* an "added ingredient" that characterizes it as a Spanish-American naturalistic work and at the same time sets it apart from other novels of the same genre.

Azevedo is indifferent to the fate of his characters. He takes an amoral stance vis-à-vis his work, and at times appears to derive pleasure from his shocking accounts of life in the Brazilian underworld. Crane depicts the awesome forces of the physical and social environment over man, and at the same time, punishes the protagonist in *Maggie* for having sinned. He does this in a manner that could accurately be described as puritanical. Gamboa is neither as amoral as Azevedo nor as punitive as Crane. Like Crane, he portrays a young woman who suffers a fall, and dies in the end. Unlike his American counterpart, however, Gamboa shows compassion toward his characters, especially at the conclusion of the novel. From the beginning, Gamboa uses the prescribed naturalistic formula of "environment over the individual" to exonerate Santa from responsibility for her predicament. He lessens the misery of her situation by rationalizing her decision to go into prostitution. When Santa is first admitted to the brothel, the author presents the first of a long list of explanations justifying her decision:

Vengo . . . porque ya no quepo en mi casa; porque me han echado mi madre y mis hermanos; porque no sé trabajar y sobre todo, porque . . . juré que pararía en esto y no lo creyeron (17).

I'm here . . . because I'm no longer welcome in my home; because my mother and bothers have thrown me out; because I don't have a job, and above all because . . . I swore I would end up here and they didn't believe me.

The blame for Santa's plight is made to fall on people other than the girl herself: her brothers and her mother. Throughout the novel, Gamboa tries to find plausible reasons to justify the protagonist's decision to become and remain a prostitute. He regards this move on her part not as something that depended on her will but rather as the result of impositions beyond her control. The author approaches the question of prostitution as though streetwalking were the only option available to Santa, which it is not, as the protagonist herself makes clear. Gamboa portrays the protagonist as an innocent girl who falls from grace and now finds herself battling against forces that completely overwhelm her. Faced with such a bittersweet description, one cannot help but feel compassion for Santa. Along with her blind friend, Hipólito, she is one of the few characters in the novel to elicit genuine concern and sympathy. The portrayal of Santa at this point stands in stark contrast to the way Gamboa describes her later as a promiscuous and successful prostitute. The author's desire to exculpate Santa for having gotten herself into such a terrible predicament is evident in many passages throughout the novel. For example, shortly after her arrival at Elvira's brothel, Santa tries to run away from her new home environment:

Por segunda vez en su trágica jornada, la ganó la tentación de marcharse, de huir, de retornar a su pueblo y a su rincón, con su familia, sus pájaros, sus flores . . . donde siempre había vivido, de donde nunca creyó salir (21).

> For the second time in her tragic journey, [Santa] was tempted to
> leave, to flee, to return to her little village and home, to her family,
> her birds, her flowers . . . where she had always lived, [the haven]
> she never thought she would leave.

Later, reflecting on her condition, Santa feels miserable for having
allowed herself to sink to such a level:

> Tan miserable y abandonada se sintió, que escondió el rostro en la
> almohada, tibia de haber sustentado su cabeza, y se echó a llorar
> mucho, muchísimo con hondos sollozos que la sacudían el encor-
> vado y hermoso cuerpo; un raudal de lágrimas que acudían de una
> porción de fuentes; de su infancia campesina, de unas miajas de
> histerismos y del secreto duelo que vivía por su desdichada pureza
> muerta (22).

> She felt so miserable and abandoned that she hid her face in her
> pillow, not willing to hold her head up high, and she began to weep
> copiously, with deep sobs that made her entire curvaceous and
> lovely body tremble; a torrent of tears that sprung from many
> sources; from her childhood in the countryside, from traces of
> hysteria, and from the secret pain that she had to endure because of
> her wretched, lost chastity.

Gamboa presents the drive that forces Santa into disagreeable
situations sometimes as a person — mother, brothers, procuresses — and
at other times as nature. The transfer of culpability may, for example,
take place between the protagonist and something as impersonal as the
rain:

> Un gran trueno celeste, anunciador del aguacero que se echaba
> encima de la ciudad, la estremeció; y volviendo la cara a la puerta

de la calle, que le quedaba a un paso, se asió la falda de seda y se adelantó a la salida, guiada por un deseo meramente animal e irreflexivo de correr y correr hasta donde el aliento le alcanzara, y hasta donde, en cambio, el daño que se le antojaba inminente no pudiera alcanzarla. . . . Mas, a tiempo que se adelantaba, la lluvia desatóse iracunda, rabiosa, azotando paredes, vidrios y suelos con unas gotazas que al caer o chocar contra algo, sonaban metálicamente, salpicaban, como si con la fuerza del golpe se hicieran pedazos (30).

A resounding thunder, herald of the storm which was about to fall on the city, shook [Santa]; and turning toward the main door that lay but a few feet from her, she tidied up her silk dress and made her way to the exit, guided by an impetuous and purely animal desire to run and run as far as her breath would take her, far away, where the harm that she perceived as imminent could no longer reach her. . . . However, as she approached [the door], the rain fell irascibly, furiously, whipping the walls, windowpanes, and the ground with raindrops so big that they sounded metallic as they hit something, spattering, as if the force with which they fell tore them to pieces.

It is ludicrous, to be sure, but what Gamboa in effect seems to be saying here is that Santa became a prostitute because on her first night in the brothel she tried to run away, but it was raining so hard that she could not leave. These oppressive forces — family, nature, social environment — may be viewed as naturalistic symbols for the insurmountable barriers that a Mexican girl might encounter as she tried to battle the elements that threatened to destroy her. However, one detects a certain heavy-handedness on the part of the author as he explores the factors that lead Santa into prostitution. This heavy-handedness makes it difficult to dismiss my argument that at this point in the novel the author is engaged in an *un*-naturalistic attempt to present Santa in a morally acceptable light. He seeks to accomplish this by exonerating the protagonist from any blame or responsibility for her predicament. Gamboa portrays Santa as an unfortunate individual who is dragged into prostitution against her will by forces beyond her control:

> Santa, impotente para subtraerse al influjo incontrastable que Elvira ejercía en su voluntad, desprendióse del piano y se aproximó al personaje. . . .   Traigo mucha plata en la cartera y en el chaleco . . . para ti toda si duermes conmigo esta noche. . . . ¿Qué dices? !Que sí! le murmuró Santa, intimada por Elvira, que antes de retirarse detúvose a mirarla (35).

> Unable to extricate herself from the powerful influence that Elvira exerted on her, Santa left the piano, and walked toward the customer. . . . I have lots of money on me . . . all for you, if you agree to sleep with me tonight. . . .   What do you say? Yes, muttered Santa, prodded by Elvira, who, before leaving [the room], stopped to give [the girl] one long, hard look.

To be sure, the portrayal of an individual caught in the grip of deadly environmental forces or harmful personal influence is characteristic of naturalistic novels as a whole. However, Gamboa seems to go out of his way as he attempts to exonerate Santa from the fate that has befallen her. In many passages, the author seeks openly to elicit sympathy for the protagonist. Of her first night at the brothel, when Santa is forced by Elvira to sleep with a drunken customer whom the protagonist loathes, Gamboa writes:

> Santa apagó su lámpara y principió a desvestirse, regocijada con la idea que esa primera noche nadie se adueñaría de ella. De pronto y a pesar de las tinieblas de la estancia, llevóse la mano al cuello

y se subió el camisón, cual si temiese que la sorprendieran. Aguardó un momento, y la respiración acompasada del gobernador la tranquilizó; soltóse el camisón y, devotamente, se sacó un viejo escapulario que ya no podría llevar más, que tenía que ocultar ¡pobre trapo desteñido y roto como su pureza, testigo íntimo de sus épocas de dicha, guardián de reliquias que no habían sabido protegerla, compañero de sus suspiros de doncella y de sus palpitaciones de enamorada! . . . Castamente, lo besó muchas veces, como besamos lo que no hemos de volver a ver (37-38).

Santa put out the light, and began to undress, rejoicing in the idea that on her first night [at the brothel] nobody would take possession of her. Suddenly, and despite the darkness of her quarters, she raised one hand to her neck, and lifted her nightgown, as though she feared someone might catch her off guard. She waited a while, and the rhythmical breathing of the [sleeping] governor calmed her somewhat; she dropped her nightgown, and, devoutly, took out an old scapulary which she no longer could wear, which she had to hide; a scruffy-looking rag, discolored and torn like her chastity, an intimate reminder of happier times, guardian of relics that hadn't known how to protect her, companion of her childhood dreams and adolescent aspirations. . . . She chastely kissed it several times, as one kisses that which one will never see again.

Even when Gamboa portrays Santa as an experienced prostitute, he does so with some reticence, interjecting observations that reflect her misery at having to lead a life that she finds unpalatable:

En los instantes . . . en que oleadas de remordimiento la asaltaban y entristecían, entraba en fulgaces coloquios consigo misma; pero por mucho que volvía el rostro dispuesta a pedir auxilio, a modo de persona que se ahoga, sólo contemplaba a entrambas orillas de su vivir, gente que se encogía o que se esforzaba porque de una vez se ahogara y con ello desapareciese la tentación lindísima de su cuerpo . . . remordimientos . . . recuerdos de su catecismo, de su niñez y de su madre . . . víctima de sus propios instintos . . . ¿dónde finalizaría con semejante vida? . . . pues en el hospital y en el cementerio (75).

In the moments . . . when waves of remorse overtook and saddened her, [Santa] would go into brief dialogues with herself; but as much as she turned [to people], ready to ask for help, as a drowning person would, she only found in her world individuals who either withdrew from her, or who tried to help [fearing that] if she [killed herself], the beautiful temptation of her body would disappear [as well] . . . remorse . . . memories of her catechism, of her childhood and her mother . . . a victim of her own instincts . . . where would she end up with such a life? . . . certainly, in the hospital and the cemetery.

Obviously, Gamboa could not possibly go through the entire novel portraying Santa as an innocent or reluctant courtesan. Given the mores of his time, that would be a contradiction in terms. Moreover, he would be deviating too far from the model of the *roman expérimental*. Therefore, by the second half of the novel, he starts to move away from his initial position, and begins to portray Santa as a promiscuous and willing prostitute:

> Santa, en pleno período de dominio y boga, en pleno período triunfal de su carne dura, de su carne joven, de su carne al alcance de cuantos anhelaban probarla, llegaba de las últimas a estos bailes, escoltadas por brillante cauda de gomosos (109).
>
> Santa considerábase reina de la eterna ciudad corrompida; florescencia magnífica de la metrópoli secular y bella, con lagos para sus arrullos y volcanes para sus iras, pero pecadora, cien veces

pecadora; manchada por los pecados de amor de conquistadores brutales, que indistintamente amaban y mataban; manchada por los pecados de amor de varias invasiones de guerreros rubios y remotos, forzadores de algunas de sus trincheras; . . . manchada por los pecados complicados y enfermizos del amor moderno. . . . Santa sentíase emperatriz de la ciudad históricamente imperial, supuesto que todos sus pobladores hombres, los padres, los esposos y los hijos, la buscaban y la perseguían, la adoraban, proclamábanse felices si ella les consentía arribar, en su cuerpo de cortesana, al anhelado puerto, al delicioso sitio único en que radica la suprema ventura terrenal y efímera (119).

During the time she was the toast of the brothel, during the time her young and firm body was at the disposal of all those eager to try it, Santa would be seen in many balls, always followed by a long string of [admirers].

Santa considered herself sovereign of that iniquitous and corrupted city; a beautiful flower [growing] in that secular and pleasant metropolis, with lakes for her lullabies and volcanos for her fits of temper, but a sinner [nonetheless], sinner one hundred times over; sullied by the carnal sins of brutal conquerors who would make love and kill indiscriminately; tainted by the sexual vices of several invasions of blond and exotic warriors, who would demand from Santa what she had never delivered before; . . . blemished by the complex and sickly sins of modern love. . . . Santa felt she was the empress of that imperial city, because its male inhabitants, fathers, husbands, and sons all sought her company and coveted her, they adored her, proclaiming their joy if she let them mount her, [and enjoy] her gracious courtesan's body, [specifically] the much craved harbor, the delectable site that houses the supreme and ephemeral earthly happiness.

The author seems to be going the opposite way now. Instead of attenuating Santa's concupiscence and promiscuity with redeeming positive remarks, he actually highlights her depraved condition. The passage in which Santa comes close to being rescued from prostitution by one of her live-in lovers, the Andalusian bullfighter, illustrates this point. Here, the protagonist wastes an ideal opportunity to have a home of her own and lead a respectable life. Gamboa juxtaposes the propriety and wholesomeness of Santa's new home environment with the protagonist's sordid predispositions in order to better delineate the predicament at the heart of the novel:

> El amancebamiento de Santa desenvolvióse tranquilo. Quietamente deslizábanse las semanas unas tras otras, en la insípida atmósfera de la [pensión] (208).
> Santa se [había] cansado de él; [lo había] dejado sin odios, al contrario, más también sin penoso esfuerzo (209).
> Era verdad. Aquel ensayo de vida honesta la aburría, probablemente porque su perdición ya no tendría cura porque se habría maleado hasta sus raíces, no negaba la probabilidad, pues en los meses que la broma duraba, tiempo sobraba para aclimatarse (210).
> Un domingo traicionero, Santa traicionó a "El Jarameño" entregándose cínicamente a Ripoll (211).

> Santa's illicit union developed peacefully. The weeks passed quietly, one after the other, in the insipid environment of the [boarding house].
> Santa got tired of [El Jarameño], she didn't feel any hate when she left him, on the contrary, but she didn't have to make any painful effort either.
> It was true. That attempt at leading a decent life bored her, probably because she was already beyond help, for she had been corrupted through and through, [and] she didn't deny that possibility, because during the two months that "the joke" lasted,

she had plenty of time to get acclimated. . . .

On a fateful Sunday, Santa cheated on El Jarameño by cynically agreeing to have sex with Ripoll.

Here, Gamboa depicts Santa as a prostitute caught hopelessly in the grip of her life of promiscuity and vice. Once ousted from El Jarameño's home, Santa returns to Elvira's brothel at once. There is no question in her mind that this is the right thing to do. It never occurs to her that she has other alternatives. In this respect, the second part of the novel stands in stark contrast to the first, in which Santa tries several times to leave the life of prostitution, although to no avail. At this point in the novel, Santa comes the closest to other naturalistic characters such as Nana and Pombinha. All three women are prostitutes, and none of them wastes any time making excuses for their lives of vice. Rather, they try to survive as best they can. To Santa, survival means going back to the brothel:

> Derechamente, sin asomos de titubeos ni vacilaciones, como golondrina que reintegra al polvoriento alero donde quedó su nido desierto resistiendo escarchas y lluvias, así Santa enderezó sus pasos fugitivos a la casa de Elvira, sin ocurrirle que sobraban recursos más seguros y más honestos, sobre todo; sin rememorar sus proyectos bordados hacía algunos meses, cuando la muerte de su madre habíala estrujado el espíritu y prometídole, con el abandono del vicio, una resurección de alma y cuerpo. Nada de eso (213).

Straight [as an arrow], without any trace of hesitation, like the swallow that returns to the dusty gable-end where its deserted nest lay, overcoming rain and snow, Santa directed her quick steps toward Elvira's [brothel], without it even occurring to her that there were more reliable and especially more decent ways to earn a living; without remembering the projects that she had devised a few months ago, when her mother's death left her spirit crushed, and prompted her to promise to resurrect her [own] body and soul. [However, she did] nothing of the kind.

When Rubio, her second and last live-in lover, asks Santa to become his mistress, she accepts his offer gladly. On the surface, she gives the impression of making a sincere attempt at living honorably as a "dueña y señora de una casita suya, con criadas de ella y muebles de ella y todo de ella, en cuenta, unos pájaros que se prometía colgar en los corredores para que con gorjeos alegraran la vivienda y en la morada evocaran placenteros recuerdos de días desaparecidos y felicidades difuntas" (268-269). [Lady and ruler of her own home, with her own servants and furnishings, and all her things, including some birds whose cages would be hung in the hallways in order to cheer up the place with their singing and bring back pleasant memories and the erstwhile happiness of days long gone by]. However, this second attempt at leading a respectable life away from prostitution is of even shorter duration than her idyll with El Jarameño. Gamboa suggests that at this stage in her life, Santa is hopelessly addicted to alcohol and the vices of prostitution. She is depicted as a woman destined to remain a prostitute for the rest of her life, sinking increasingly lower into the bowels of the underworld:

> Por alcohólica, por enferma y por desgraciada engañó a Rubio con frenesí positivo, sin parar, donde se podía, en la calle, en el baño, en los carruajes de punto, en la mismísima vivienda. Y antes y después del engaño reincidente, bebía, bebía. . . . En ocasiones, se quejaba, reapareciéndole los dolores alarmantes y raros. . . . Cuando al fin Rubio se enteró, al cabo de varios perdones y participaciones en excesos alcohólicos, cuando la expulsó despiadada y brutalmente, Santa estaba borracha. Al cochero, que le propuso al reconocerla llevarla a casa de Elvira, le contestó riendo y tambaleando: No, allí no . . . llévame a otra, hombre, de tantísimas que

hay, pero que sea de a ocho pesos, siquiera . . . ¡todavía los valgo! (278).

Due to her alcoholism, her sickness, and wretchedness, she cheated on Rubio with a vengeance, without a break, wherever she could, in the streets, in the public bath houses, on streets cars, even in her own home. And before and after the deception which she couldn't help but relapse into, she would drink copiously. . . . Sometimes she would complain of pains and aches that returned increasingly stronger. . . . When Rubio finally caught on, after having several times forgiven her and taken part in her drinking sprees, when he threw her out forcefully and heartlessly, she was drunk. To the coachman who, upon recognizing her, suggested that she be taken to Elvira's brothel, she replied laughing and staggering: No, not there . . . take me to another [brothel], man, there are so many of them, but one where customers are charged at least eight pesos. . . . I'm still worth that!

Santa becomes more like Pombinha. On the surface, Gamboa and Azevedo appear to be following the same path. That, however, is not the case. Gamboa portrays Santa the way he does for reasons altogether different from those that lead Azevedo to take an amoral stance vis-à-vis his literary creation. In the second half of *Santa*, one detects a drastic change in the way Gamboa depicts the protagonist. The first part of the novel outlines the predicament of a young woman who is dragged into prostitution, practically against her will. The second part introduces a Santa who differs markedly from the naive girl presented earlier. Now, she is as depraved as any of her many customers. To many critics, this change conforms to the naturalistic notion of the environment's ability to shape and destroy lives. Santa can be seen as the proverbial "human insect," caught in the grip of forces and drives that she can neither understand nor control. However, this view focuses on naturalistic themes sometimes at the expense of other important patterns and elements in the novel. Contrary to what critics like Mena propose, there is more to *Santa* than merely naturalistic themes and formulas.

The fact that Santa undergoes a drastic change in the second half of the narrative reflects the extent to which Gamboa may have been following naturalistic tenets. However, this transformation may also point to a desire on the part of the author to make credible a final redemption of Santa's sins. This could be attained by a cathartic and poignant finale. In order to accomplish this, Gamboa is compelled to portray Santa as a depraved prostitute who seems to enjoy her sexual exploits.

The tale of an innocent country girl who is seduced, and then is rejected by lover and family alike to die diseased and abandoned would betray a puritanical callousness bordering on sadism if it were to close tersely with the protagonist's death, as *Maggie* does. This would be especially true if such a story were to come from a writer steeped in the Catholic tradition like Gamboa. To Gamboa, no purpose would be served if Santa were to die disfigured and neglected. Consequently, he permits the protagonist to change and develop into a successful prostitute. She also appears to enjoy her success and the influence derived from her position as a courtesan to the rich and powerful. By giving his protagonist this life, the author allows for the possibility that Santa may eventually be punished for her sins. Gamboa goes on to structure his novel in such a way as to make plausible the subsequent implementation of this development. The author would be left with few reasons to punish Santa with disease, abandonment, and death, if she had not become so depraved and had not enjoyed her exploits so licentiously. By positing a cruel punishment for the protagonist as something feasible and believable, the author makes it possible for Santa to receive divine mercy and forgiveness, if she should reflect and repent. She does both:

[Santa] sentíase lo que en realidad era: un pedazo de barro humano; de barro pestilente y miserable que ensucia, rueda, lo pisotean y se deshace (124).

Su instinto sugeríale a Santa el encaminarse a un templo. . . . Habíanla ganado tales ansias de cambiar de vida . . . sí, de cambiar de vida ¿por qué no? . . . ¿o sólo de eso se podía vivir? . . . ¿Cómo de muy diversos modos vivía tanta mujer, hasta con criaturas de nutrir y abandonadas igualmente de sus seductores? . . . Pues a imitarlas y a pegarse al trabajo, que fuerzas y salud poseía de sobra. ¿De qué trabajaría? . . . ¿de planchadora? ¿de lavandera? . . . De lo que se presentara, en cualquier oficio. . . . Y prosiguió bordando el plan de toda una existencia de arrepentimiento y enmienda, con la que se regeneraría poquito a poco, mucho más despacio que cuando se envileciera, pero lográndolo al cabo por remate a sus empeños (128-129).

[Santa] . . . realized what she really was: a piece of human dirt; of a disease-ridden and wretched dirt that is defiled, trampled upon, and destroyed.

Her instinct led her to a church . . . the desire to change her way of life had overtaken her . . . yes, to change her life, and why not? . . . was that the only way she could earn a living? . . . Didn't many other women have [decent] employment, even those who were abandoned by their lovers with babies to look after? So, [Santa] could follow their example and get herself a good job since she was still strong and healthy. What would she work as? . . . pressing clothes? as a laundress? . . . [She would take] whatever came her way, whatever job. . . . And she went on to devise the plans for a whole lifetime of repentance and rehabilitation, which she would accomplish little by little, more slowly than when she debased herself, but attaining her goal in the end as the result of her determination.

When confronted with the magnitude of her predicament, Santa, like Maggie, turns to religion for understanding and forgiveness:

> Santa, en éxtasis, pidió mentalmente la muerte, olvidada de su vida y de sus manchas. Morir ahí, en aquel instante, frente por frente del Dios de las bondades infinitas, y de los misericordiosos perdones (132).

> In ecstasy, Santa mentally asked to die, forgetting her life and her blemishes. To die right there, in that very instant, face to face with the god of infinite goodness and of compassionate mercy.

Like Maggie, Santa does not find compassion or redemption with institutionalized religion. As a result, she looks for it elsewhere. Santa's search remains constant throughout the latter part of the novel, and eventually takes the protagonist to Hipólito:

> Se amarían . . . era infalible y era misericordioso: todos aman, todo ama, hasta los insectos, hasta los seres más débiles y desgraciados. . . . Sí, ese día amanecería, tendría crepúsculos, saldría el sol entre nublazones de oro y se hundiría entre los opalos de la tarde. ¿Qué importaba que el cuerpo de él fuese deforme y que el de ella se hallara marchito por todas las lascivias? . . . El amor hermosearía el cuerpo del hombre y limpiaría el cuerpo de la hembra, y ya redimidos, caminarían gozosos rumbo a la Sión de las almas, sin memorias de lo pasado, dejando la carne en las zarzas, para las fieras. . . . El mal no existía, el mal acabaría, el mal acaba. . . . Santa se bañaría en el Jordán del arrepentimiento y saldría más blanca que los armiños blancos (237-238).

> They would love each other . . . it was inevitable and redemptive: we all love, everything loves, even the insects, even the weakest

and most wretched of creatures. . . . Yes, this day would come, and there would be a [beautiful] twilight, the sun would come out from golden clouds and would sink between the opals of the evening. What difference did it make that his body was deformed and that hers had become withered due to the lasciviousness that it had suffered? . . . Love would restore beauty and grace to his body, and would cleanse hers, and the two, already redeemed, would walk joyfully toward the Zion of souls, without any memories from the past, leaving their physical body by the wayside, for the wild beasts. . . . Evil wouldn't exist [there], evil would come to an end, evil does come to an end. . . . Santa would bathe in the Jordan of repentance, and would come out whiter than a white ermine.

Santa is given several chances to reform herself before she sinks to the lowest levels of the underworld. However, for some reason she never takes advantage of any of these opportunities. She actually wastes them by cheating on both men who try to take her away from prostitution. It seems as though to Gamboa a genuine redemption is valid only if earned by the person to be redeemed. Santa cannot have other people — family, lovers, friends — walk her path or carry her load for her. She must do it herself if she is to receive divine clemency and salvation. Gamboa, however, does not stop there. He goes to the opposite extreme, and chooses for Santa a road that is harsh at best and horrifying at worst. Not only is Santa not allowed to be rescued by her two pleasant and worldly lovers, she is forced to traverse the most squalid brothels of Mexico City only to be saved at the end by the least physically attractive character in the entire novel, Hipólito. The religious symbolism is apparent in many parts of *Santa*, and a careful reader should have little difficulty in recognizing Hipólito as a Christ-figure.

Obviously, Gamboa is a naturalistic writer. But he is also a Mexican responding to cultural directives that may be as strong and important an influence on his writing as the aesthetic tenets of European Naturalism. Unlike Crane or Azevedo, Gamboa infuses his work with religious images and symbols that create an atmosphere conducive to bringing the novel to a redemptive close. Echoing traits of the mystic tradition in Hispanic culture, after having subjected Santa to extreme suffering and a brutal cleansing of her sins, Gamboa turns his protagonist to death, to the transcendence of the actual world, as the only way out of her torment:

> Uno de los cuartetos contenía ofrecimientos tan misericordiosos:
> " . . . dicen que los muertos, reposan en calma,
>   que no hay sufrimiento en la otra mansión. . . ."
> que Santa los repetía sin descanso, obsesionada ya por la muerte, creyendo a pie juntillas en la garantía de los versos sepulcrales. Sin aquel entusiasmo ni aquella devoción con que decía lo primero, cantaba el resto por no truncar la estrofa:
> " . . . que si el cuerpo muere, jamás muere el alma,
>   y ella es la que te ama con ciega pasión. . . ." (307-308)

> One of the quatrains contained such merciful offerings:
> " . . . it is said that the dead rest peacefully,
>   that there is no suffering in the other world. . . ."
> which Santa repeated over and over again, already obsessed with dying, believing wholeheartedly in the promise of these funereal verses. Without the enthusiasm or devotion with which she recited the first lines, she uttered the rest only to complete the stanza:
> " . . . that if the body dies, the soul lives forever,
>   and [the soul] is the one that loves you with blind
>   passion. . . .

Santa goes full circle from being an innocent country girl to a reluctant prostitute, to a concupiscent whore, to a contrite harlot, only to die a purified and dignified human being in the end: "El sufrimiento, el amor y la muerte habían purificado a Santa" (341-342). [Suffering, love, and death had purified Santa]. The road that Santa traverses as her grim story unfolds eventually takes her back to her idyllic Chimalistac. The circle is finally closed as Hipólito and his *lazarillo* [blind man's guide] bury her body in the little village where she had enjoyed an innocent and pristine childhood:

> Y allá, en el risueño cementerio de Chimalistac, del pueblecito en que se metió la cuna blanca de Santa, allí la enterraron Hipo y Jenaro, en el simpático cementerio derruido, siempre abierto y siempre aplacible, en cuyos bardales desmoronados, los lagartos toman el sol y corretean, las hormigas trabajan y las abejas anidan; en cuyos árboles copudos y viejos dan sus pájaros moradores, estupendos concertantes de gorjeos (342).

> And there, in the cheerful cemetery of Chimalistac, in the little village where Santa's white cradle was laid down to rest, there Hipólito and Jenaro buried her, in the pleasant, neglected cemetery, always open and always quiet, on whose dilapidated walls the lizards sunbathe and chase one another, the ants work, and the bees build their hives; in whose old and bushy trees the local birds put on outstanding twittering concerts.

At the end of the novel, one finds another trait that sets Gamboa apart from other naturalists such as Crane or Azevedo. In *Maggie*, Crane tells of the girl's suicide, and closes the novel with the terseness and detachment that have come to characterize many of his works, especially his Bowery tales. In *O Cortiço*, the last image of Pombinha stands in stark contrast to that of Maggie. The former is alive, successful, and having a grand time as a prostitute: "Agora as duas cocotas [Pombinha e Léonie] eram vistas por toda parte onde houvesse prazer" (*O Cortiço*

155). [Now the two coquettes Pombinha e Léonie were seen everywhere where there was pleasure]. While it is true that Santa dies, it is not at all in the same way that Maggie does. Between the days when Santa is the toast of her brothel and the time when she finds herself transfigured and abandoned in the most squalid whorehouses of Mexico City, there is a long period of suffering. During this period, Santa reflects on her predicament in a characteristically Catholic fashion. Subsequently, she repents, and thus becomes eligible to receive divine mercy and forgiveness. This clemency is bestowed upon her through Hipólito. As a Christ-figure, the blind piano player suffers his own ordeal. He desires Santa, but refuses to have her in the same way that her customers and lovers do, so that she may be redeemed and saved. To be sure, he rapes her in a fit of rage. Later, however, he acknowledges his dastardly transgression, and eventually earns Santa's trust and affection once again. Gamboa closes the novel with a reference to Hipólito's love for Santa that is at once lyrical and cathartic:

> Y sucedió una vez, cuando Hipólito ya no tenía qué dar a Santa, — ni lágrimas, porque se las había dado todas — que de tanto releer en alta voz el nombre entallado en piedra: ¡Santa! . . . ¡Santa! . . . vínole a los labios, naturalmente, una oración. [A Santa y a Hipólito] sólo les quedaba Dios. ¡Dios queda siempre! Dios recibe entre sus divinos brazos a los desgraciados, a los que apestan y manchan, a . . . los que padecen de hambre y sed de perdón . . . ¡A Dios se asciende por el amor y por el sufrimiento! . . . Y seguro del remedio, radiante, en cruz los brazos y de cara al cielo, encomendó [Hipólito] el alma de la amada, cuyo nombre puso en sus labios la plegaria sencilla, magnífica, excelsa, que nuestras madres nos enseñan cuando niños, y que ni todas las vicisitudes juntas nos hacen olvidar:
>
> Santa María, Madre de Dios, . . . principió muy piano, y el resto de la súplica subió a perderse en la gloria firmamental de la

tarde moribunda:

Ruega, Señora, por nosotros, los pecadores . . . (344-345).

Once, when Hipólito no longer had anything to give Santa — not even tears, because he had shed as many as he could for her — on account of repeatedly reading aloud the name engraved in stone: Santa! . . . Santa! . . . there came to his lips, effortlessly, a prayer. . . . [Hipólito and Santa] had only God to turn to. He is always there [when one needs him]. God receives with open arms the wretched, those who are blighted and tainted, those . . . who yearn for forgiveness. . . . Through love and suffering, one is able to ascend to the kingdom of God! . . . And certain of the power of his prayer, beaming with joy, his arms stretched out in the shape of a cross, and his face turned upward to the heavens, [Hipólito] entrusted the soul of his beloved [to God]. [Santa], whose name placed on his lips the simple, magnificent, and lofty prayer which our mothers teach us when we are young, and which not even the worst vicissitudes can make us forget:

Holy Mary, mother of god, . . . he began very gently, and the rest of his prayer soared up to the heavens, fading away into the celestial glory of that late afternoon:

Pray for us, sinners. . . .

In her article, "Función del prostíbulo en *Santa* y *Juntacadáveres*," Ana María Alvarado touches briefly on Gamboa's use of names and plot developments that have clear religious connotations. The name of the protagonist, Santa [saint], itself is an indication of the extent to which the author is responding to a cultural tradition that places great significance on religion. Even if this religious quality may sometimes manifest itself in the form of irony or criticism toward institutionalized religion, it is nevertheless pervasive throughout the novel. Furthermore, it is used as a positive device to transcend the very predicament and suffering against which it is juxtaposed and by which it is criticized. One of the more charged scenes in *Santa* is the one in which the protagonist tries to go into a church to pray for her dead mother. According to Alvarado, "hay una enorme carga emotiva que se traduce en crítica hacia la iglesia, que condena en vez de salvar, que es su función ante la sociedad."[11] [There is a great deal of emotional tension, which is articulated as criticism toward the church, which condemns when it should rescue, which is its function before society]. *Santa* chronicles in vivid and sometimes shocking detail the descent of this woman "de nombre demasiado simbólico"[12] [with an overtly symbolic name], to present at the end a cathartic denouement in which the protagonist is finally redeemed, forgiven, and at last able to rest:

> En la muerte de Santa, halló Hipólito su purificación. Ella volvió al lugar de partida, lejos de la vida de la ciudad y de la sociedad que corrompen y que tanto mal le habían hecho. . . . Dos veces solamente amó Santa: la primera vez en la inocencia que le abrió las puertas a la realidad de la vida; la segunda en los umbrales de la muerte. El segundo amor le reintegró la pureza que el primero le había quitado. El primero la mancilló, el segundo . . . la adoró como a una santa. Hipólito la redime en la muerte.[13]

> In Santa's death, Hipólito found his purification. She returned to the starting point, far away from city life and the society that corrupt and that had done her so much harm. . . . Only twice did Santa love: the first time with the innocence that opened [her eyes] to the reality of life; the second time just before death. The second love restored to her the purity that the first had taken away. The first crushed her, the second . . . adored her as one would a saint. Hipólito redeems her in death.

Like many of Emilia Pardo Bazán's novels, *Santa* belongs in the general corpus of works that have come to be associated with the "Catholic" Naturalism, sometimes referred to as the "shy" Naturalism, of Spain and Spanish America. We can detect in Gamboa's fiction, as well as in the fiction of most other naturalists in the Hispanic world, a propensity to depict the human drama as something more than just the result of impersonal forces, blind instinct, or unbridled concupiscence. *Santa* is a prime example of a Hispanic naturalistic novel whose language, imagery, and theme at times seem to conspire against the stated goals of the *roman expérimental*, after which it is modeled. In his unwillingness to accept wholeheartedly the idea that the individual is inevitably condemned to a predetermined fate and a life of suffering, Gamboa's loyalty to principles that run counter to naturalistic literary ideology becomes apparent. His brand of naturalistic fiction is unique in the Americas in that with it the author sought to bridge two very different and distant worlds: the intellectual milieu of European letters and the social and religious ambience of his native Mexico, both of which are treated with mastery, candor, and understanding in *Santa*.

Notes

[1] Manuel González, *Trayectoria de la novela en México* (México: Ediciones Botas, 1951) 66-78.

See also Kessel Schwartz, *A New History of Spanish-American Fiction*, vol. 1 (Coral Gables, Florida: University of Miami Press, 1972) 105-106.

[2] González, *Trayectoria* 72.

See also R. Anthony Castagnaro, *The Early Spanish-American Novel* (New York: Las Américas, 1971) 60-61.

[3] Francisco Mena, "Federico Gamboa y el naturalismo, como expresión ideológica y social," *Explicación de textos literarios* 2 (1976): 207-214.

[4] Mena, "Gamboa" 75.

[5] For an assessment of the moralizing strain in *Santa*, see María-Guadalupe García-Barragán, "*Santa*, La novela olvidada que vuelve: Sus símbolos e influencias sobre la literature actual," *Proceedings of the Pacific Northwest Conference on Foreign Languages* 25 (Corvalis: Oregon State University Press, 1974): 184-188. García-Barragán argues that "*Santa* . . . sí es un libro moralizador porque intenta hacer detestar el vicio de la carne mostrando sus terribles estragos morales y físicos en el personaje de la heroína y en su temprana y dolorosa muerte" (184). [*Santa* . . . is indeed a moralizing book because it aims to foment hatred for the sins of the flesh by revealing the terrible moral and physical havoc visited on the protagonist and her early and painful death]. Gamboa himself sheds some light on his intent in *Santa*, when,

quoting a much admired fellow naturalist from France, Edmond de Goncourt, he writes in the preface to his novel that, like Goncourt's *La fille Elise, Santa* is the story of a chaste and innocent girl. To be sure, Gamboa's novel has passages that strike even our post-modern sensibility as erotic and sensational. Yet, as will be demonstrated later, even here the author "guarda cierto recato o discreción aun en las escenas más escabrosas" (184) [maintains a certain modesty or discretion even in the crudest scenes].

See also Seymour Menton, "Federico Gamboa," in *Latin-American Writers*, vol. 1, ed. Carlos A. Solé and Maria Isabel Abreu (New York: Charles Scribner's Sons, 1989) 373. Commenting on *Santa*, Menton observes that "Gamboa's lip service to heredity is totally gratuitous. He would have the reader believe that Santa quickly adjusted to the nocturnal life of Mexico City because of the vice of some unknown ancestor. . . . The novel ends on a religious albeit incongruent note, [and] despite its crude naturalism, *Santa* is an edifying, moral novel" (373).

[6] Federico Gamboa, *Santa* (México: Ediciones Botas, 1960) 67. All subsequent quotations from *Santa* are from this edition. Citations by page number appear in parentheses in the text.

[7] "Poetics," *Crowell's Handbook of Classical Literature*, 1964 ed.

[8] Many Spanish and Spanish-American naturalistic writers had a difficult time reconciling their Christian beliefs with the grim view of the individual in the harsh world of the *roman expérimental*. Federico Gamboa in Mexico and Emilia Pardo Bazán in Spain exemplify perhaps more poignantly than any other novelist of their generation the nature and extent of this dilemma. On the one hand, they embrace willingly the teachings of Zola and the other French naturalists. On the other hand, however, they are unable to let go completely of certain religious beliefs that run counter to naturalistic literary ideology. This tension is apparent in novels such as *Santa* and *Los pazos de Ulloa*. On the question of Spanish and Spanish-American Naturalism vis-à-vis Catholicism and Hispanic culture, see:

M. Gordon Brown, "La condesa de Pardo Bazán y el naturalismo," *Hispania* 31 (1948): 152-156.

Gifford Davis, "The Critical Reception of Naturalism in Spain before *La cuestión palpitante*," *Hispanic Review* 22 (1954): 97-108.

Harry L. Kirby, "Pardo Bazán, Darwinism, and *La madre naturaleza*," *Hispania* 47 (1964): 733-737.

Guillermo Ara, *La novela naturalista hispanoamericana* (Buenos Aires: Eudeba, 1965).

Jorge Campos, "El naturalismo mejicano: Federico Gamboa," *Ínsula* 20 (1965): 21.

Walter Pattison, *El naturalismo español: historia de un movimiento* (Madrid: Gredos, 1965). See especially Chapter 9, "Hacia un naturalismo espiritual" (140-165).

Fernando José Barroso, "La intención naturalista y reformadora en la novelística de Emilia Pardo Bazán," Ph.D. dissertation, University of Virginia, 1970.

Carlos Feal Deibe, "Naturalismo y antinaturalismo en *Los pazos de Ulloa*," *Bulletin of Hispanic Studies* 48 (1971): 314-327.

Alexander Hooker, *La novela de Federico Gamboa* (Madrid: Editorial Playor, 1971) 36.

Fernando Barroso, *El naturalismo de la Pardo Bazán* (Madrid: Playor, 1973).

Gifford Davis, "Catholicism and Naturalism: Pardo Bazán's Reply to Zola," *Modern Language Notes* 90 (1975): 282-287.

Emilio González López, "Doña Emilia Pardo Bazán y el naturalismo español en la narrativa: *Los pazos de Ulloa, La madre naturaleza, Un destripador de antaño* y otros cuentos," *Sin Nombre* 7 (1976): 62-67.

Michael E. Gerli, "Apropos of Naturalism and Regionalism in *Los pazos de Ulloa*," *South Atlantic Bulletin* 42 (1977): 55-60.

Mariano López, "Naturalismo y espiritualismo en *Los pazos de Ulloa*," *Revista de Estudios Hispánicos* 12 (1978): 353-371.

Ana María Alvarado, "Función del prostíbulo en *Santa* y *Juntacadáveres*," *Hispanic Journal* 2 (1980): 57-68.

Maurice Hemingway, "Grace, Nature, Naturalism, and Pardo Bazán," *Forum for Modern Language Studies* 16 (1980): 341-349.

R. C. Boland, "The Antithesis Between Religion and Nature in *Los pazos de Ulloa*: A Different Perspective," *Revista Canadiense de Estudios Hispánicos* 5 (1981): 209-215.

Maurice Hemingway, *Emilia Pardo Bazán: The Making of a Novelist* (Cambridge: Cambridge University Press, 1983).

David Goldin, "The Metaphor of Original Sin: A Key to Pardo Bazán's Catholic Naturalism," *Philological Quarterly* 64 (1985): 37-53.

João Sedycias, "Crane, Azevedo, and Gamboa: A Comparative Study," Ph.D. dissertation, State University of New York at Buffalo, 1985.

Mercedes Tasende-Grabowski, "Otra vez a vueltas con el naturalismo," *Hispania* 74 (1991): 26-35.

[9] John Englekirk, ed., *An Outline History of Spanish-American Literature* (New York: Appleton-Century-Crofts, 1965) 90.

[10] Hooker, *Novela* 36.

[11] Alvarado, "Función" 57-68.

[12] Alvarado, "Función" 60.

[13] Alvarado, "Función" 61.

Part Two

A Girardian Exegesis of the *Roman Expérimental*

Chapter 4

René Girard and the Concept of Mimetic Desire

Maggie, *O Cortiço*, and *Santa* are naturalistic novels ostensibly concerned with questions of survival. They deal with the dilemmas confronting members of the lower class, and seek to analyze objectively and truthfully the darkest aspects of their characters' lives. All three novels demonstrate the subordinate relation of the individual to his or her social and physical environment, and depict human free will as having little bearing on the characters' destinies.

The naturalistic novel, in Europe as well as in the Americas, has historically been viewed as a literary genre that does not offer scope for great depth of characterization. In principle, the *roman expérimental* is not expected to dwell on the psychology of its characters nor serve as the medium for introspection or metaphysical exploration.[1] Yet, *Maggie*, *O Cortiço*, and *Santa* do reveal a metaphysical dimension, and owe much of their appeal to the conflictive and, at times, violent dynamics of complex psychological structures. Foremost among these structures are several love triangles, or situations involving three or more characters, all vying for a common object of desire. These situations are presented in various configurations and with varying degrees of virulence and intensity. An exploration of the mechanics of these triangles and the role that they play in *Maggie*, *O Cortiço*, and *Santa* will shed light on some important aspects of these novels. Literary and psychological constructs such as Denis de Rougemont's concept of passionate love[2] and René Girard's theory of mimetic desire[3] can be used profitably in an interpretation of Crane, Azevedo, and Gamboa as we seek to open a new avenue into the origins and development of the crises that figure so prominently in New World naturalistic fiction.

As I have stated in the preface, the critical approach used in this study combines René Girard's theory of mimetic desire with a traditional examination of language, theme, and structure.[4] While the precepts associated with the traditional analysis of character and plot should be familiar to most readers,[5] Girard's theory may not. Therefore, this chapter is devoted to an analysis of his theory of mimetic desire. Included in this analysis is a review of ancillary material that relates to Girard's model such as Rougemont's notion of passionate love and Freud's formulation of human desire in terms of postponement and obstruction.

At the heart of Girard's theory is the concept of mimetic desire, which he describes as a desire based on someone else's desire. In a mimetic triangle, the individual who desires (i.e., the subject) takes interest in certain objects only because he believes these objects to be desired by somebody else (i.e., the mediator, also referred to as the Other). Here, an individual's desire is defined according to another, as opposed to a desire according to oneself. The subject's aim is to usurp the qualities associated with another (the mediator) who is regarded as having the spontaneity and independence which the subject treasures and wants for himself. Mimetic or mediated desire is never expressed as a linear or simple movement of a subject toward a desired object. By coveting the object of another's desire, the subject seeks to appropriate the greater autonomy that he perceives in this Other (the mediator) who becomes his role model. He tries to accomplish this appropriation by desiring what the model desires and by wanting to possess what the model possesses. Girard points out that there is an unmediated variant of desire, which he calls love-passion, but he makes clear the distinction between the two forms:

> Passion . . . is the opposite of vanity. . . . The passionate person . . . is distinguished by his emotional autonomy, by the spontaneity of his desires, by his absolute indifference to the opinion of Others. The passionate person draws the strength of his desire from within himself and not from Others. . . . True love . . . does not transfigure. The qualities which this love discovers in its object, the happiness it expects from it, are not illusory. Love-passion is always accompanied by esteem. . . . It is based on a perfect agreement among reason, will, and sensibility (19).

According to Girard, all forms of desire other than unmediated love-passion originate in another desire: "at the origin of a desire there is always the spectacle of another real or illusory desire" (105). The mimetic triangle usually develops around an object of desire that in the eyes of the subject and mediator is at once unique and alluring. The special qualities of this object are not so much attributes of the object proper but rather its uniqueness is determined by the position that the object occupies in the mimetic structure vis-à-vis the other two players. The triangle that gives rise to mediated desire does not have an ontological reality of its own. The structures that make up the triangle are not integrated into a uniform unit, in the way of a gestalt. Rather, these structures are inter-subjective, and, as such, cannot be localized. In effect, the triangle has no reality independent of the interpersonal tensions that give rise to it. It is, as Girard puts it, a "systematic metaphor, systematically pursued" (2).

In *Deceit, Desire, and the Novel*, Girard sketches a brief history of desire and comments on the way in which passion has affected society and has been perceived by men and women throughout the ages. He criticizes the modernist notion of individual autonomy and spontaneity of desire, and locates our age at a dangerous crossroads. William Johnsen sums up Girard's position thus:

> In the world before the Enlightenment man openly copied the desires of models who inhabited the transcendent world of the gods, royalty, or literature. The crisis of modernism is the promethean promise to deliver autonomy from the gods, mediators external to man's world, unto man himself. Each subject privately discovers that he is no god, but blames himself, not the promise. He feels that he alone is incapable of autonomy, and must therefore secretly imitate [what he believes to be] the autonomous desires of Others, masking his discipleship as an originality powerful enough to enslave others. The illusion of divine autonomy promised to an enlightened world is thus perpetuated; men become gods in the eyes of each other, while remaining disciples in their own eyes.[6]

Girard identifies the main character in Cervantes's *Don Quijote* as the archetypal hero whose individuality has been relinquished to his model, the mediator of his desire. In the case of don Quijote, his model is the great hero of chivalric romances, Amadis of Gaul. As Girard observes:

> Don Quijote has surrendered to Amadis the individual's fundamental prerogative: he no longer chooses the objects of his own desire — Amadis must choose for him. [In *Don Quijote*], the disciple pursues objects which are determined for him by . . . the mediator of [his] desire (1-2).

In addition to origin, another central element in Girard's theoretical construct is the notion of rivalry and conflict. The distance between subject, mediator, and object of desire determines whether their relationship is one of reverence and peace or contempt and turmoil. The smaller the space separating subject and mediator, the greater the chances for rivalry and violence between the two. Working from this premise, Girard divides mimetic desire into two kinds, one based on *external* and another based on *internal* mediation. External mediation involves a situation in which the distance between subject and mediator is sufficient to eliminate the possibility of contact and strife between the two. Internal mediation, on the other hand, refers to a volatile state of affairs where this distance is small enough to allow for subject and mediator to come in contact and, consequently, for rivalry and violence to arise. However, the strife between subject and mediator does not ensue because of proximity alone. Girard accounts for the appearance of violence as the result of two separate but related actions. First, he notes that the mediator becomes an obstacle to the subject as the subject seeks to appropriate those objects that he finds desirable:

> In most . . . desires, the mediator himself desires the object, or could desire it: it is even this very desire, real or presumed, which makes this object infinitely desirable in the eyes of the subject. The mediation begets a second desire exactly the same as the mediator's. This means that one is always confronted with two competing desires. The mediator can no longer act his role of model without also acting or appearing to act the role of obstacle. Like the relentless sentry of the Kafka fable, the model shows his disciple the gate of paradise and forbids him to enter with one and the same gesture (7).
>
> The impulse toward the object is ultimately an impulse toward the mediator; in internal mediation this impulse is checked by the mediator himself since he desires, or perhaps possess, the object. Fascinated by his model, the disciple inevitably sees, in the mechanical obstacle which he puts in his way, proof of the ill will borne him. Far from declaring himself a faithful vassal, he thinks

only of repudiating the bonds of mediation. But these bonds are stronger than ever, for the mediator's apparent hostility does not diminish his prestige but instead augments it. The subject is convinced that the model considers himself too superior to accept him as a disciple. The subject is torn between two opposing feelings toward his model — the most submissive reverence and the most intense malice. This is the passion we call *hatred*.

Only someone who prevents us from satisfying a desire which he himself has inspired in us is truly an object of hatred. The person who hates first hates himself for the secret admiration concealed by his hatred. In an effort to hide his desperate admiration from others, and from himself, he no longer wants to see in his mediator anything but an obstacle. The secondary role of the mediator thus becomes primary, concealing his original function of a model scrupulously imitated.

In the quarrel which puts him in opposition to his rival, the subject reverses the logical and chronological order of desires in order to hide his imitation. He asserts that his own desire is prior to that of his rival; according to him it is the mediator who is responsible for the rivalry. Everything that originates with this mediator is systematically belittled although still secretly desired. Now the mediator is a shrewd and diabolical enemy; he tries to rob the subject of his most prized possessions; he obstinately thwarts his most legitimate ambitions (10).

The rivalry between subject and mediator intensifies as the distance between the three corners of the triangle decreases. This situation is further compounded by what Girard calls double mediation, a state of affairs in which subject and mediator can exchange places without causing any change in the mimetic structure itself. In double mediation, the actions of one are mirrored and repeated in the moves of the other:

The closer the mediator gets to the desiring subject, the more the possibilities of the rivals merge and the more insuperable becomes the obstacle they set in each other's way (26).

Metaphysical desire is always contagious. It becomes even more so as the mediator draws nearer to the hero. Contagion and proximity are, after all, one and the same phenomenon. Internal mediation is present when one "catches" a nearby desire just as one would catch the plague or cholera, simply by contact with an infected person. In the world of internal mediation, the contagion is so widespread that everyone can become his neighbor's mediator without ever understanding the role he is playing. This person who is a mediator without realizing it may himself be incapable of spontaneous desire. Thus he will be tempted to copy the copy of his own desire. What was for him in the beginning only a whim is now transformed into a violent passion. We all know that every desire redoubles when it is seen to be shared. Two identical but opposite triangles are thus superimposed on each other. Desire circulates between the two rivals more and more quickly, and with every cycle it increases in intensity like the electric current in a battery which is being charged. We now have a subject-mediator and a mediator-subject, a model-disciple and a disciple-model. . . . Each imitates the other while claiming that his own desire is prior and previous. Each looks on the other as an atrociously cruel persecutor. All the relationships are symmetrical; the two partners believe themselves separated by a bottomless abyss but there is nothing we can say of one which is not equally true of the other. There is a sterile opposition of contraries, which becomes more and more atrocious and empty as the two subjects approach each other and as their desires intensify (99-100).

Because the subject and the mediator eventually vie for the same object, the mediator is unable to play the role of instigator of desire without also acting as obstacle to the subject that he mediates. His is a dual role. He is both the model that the subject admires and the hated rival that stands in the subject's way. The relationship between the two is at once ambivalent and contentious. Because of decreasing distances, mimetic desire is bound to intensify to mimetic rivalry. The closer the two subject-mediators get, the more forcefully they try to convince themselves that their relationship to the object of desire is independent of the rival. As long as they believe in the spontaneity and chronological priority of their desire over the other, they will find themselves trapped in a violent reciprocity. They can only become more like each other as they try to assimilate the illusion of each other's superior difference:

> The players are *partners*, but they only agree to disagree. . . . Each one holds the Other responsible for the misfortunes which falls upon him. This is truly double mediation, equal cause of suffering for all; it is a sterile conflict from which the players, who have come together of their own accord, cannot withdraw (103).
>
> The more intense the hatred the nearer it brings us to the loathed rival. Everything it suggests to one, it suggests equally to the other, including the desire to *distinguish oneself* at all costs (100).

The more they try to distinguish themselves from their rival, the more the two subject-mediators come to resemble each other. They are consumed by the same self-defeating mission. The model becomes an obstacle, though without ceasing to be the arbiter and instigator of the subject's desire. Actually, the subject grows more fascinated as the model becomes a greater obstacle. And the greater this fascination, the more the model becomes associated as an obstacle and, by extension, with the desired object. Expounding on a central theme in Rougemont's *Love in the Western World*, Cesáreo Bandera points out that the subject of desire grows more passionate about those objects that are denied him than about those that are not. The harder it is for the subject to get to the object of his desire, the more ardently he will long for it. Ultimately, the subject will strive toward an object infinitely removed from him, because only there can such an object shine in its infinite splendor. However, that infinite distance is at the same time an insurmountable obstruction.[7] The more difficult the obstacle separating subject and object, or lover and beloved, the more it is preferred. The insurmountable barrier that the subject seeks is the most suited for intensifying passion. At this extreme, Rougemont notes, the subject's wish to be parted from the object of his desire assumes an emotional value greater than passion itself.[8] Other students of human psychology, such as Sigmund Freud, have also taken note of the problematic position of desire vis-à-vis obstructions that play the dual role of intensifying and at the same time thwarting passion. In his article "On the Universal Tendency to Debasement in the Sphere of Love," Freud argues that

> The psychical value of erotic needs is reduced as soon as their satisfaction becomes easy. An obstacle is required in order to heighten libido; and where natural resistances to satisfaction have not been sufficient, men have at all times erected conventional ones so as to be able to enjoy love. This is true both of individuals and of nations. In times during which there were no difficulties standing in the way of sexual satisfaction, such as perhaps during the decline of the ancient civilizations, love became worthless and life empty, and strong reaction-formations were required to restore indispensable affective values. In this connection it may be claimed that the ascetic current in Christianity created psychical values for love which pagan antiquity was never able to confer on it. This current assumed its greatest importance with the ascetic monks, whose lives were almost entirely occupied with the struggle against libidinal temptation.[9]

Like Girard's model of mimetic desire, Rougemont's notion of passionate love involves a longing that thrives on want, postponement, and incompletion. In both cases, the obstacle separating subject and object of desire is arbitrary. It is often an imagined wall created by the subject in order to heighten his own passion. Rougemont contends that it is the arbitrary character of the obstructions introduced into a work of fiction that shows what that work is really about. The events narrated are but images or projections of a longing and of the obstacles in the plot that run counter to this longing. The intensity of the subject's passion is directly proportional to the magnitude of the obstacle that he sets in his own way. There is a point in the development of this kind of desire in which the obstruction that the subject creates no longer is used simply to stir up passion but becomes in itself the goal pursued for its own sake. Taken to its logical conclusion, we can see that the obstacles that the subject seeks and by which his desire is intensified point to an implicit wish to die.   Death, more than any other stumbling block, is the insurmountable obstacle *par excellence.* Death represents the absolute obstruction, and at the same holds the irresistible promise of total passionate bliss and transfiguration. Also, as the ultimate and unstated goal of passion, death kills desire in a final act of simultaneous fulfillment and destruction.[10] Thus, it is not surprising that most of the great love stories of the West should end in death. *La Celestina* (the story of Calisto and Melibea), *Tristan and Iseult,* and *Romeo and Juliet* all deal with the themes of transfiguring passion and death, and lend themselves particularly well to an exegesis of the kind proposed by Rougemont. These are only three in a long list of works characteristic of a genre that figures prominently in all Western literatures:

> One thing the tremendous vogue of romantic novels makes
> immediately clear: the chord that awakens in us the most sonorous
> echoes, has for its tonic and dominant, so to speak, the words

"love" and "death." . . . Happy love has no history. Romance only comes into existence where love is fatal, frowned upon and doomed by life itself. What stirs lyrical poets to their finest flights is neither the delight of the senses nor the fruitful contentment of the settled couple; not the satisfaction of love, but its passion. And passion means suffering.[11]

Rougemont's construct is useful to the student of literature and psychology because it addresses and formalizes the fascination that the lovers have for each other, and, more importantly, for love itself. They are consumed by a desire that rules their lives and compels them to act against reason. This passion eventually causes their death. Rougemont cautions that "to love passion for its own sake has been to love to suffer and to court suffering. . . . Hardly anything could be more tragic [than a desire] that sears us and annihilates in its triumph."[12] In Girard's model as well as in Rougemont's, the reader comes face to face with a fascination so fierce and irrational as to verge on the pathological. Girard describes the impasses that the two subject-mediators bring upon each other as "una especie de nudo corredizo en que el deseo se ahoga y que el mismo aprieta sin cesar"[13] [a kind of hangman's noose with which desire strangles itself and which it itself tightens relentlessly]. Focusing on the pathological nature of the disorder that besets the two rivals, Girard observes:

A la conversión del modelo en obstáculo sucede la conversión del obstáculo en modelo, una verdadera pasión por el obstáculo, lo que la psiquiatría llama masoquismo, que se agranda, se invierte, se redobla y se exaspera en la difuminación [sic] cada vez más completa del objeto y en la creciente reciprocidad de ambos mediadores-obstáculos, los dobles.[14]

The conversion of model into obstacle is followed by the

transformation of obstacle into model, a real passion for the obstacle, what in psychiatry is called masochism, [an obsession] that grows more acute, reverses itself, intensifies, and despairs at the increasingly more complete stumping of the object and at the growing reciprocity of both mediator-obstacles, the doubles.

If the subject of mimetic desire is able to recognize the role that imitation plays in the birth and development of his passions, he may be able to free himself from the bonds of mediation by renouncing either the desire itself or his pride. If he refuses to renounce either, Girard notes, then the disease that afflicts the subject grows more serious as the distance between himself and his mediator diminishes:

> The ontological sickness grows more and more serious as the mediator approaches the desiring subject. Its natural end is death. The power of pride cannot but end in the fragmentation and ultimately in the complete disintegration of the subject. The very desire to unify oneself disperses, and here we have arrived at the definitive dispersion. The contradictions caused by internal mediation end by destroying the individual. Masochism is followed by the last stage of metaphysical desire, that of self-destruction, physical self-destruction (279).

Elaborating further on a point explicated in Rougemont's pioneering study on love in the West, Girard asserts that the truth about desire is not to be found in any grandiose, romantic fulfillment of its goals. Rather, this truth manifests itself in death:

> The truth of metaphysical desire is death. This is the inevitable end of the contradiction on which that desire is based. Novels are full of signs announcing death. But the signs remain ambiguous so long as the prophecy is not fulfilled. As soon as death is present it lights

up the path behind it; it enriches our interpretation of the mediated structure; it gives their full meaning to the many aspects of metaphysical desire (282).

However, Girard maintains that while mimetic desire in literary fiction eventually leads to death when it is allowed to run its full course, death is not necessarily the ultimate message of the novel.[15] To be sure, in the case of the subject who refuses to renounce his desire or his pride, death becomes the only alternative. But it is in death that he is able to put an end to his agony:

> The ultimate meaning of desire is death but death is not the novel's ultimate meaning. The demons like raving madmen throw themselves into the sea and perish. But the patient is cured (290).

It is at the time of death that the subject is at last set free from mimetic desire. According to Girard, it is at this point, when the subject is face to face with his demise, that he recants his pathological longing and his pride. He withdraws from the lie of mimetic desire, and by doing so adds to what Girard calls "the unity of novelistic conclusions." Having renounced desire and repudiated his mediator, the subject is able at last to set himself free:

> Repudiation of the mediator implies renunciation of divinity, and this means renouncing pride. The physical diminution of the hero both expresses and conceals the defeat of pride. . . . In renouncing divinity the hero renounces slavery. Every level of his existence is inverted, all the effects of metaphysical desire are replaced by contrary effects. Deception gives way to truth, anguish to remembrance, agitation to repose, hatred to love, humiliation to humility, mediated desire to autonomy, deviated transcendency to vertical transcendency. This time it is not a false but a genuine

conversion. The hero triumphs because he is at the end of his resources; for the first time he has to look his despair and his nothingness in the face. But this look which he has dreaded, which is the death of pride, is his salvation (294).

Based on this view of desire, Girard divides works of fiction into two distinct categories. The first group comprises those works that reveal the imitative nature of desire and the role that mimetic desire plays in literature. The second group encompasses those works that only reflect the presence of mimetic desire, without disclosing much about its nature. To Girard, "novelistic" works are superior to their romantic counterparts because they are able to tell the truth about mimetic desire and about literary fiction itself. In this light, literature is viewed as a potent drug. It addicts and deceives when it only reflects mediation but sets one free from the illusions of mimetic desire when it reveals the truth of mediation. The dynamics of concealment and disclosure figure prominently in literature, and are central to Girard's model as well. By using and exposing mimetic desire, "novelistic" works of fiction are able to tell less of a lie than their romantic counterparts. They do this by not attempting to disguise the purely rhetorical nature of the devices that they use to reveal the truth of mediation. Commenting on Cervantes's *Don Quijote*, Bandera provides an insightful examination of the problem of concealment and disclosure of desire in literature. Bandera compares literary fiction to historical discourse, and questions whether the two are able to convey the same truth:

> The individual imagination of the author originates in and is a function of a rather intricate network of interpersonal relationships to which it always points and which it inevitably assumes. No imaginary or fictional point of view is ever spontaneously generated, it is always determined, either positively or negatively,

by other points of view. Literary fiction does not reflect true reality . . . but only a historical reality that has already been fictionalized, where people are already fighting over points of view, which are not real points of view . . . but only desires nourished and kept alive by the fighting itself. In other words, literary fiction only reflects the historical precondition of its own existence. In the mirror that it holds up to history only its own image is reflected. Therefore, although the fiction inevitably lies, the lie it tells is our own lie. In this sense, and only in this sense, it tells the truth.[16]

Here, Bandera is referring to "novelistic" fiction when he states that literature can tell the truth, this truth being that of the mechanism of desire. However, Girard is quick to point out that only a few novelists are able to grasp the true nature of desire, and even fewer succeed in revealing its mimetic mechanism in their fiction. In most works of fiction, one does not encounter the same degree of complexity and disclosure found in "novelistic" writers such as Cervantes or Dostoyevsky. This is usually the case when the author is only able to reflect the presence of mimetic desire and does not have either the artistic ability or the psychological wherewithal to reveal it in its entirety. This also happens when the writer's perception of desire is still formulated in terms of subject and object alone.

Girard's examination of the theme of desire in literature has been hailed as one of the most innovative models in literary analysis in the last few decades. His theory is particularly germane to psychological approaches to the novel and the comparative study of the themes of eros and thanatos. As the following chapters will show, the models proposed by Rougemont and Girard lend themselves particularly well to an interpretation of *Maggie, O Cortiço,* and *Santa* because they treat and cogently formalize the desire at the heart of many of the conflicts and crises in these three novels.

Notes

¹ Olívio Montenegro, *O romance brasileiro: As suas origens e tendências* (Rio de Janeiro: José Olympio, 1938) 63-64.

Malcolm Cowley, "'Not Men': A Natural History of American Naturalism," *The Kenyon Review* 9 (1947): 414-435.

Rod Horton and Herbert Edwards, *Backgrounds of American Literary Thought* (New York: Appleton-Century-Crofts, 1952) 246-247.

José Osório de Oliveira, *História breve da literatura brasileira* (Lisboa: Editorial Verbo, 1964) 93.

Guillermo Ara, *La novela naturalista hispanoamericana* (Buenos Aires: Eudeba, 1965) 56.

Sérgio Milliet, introduction, *O cortiço*, by Aluísio Azevedo (São Paulo: Livraria Martins Editora, 1967) 14.

Sydney Krause, "The Surrealism of Crane's Naturalism in *Maggie*," *American Literary Realism* 16 (1983) 253.

² Denis de Rougemont, *Love in the Western World*, trans. Montgomery Belgion (Princeton, New Jersey: Princeton University Press, 1983). Rougemont's landmark study on love in the West was originally published in Paris as *L'amour et l'occident* in 1939, and was subsequently translated into English and published in the U.S. as *Love in the Western World* in 1940.

See also Denis de Rougemont, *Love Declared: Essays on the Myths of Love*, trans. Richard Howard (New York: Pantheon Books, 1963).

³ René Girard, *Deceit, Desire, and the Novel: Self and Other in Literary Structure*, trans. Yvonne Freccero (Baltimore, Maryland: Johns Hopkins Uni-

versity Press, 1980). All subsequent quotations from *Deceit, Desire, and the Novel* are from this edition. Citations by page number appear in parentheses in the text.

See also Ruth El Saffar, "Unbinding the Doubles: Reflections on Love and Culture in the Work of René Girard," *Denver Quarterly* 18 (1984): 6-22. In this cogent treatment of the question of love and culture in post-structuralist literary criticism, Ruth El Saffar, arguably one of Girard's most rigorous and insightful critics, remarks that she has been following closely Girard's work for the past twenty years because "it addresses powerfully and insightfully the issues of our times" (6). El Saffar points out that "Girard's emphasis on literature as vital, revelatory, expressive not just of its own internal coherences or of a particular author's time and place, but of essential human structures, has always seemed salubrious [and] bracing." Also, El Saffar has found Girard's reading of the literary work "as a vehicle of discovery for the author as well as for the reader" both cogent and engaging (6).

Recent critics who have used Girard's models of mimetic desire and ritual violence in their analyses of literature and culture include Cesáreo Bandera, "Cervantes frente a don Quijote: violenta simetría entre la realidad y la ficción," *Modern Language Notes* 89 (1974): 159-172.

Cesáreo Bandera, "Literature and Desire: Poetic Frenzy and the Love Potion," *Mosaic* 8 (1975): 33-52.

Cesáreo Bandera, *Mímesis conflictiva* (Madrid: Gredos, 1975).

Cesáreo Bandera, "Conflictive Versus Cooperative Mimesis: A Reply to Ciriaco Morón-Arroyo," *Diacritics* 9 (1979): 62-70.

Cesáreo Bandera, "Cervantes's *Quijote* and the Critical Illusion," *Modern Language Notes* 94 (1979): 702-719.

Alan Williams, "Deceit, Desire, and Film Narrative," *Cine-Tracts* 4 (1981): 38-49.

David Savran, "The Girardian Economy of Desire: Old Times Recaptured," *Theatre Journal* 34 (1982): 40-54.

Bruce Bassoff, *The Secret Sharers: Studies in Contemporary Fictions* (New York: AMS Press, 1983).

Jostein Boertnes, "The Last Delusion in an Infinite Series of Delusions:

Stavrogin and the Symbolic Structure of *The Devils*," *Dostoyevsky Studies* 4 (1983): 53-67.

Douglas B. Wilson, "The Commerce of Desire: Freudian Narcissism in Chaucer's *Troilus and Cryseyde* and Shakespeare's *Troilus and Cressida*," *English Language Notes* 21 (1983): 11-22.

Robin Beaty, "The Dissenter's Search for the 'Unknown Desire': Romantic Denial and Novelistic Truth in the Novels of D. H. Lawrence," Ph.D. dissertation, Rutgers University, 1984.

Vincent P. Ciminna, "Violence and Sacrifice: An Analysis of Girard's Interpretation of Ritual Action," Ph.D. dissertation, New York University, 1984.

Beatrice Marie, "*Emma* and the Democracy of Desire," *Studies in the Novel* 17 (1985): 1-13.

João Sedycias, "Crane, Azevedo, and Gamboa: A Comparative Study," Ph.D. dissertation, State University of New York at Buffalo, 1985.

Victor L. Tremblay, "Structures mythiques du romanesque traditionnel dans la littérature québécoise: Application psycho-sociale et littéraire des théories de René Girard, de Gilbert Durand, et de Mikhael Bakhtine," Ph.D. dissertation, University of British Columbia, 1985.

Charles R. McCreary, "L'échange et le désir: Une analyse de quatre pièces de Racine," Ph.D. dissertation, Northwestern University, 1986.

Timothy J. Mitchell, "Scapegoating and Sociocentrism in the Folk Rituals of Spain," Ph.D. dissertation, State University of New York at Buffalo, 1986.

D. S. Neff, "Two Into Three Won't Go: Mimetic Desire and the Dream of Androgeny in *Dancing in the Dark*," *Modern Fiction Studies* 34 (1988): 387-403.

João Sedycias, "Violent Symmetries: Self and Other in Aluísio Azevedo," in *Studies in Modern and Classical Languages and Literatures I*, ed. Fidel López Criado (Madrid: Orígenes, 1987): 83-90.

Debra D. Andrist, *Deceit Plus Desire Equals Violence: A Girardian Study of the Spanish Comedia* (New York: Peter Lang, 1989).

James G. Williams, *The Bible, Violence, and the Sacred: Liberation from the Myth of Sanctioned Violence* (San Francisco: Harper and Row, 1991).

Robert Hamerton-Kelly, *Sacred Violence: The Hermeneutic of the Cross in the Theology of Paul* (Minneapolis, Minnesota: Fortress Press, 1992).

[4] The interpretive model used in the second part of my study is derived almost entirely from Girard's first book dealing with mimetic desire, *Mesonge romantique et vérité romanesque*, originally published in Paris in 1961 and subsequently translated into English and published in the U.S. as *Deceit, Desire, and the Novel: Self and Other in Literary Structure* in 1965. Later works by Girard that concentrate on culture and violence, such as *Violence et le sacré* (Paris, 1972) and *Des choses cachées depuis la fondation du monde* (Paris, 1978) [published respectively in the U.S. as *Violence and the Sacred* (1977) and *Things Hidden Since the Foundation of the World* (1987)], *To Double Business Bound: Essays on Literature, Mimesis, and Anthropology* (1978), and *The Scapegoat* (1986) were not included in the present study because, to me, they represent a departure from Girard's earlier criticism, and illustrate the point at which his system appears to break down.

See also Richard Macksey, review of *A Theater of Envy: William Shakespeare*, by René Girard, *Modern Language Notes* 106 (1991): 1118-1121. With the possible exception of his most recent book, *A Theater of Envy: William Shakespeare* (1991), which marks the critic's return to the analysis of canonical literature, much of the criticism that Girard has produced since the publication of *Deceit, Desire, and the Novel* deals with the origins and dynamics of human culture, specifically with myth, violence, and the scapegoat mechanism. In his review of *A Theater of Envy*, Richard Macksey observes that "among literary critics . . . the complaints are often that [Girard] has . . . ceased to 'do literature' . . . [that] he has betrayed the specificity of literature and, by insisting on its referentiality and explanatory function, abandoned the 'text'" (119).

Hayden White, "Ethnological 'Lie' and Mythological 'Truth'," *Diacritics* 8 (1978): 2-9.

Hans Kellner, "Triangular Anxieties: The Present State of European Intellectual History," in *Modern European Intellectual History*, ed. Dominick LaCapra and Steven Kaplan (Ithaca, New York: Cornell University Press,

1982): 111-136.

Toril Moi, "The Missing Mother: The Oedipal Rivalries of René Girard," *Diacritics* 12 (1982): 21-31.

El Saffar, "Unbinding the Doubles." Most of all, Girard has been criticized for turning wistfully to a supposedly more stable "scientific" foothold in his attempt to legitimize the historical and anthropological applications of certain key theoretical constructs expounded in *Violence and the Sacred, Things Hidden Since the Foundation of the World, To Double Business Bound,* and *The Scapegoat.* Along with Hans Kellner, Toril Moi, and Ruth El Saffar, Hayden White has provided one of the more exacting and perspicacious readings of Girardian criticism to date. White criticizes Girard for assuming that history or science can afford a secure base on which to stand in the intricate endeavor of interpreting literary texts. History, White contends, cannot be used legitimately as background or context by the literary critic, just as the "truths" gleaned from literary texts do not provide sufficiently solid grounds from which to launch an authoritative commentary on anthropology, history, human behavior, or politics, as Girard has attempted to do. However, this is not to say that literary fiction is produced and survives in a vacuum, without any connection to the culture, life, or times of the author. On the contrary, literature reflects in its own unique way certain relevant aspects of the personal and cultural milieu out of which it is born. Conversely, history, anthropology, or psychology can aid in our understanding of literary texts, but not to the extent that Girard boldly claims in his later work.

In his article "Triangular Anxieties: The Present State of European Intellectual History," Kellner points out that the tacit claim that the individual text, which is inherently problematic, can be explained by an allegedly more secure historical or scientific context is central to Girard's concept of communal rivalry and violence (133). This claim, Kellner charges, is fallacious. White, too, correctly argues in his article "Ethnological 'Lie' and Mythical 'Truth'" that "it is one thing to interpret literary texts and quite another to purport to construct a comprehensive philosophy of history and theory of society, laying claim to the authority of science, as Girard has done. This is not because literature inhabits a realm of fantasy and history is comprised of facts, or because art is one thing and society another. Rather, it is because our interpretations of history and society can claim no more authority than our interpretations of literature can claim" (9). Kellner concurs with White and buttresses White's position by demonstrating that the above passage "makes plain the illegitimacy of using the *product* of an allegorizing process as the scientific foothold for another allegorizing process" (134). The point here, Kellner maintains, is not that literary interpretation is somehow less authoritative than historical or scientific discourse or that it lacks standards of choice. Rather, it is that "Girard has failed to face the consequences of allegory, and instead is trying to escape into a 'reality' of 'context.' . . . What [Girard] assumes to be [his] secure foothold is itself an allegorical construction" (134). Girard seems to be unable, or unwilling, to self-consciously demonstrate "the allegorical base upon which [he] envisions the process of interpretive reading erecting itself" (134).

For further criticism of Girard's theories and applied criticism, see Robert J. Nelson, "Ritual Reality, Tragic Imitation, Mythic Prayer," *Diacritics* 6 (1976): 41-48.

Paul Dumouchel, *L'enfer des choses: René Girard et la logique de l'économie* (Paris: Seuil, 1979).

William Johnsen, "René Girard and the Boundaries of Modern Literature," *Boundary 2* 94 (1979): 277-288.

Ciriaco Morón-Arroyo, "Cooperative Mimesis: Don Quixote and Sancho Panza," *Diacritics* 8 (1978): 75-86.

Ciriaco Morón-Arroyo, "On Cervantes and Calderón: A Repl(a)y," *Diacritics* 9 (1979): 71-79.

François Chirpaz, *Enjeux la violence: Essai sur René Girard* (Paris: Cerf, 1980).

Thomas Jeffers, "Violence is *Our* Property: The New Work of René Girard," *The Michigan Quarterly Review* 19 (1980): 421-426.

Sarah Kofman, "The Narcissistic Woman: Freud and Girard," *Diacritics* 10 (1980): 36-45.

Michel Deguy and Jean-Pierre Dupuy, eds., *René Girard et le problème du mal* (Paris: B. Grasset, 1982).

Jean-Baptiste Fages, *Comprendre René Girard* (Toulouse: Privat, 1982).

William E. Cain, *The Crisis in Criticism: Theory, Literature, and Reform in English Studies* (Baltimore, Maryland: Johns Hopkins University Press, 1984) 224-229.

Alberto Carrara, *Violenza, sacro, rivelazione biblica: il pensiero di René Girard* (Milano: Vita e Pensiero, 1985).

Paul Dumouchel, *Violence et vérité autour de René Girard* (Paris: B. Grasset, 1985).

Christine Orsini, *La pensée de René Girard* (Paris: Editions Retz, 1986).

Paul Dumouchel, ed., *Violence and Truth: On the Work of René Girard* (Stanford, California: Stanford University Press, 1988).

Paisley Livingston, *Models of Desire: René Girard and the Psychology of Mimesis* (Baltimore, Maryland: Johns Hopkins University Press, 1992).

Andrew J. McKenna, *Violence and Difference: Girard, Derrida, and Deconstruction* (Urbana: University of Illinois Press, 1992).

[5] "Explication," *Dictionary of World Literary Terms*, 1970 ed. While not being an *explication de texte* in the strict sense of the word, the critical method used in the first part of my study has a good deal in common with this literary approach, which is defined as "a detailed examination and explanation of a work, or of a minute passage thereof. It may seek to elucidate the author's meaning, as by clearing away difficulties, or to disclose latent meanings, perhaps not conscious in the author or fresh for the critic's time. Partly a practice carried over from the study of works in a foreign language, or the French *explication de texte*, it was given prominence in the New Criticism" (110).

See also "Explication de texte," *A Handbook to Literature*, 1985 ed.

Wilfred L. Guerin, *A Handbook of Critical Approaches to Literature* (New York: Harper and Row, 1979) chapters 1 and 2.

[6] Johnsen, "Boundaries" 278.

[7] Bandera, "Frenzy" 42.

[8] Rougemont, *Love in the Western World* 44.

[9] Sigmund Freud, "On the Universal Tendency to Debasement in the Sphere of Love," *The Standard Edition of the Complete Psychological Works of Sigmund Freud*, vol. 11, trans. Alan Tyson (London: Hogarth Press, 1975): 187-188.

[10] Rougemont, *Love in the Western World* 46.

[11] Rougemont, *Love in the Western World* 15.

[12] Rougemont, *Love in the Western World* 50.

[13] René Girard, foreword, *Mímesis conflictiva*, by Cesáreo Bandera (Madrid: Gredos, 1975) 10.

[14] Girard, *Mímesis* 10.

[15] Girard uses the term "death" in *Deceit, Desire, and the Novel* not in its usual sense but rather in a Christian context, as an end that allows for a new beginning. Commenting on the transformation of two central characters in Dostoyevsky's *The Brothers Karamazov*, he writes: "Rashkolnikov and Dmitri Karamazov do not die a physical death but they are nonetheless restored to life. All Dostoyevsky's conclusions are fresh beginnings; a new life commences, either among men or in eternity" (291).

[16] Bandera, "Illusion" 717-718.

Chapter 5

Mimesis and Crisis in *Maggie*

Maggie's downfall and eventual destruction has often been viewed in part as the result of her inability or unwillingness to recognize the true nature of the world in which she lives. Among the critics who subscribe to this view is Robert Stallman, who observes that reality in *Maggie* is invariably depicted as something grim and sordid, from which the protagonist seeks to escape through her transcendent dreams.[1] Stallman points out that Maggie is unable to perceive correctly the nature of her environment because of confusion and misapprehension. She and the other characters in the novel use self-deception as an escape, a balsam with which they try to lessen the unpleasantness of their slum world. Stallman writes:

> [The characters in *Maggie*] challenge the universe, they disdain the reality of their environment under the delusion of being superior to it, they contend not against it but meanwhile against themselves, one against the other seeking release from their destiny in violence or, on the other hand, in illusions of happiness and grandeur. They escape reality in "places of forgetfulness," in saloons, hilarious halls "of irregular shape," . . . in opera and theatre, and in mission houses. . . . The confused Maggie, like the confused Emma Bovary, confounds dream and reality. . . . Confused and mixed

identity correlates in motif with the confusion between illusion and reality as exemplified by every person in the novel and as summarized in Crane's phrase "transcendental realism;" every one of these Bowery characters transcends reality in self-deluding dreams. The crossed identity of the characters and the evoked confusion of every scene in *Maggie* reflects the moral confusion of the Bowery world.[2]

However, Stallman does not pursue the problem of delusion and escapism to any considerable extent. Also, he does not see a connection between Maggie's failure to perceive the danger inherent in her penchant to escape reality by day-dreaming her way out of her real environment and her eventual demise. Instead, Stallman places the responsibility for Maggie's ruin on her milieu:

> The true villain of this comic melodrama is Maggie's environment, including the persons and institutions composing it — notably the church. . . . What Crane ridicules in *Maggie* is the cowardice of the Bowery world, on the one hand, and on the other the hypocrisy of the church and mission-house as a religious force in the netherworld of the city. Maggie is victimized not only by the collar-and-cuff factory, but also by the saloon and theatre sanctuaries, the places of escape from grim realities.[3]

Another student of Crane, Joseph Brennan, focuses on what he considers the most remarkable characteristic of *Maggie* — the insistent ironic tone.[4] Brennan notes that in *Maggie* the irony is pervasive, ranging from the inversion of a single word or phrase to the thematic idea itself. According to Brennan, Maggie is the innocent victim of the brutal forces that rule her world, a flower that "blossomed in a mud puddle," only to be sullied and trampled back into it. Yet, Brennan places some of the responsibility for Maggie's downfall on the protagonist herself:

Maggie rather pathetically attempts to improve the appearance of her home. When we study the several passages in which . . . lambrequin and blue ribbons . . . appear, it becomes clear that they are intended as symbols of Maggie herself, of her essentially feminine but somewhat romantically distorted sensibility. . . . It seems likely, too, that in the lambrequin's "immense sheaves of yellow wheat and red roses of equal size," Crane is suggesting something further about Maggie: the romantic distortion of her sensibility, which beguiles her into regarding a patent vulgarian like Pete as a "golden sun," a "knight" and "ideal man," the "lover . . . under the trees of her dream-gardens." For Maggie is no more spared by Crane's irony than the rest of his characters. Indeed, however sympathetically in other respects she may be portrayed, her tastes and mental perceptions are sometimes absurd to the point of exasperation.[5]

Brennan describes Maggie as the quintessential romantic dreamer whose unrealistic assessment of the real world proves not only dangerous but also "absurd to the point of exasperation." By implying that this distortion of Maggie's sensibility is partly to blame for her ruin, the critic suggests some deleterious element in the novel that actively contributes to the protagonist's downfall. However, he does not make an in-depth examination of this harmful agent, and refers to Maggie's culpability only in passing.

A third critic, James Colvert, observes that while Crane was aware of the role that impersonal forces play in human affairs, he was more interested in the infirmities and perversities of the human will and their effects on moral responsibility. As a result, Colvert concentrates on those aspects of *Maggie* that reinforce the characterization of the protagonist as the victim not so much of impersonal environmental forces as of a world view grounded in vanity and misinterpretation.[6] Colvert spares no criticism of Maggie's outlook on life, which in the critic's opinion can only invite disaster:

> Crane brought to bear upon his slum study essentially the same
> attitude and the same literary idea and method he applied to his
> study of "the little men"; the chief difference is that in the dark and
> grim *Maggie* he elaborated the moral consequences of the human
> perversities he comically satirized in the earlier pieces. . . . Like
> "the little men," the people in *Maggie* entertain false images of self
> which lead them into moral error. Pete, the villainous bartender,
> sees himself as a *gallant* of the most dazzling excellence; Maggie's
> brother, the brawling Jimmy, though he can ignobly take to his
> heels in a fight, is convinced that his courage is of heroic
> proportions; the yearning Maggie herself hopes that the poor little
> tinsel world of the music hall can be for her a real world; the brutal
> Mrs. Johnson believes that she is the most self-sacrificing of
> mothers. These illusions are the source of the moral outrage which
> drives Maggie to despair and suicide.[7]

The connection that Colvert makes between the deliberate misapprehension of reality and the protagonist's death is significant because it
exemplifies a basic precept of the naturalistic school. However, the
transition from viewing Maggie as a romantic dreamer to regarding her
as a sober individual capable of clear thinking and such a profound
indignation as to cause her to commit suicide is not a smooth one.
Although Colvert contends that Maggie's illusions are the source of the
moral outrage responsible for her ruin, unfortunately he does not support
this position with adequate textual evidence. In any case, Colvert
correctly places some of blame for the protagonist's death on the girl
herself. He argues that Maggie's inability or unwillingness to differentiate between the romanticized product of her imagination and the real
world contributes to her demise. Still, Colvert holds the protagonist
responsible for her own predicament only to the extent that the motif of

deliberate false self-estimate proves useful in his reading of *Maggie* as an ironic study of vanity and conceit. The theme of disillusionment resulting from conceit or dependence on fantasy in *Maggie* is elaborated further by Florence Leaver.[8] Leaver bases her critique of the novel on the notion of isolation, and argues that Crane's concept of alienation is one aspect of the author's modernity:

> It is this [sense of alienation] perhaps, as much as his style, which has made him seminal for twentieth-century writers. His isolation is akin to that of Hemingway's old waiter looking into "nada," of the wounded man "in another country," of Ole Anderson waiting for the killers, of Salinger's "catcher," of Tennessee Williams's lonely women, of Arthur Miller's pathetic Willy Loman, who paradoxically persists in preaching garrulity and being "well-liked," and of the queer of *Winesburg, Ohio*.
>
> This is the isolation known as the "lonely crowd," the isolation of modern man, who has been sent to his unconscious to understand himself and even to find his God. He has become the victim, aware or unaware, of the power of circumstance, the indifference of nature, the fading of tradition, and the weakening, if not loss, of faith. He feels terribly alone, with nowhere to go for absolutes. He is too often unsatisfied with the answers his church gives to his questions; he feels that, like the minister in Crane's *Maggie*, it steps aside. For him, increasing knowledge of the physical universe solves some problems, but creates others infinitely more frightening.[9]

Leaver's initial view of Maggie is that of a blameless young woman undeservedly punished for a transgression not entirely of her own doing. This is perhaps too simplistic an interpretation of the novel, as it leaves unanswered some important questions about the protagonist's mindset and behavior. Later, Leaver eventually comes around to address some key facets of Crane's work, thus providing a more comprehensive and realistic representation of Maggie's plight.   Specifically, the critic identifies certain harmful elements in the protagonist's physical and social environment, and argues that these influences play a major role in shaping the tragic course of her life. Leaver correctly points out that Maggie's ordeal is aggravated by her withdrawal from the world in which she is condemned to live but to which she feels she does not belong. By realizing vaguely that she has lost "the dimension of depth," and is hopelessly cut off from the finer and more pleasant environment with which she can interact only in her dreams, Maggie withdraws even further and loses contact with reality:

> Maggie's isolation consists, in the beginning of *Maggie: A Girl of the Streets,* of her being in the slum, but not of it. . . . Her pristine purity struggles pitifully at first to bring a touch of beauty into her squalid home, but only failure can result. She turns to dreams and imaginings, and dooms herself to disillusionment and death. She dreams of Pete, her seducer, as "the ideal man." . . . Later, when she has become a street-walker, her dreams exploded by shocking reality, society creates a vacuum about her; she is completely isolated. The neighbors scream derision; her mother, in a drunken fury, reviles her; her brother Jimmy, seducer of many girls, now draws away with "radiant virtue"; Pete who had ruined her, rejects her; the minister "made a convulsive movement and saved his respectability by a vigorous side-step." On her way to the river, even the men she solicits refuse her and she walks to her lonely death. She is not afraid, she is lonely and desolate.[10]

Maggie routinely turns to quixotic ideals and flights of fancy in an environment that accommodates neither. Still, even after continuous failure, she insists on substituting her romantic dreams for reality and on acting out her fantasies in the real world. By embracing a view of life that is dangerously at odds with the violent microcosm in which she must fight for survival, Maggie courts disaster and, as Leaver argues, "dooms herself to disillusionment and death."[11] Again, even though Leaver's insight is correct, she falls short of probing an important aspect of Maggie's story, namely, the psychological factors that lead the protagonist to espouse the views that ultimately bring about her downfall and destruction. The theme of alienation is further developed by William Stein, who concentrates on those aspects in *Maggie* that reinforce the view of individuals and their world as devoid of purpose.[12] Stein suggests that most of the characters in Crane's novel are pathetically estranged from the world in which they seek to enact a particular role. Their aspirations and desires are completely cut off from any realistic goal in life. Commenting on Crane's oeuvre, Stein writes:

> When the codes of values, inherited from both the past and present, no longer offer ways to order, to assort, to assimilate, and particularly *to bear* the horrors of experience, the sensitive individual engages in a distressing mode of self-questioning that runs something like this: Who am I? How does *this* I fit into *this* society in *this* world? When he discovers that he cannot answer these, he encounters the fundamental absurdity of himself and of his universe. This outcome is inescapable. If one's prior experience does not aid in adjustment to a critical moment in the present, then one has lived in a state of self-deception most of his life. What he has trusted to explain the purposes of existence is unveiled as a monstrous, diabolic lie. Unless man is this state of hopeless deracination has recourse to some stabilizing transcendental principle, he is doomed to incurable despair. The only exception to this rule, at least as Crane presents it, is the individual who denies the meaning of the terrifying revelation.[13]

Following this rationale, one can say that Maggie has been living in a state of self-deception because nothing in her prior experience can show her how to adjust to the new and more unpleasant conditions that she faces. The incongruity between what she wishes reality to be and what reality actually is alienates her from her milieu. This reading of the novel places the blame for what happens to Maggie almost entirely on the protagonist herself. Unfortunately, it does not move further to seek in the text evidence that may shed some light on the structure and dynamics of the protagonists's deliberate and fatal self-deception.

In his study of the thematic patterns in Crane's early novels, Thomas Gullason addresses questions believed to have haunted the author throughout his life, including the themes of ideals versus reality and the problem of spiritual crisis.[14] For example, the protagonist in *Maggie* illustrates the dilemma of the tragic hero who must resolve the dichotomy between his ideals and the reality of a dangerous environment. Gullason analyzes Maggie, as well as a number of Crane's early protagonists, with a certain amount of compassion:

> All are young dreamers groping somewhat blindly for a way in which to make their ideals come true. They leave their home environments hoping to find their "rightful" positions in the world. Each also has an ideal, sometimes vague love. Suddenly they are all jolted by real-life situations and they rapidly deteriorate.[15]

However, Gullason proves to be ambivalent in his depiction of Maggie. The critic is reticent when he could be more straightforward, and the tone of his initial description of the protagonist changes significantly as he probes the factors that lead Maggie to commit suicide. The compassion elicited by expressions such as "groping somewhat blindly for a way in which to make [her] ideals come true" and "[she] has an ideal, sometimes vague love" gives way at the end of his critique to the implied guilt associated with the attitude of the careless dreamer:

Maggie's romantic hopes flower in the brutal slum of Rum Alley. Faced with the prospect of a prolonged drudgery in a shirt factory or prostitution, Maggie dreams of escape from her environment and finds a "fairyland prince," Pete, who will help her find freedom as the "new" woman. Maggie magnifies, distorts Pete's charms; and after watching the action of a heroine in a play, she wonders if she too can acquire culture and refinement. She is instead acquired as Pete's mistress.[16]

Terms such as "romantic hopes," "dreams of escape," "freedom as the 'new' woman," illustrate Maggie's tragic misapprehension of reality. In the context of Crane's novel, Maggie's dreams emerge not so much as lofty and praiseworthy ideals but rather as grotesque travesties of aspirations that under different circumstances might be considered good and commendable. It seems that Maggie is made to pay an awful price for the mistake of dreaming an otherwise acceptable dream in a world that has little appreciation or use for romantic flights of fancy. Gullason, however, fails to pursue further the notion of deliberate misperception of reality and does not probe in the text for the psychopathological factors that cause such a misperception. Instead, he brings his reading of Maggie's ordeal to a close by suggesting that the reasons that lead the protagonist to commit suicide stem mainly from her growing awareness of her false illusions:

Gradually she becomes aware of her false illusions: Pete is not a knight but an artful seducer; her environment, which she thought she could surmount, bewilders and entraps her. Mocked and ostracized by her own degenerate society, Maggie becomes a reluctant prostitute. The ugly images just prior to her suicide contrast with earlier, more fanciful scenes of the ideal life she had yearned for.[17]

David Fitelson goes further than any of these critics in probing Crane's text for the structure of Maggie's vision of reality, which he regards as dual and fatal.[18] He points out that regardless of the degree to which each character in *Maggie* succeeds in the struggle for existence, the majority recognize both the absolute value of survival and the certainty that the struggle is the sole path to its attainment. Fitelson writes:

> In the specific tale of Maggie's downfall, Crane comments on this certainty by presenting the case of one who attempts to remain aloof from the struggle. It is not that Maggie totally fails to recognize the nature of the world, but that her vision is a dual one.[19]

Fitelson goes on to map out Maggie's downfall by dividing her ordeal into four different stages. At each phase of her tragic descent, the protagonist is pulled farther away from the realistic assessment of her environment toward the romantic idealization of a dream world:

> In the first stage, [Maggie] is a realist, fashioning her image of the world from the object lessons to which she is daily exposed. The other world is a vague possibility on the fringe of consciousness . . . [In] the second stage . . . there persists with her . . . a sense of the possibility of escape to the other world. In her idealization of Pete, Maggie attempts to unite the poles of her dual image. . . . Pete is admired because he represents . . . the possibility of escape and [he has] the power to deal with the world of hardships and insults on its own terms. In the third stage of her journey, Maggie suddenly loses all contact with the actual world. Unable to bear any longer the misery of her life at home . . . she gives herself physically to Pete, and from the moment she is accepted by him, her sense of the possibility of escape to the other

world dominates her awareness of [her real] world . . . When Pete leaves her . . . Maggie is not, as might be expected, jolted back to her vision of the actual world. She is now too thoroughly committed to her yearning for the other to do anything but increase desperately her efforts to reach it. . . . In the fourth stage of her journey, Maggie at first appears to have returned with a vengeance to her vision of the actual world. At last, it would seem, she has come to accept the certainty that its laws are inexorable, and in conducting her life in accordance with those laws she appears to have been eminently successful. [But] all is not as it appears . . . what actually confronts us in this remarkable reversal of vision and behavior is another instance of irony. [Maggie] has retained a fatal measure of her vision of the other world, and now it appears to her [that] escape to it can be accomplished only by means of a forcible exit from the actual one. Consequently, on a rainy night . . . she jumps in the river and drowns.[20]

Fitelson provides a lucid and compelling interpretation of *Maggie*. He is particularly attentive to the nuances and structural correlations in the text, which are often obscured by the novel's strident and excessively violent language. The critic pursues these patterns systematically, and succeeds in shedding new light on Crane's work. However, like the other Crane scholars examined here, Fitelson does not provide sufficient textual evidence to account for Maggie's dual and fatal vision. He correctly observes that Maggie deliberately views her slum world as something other than the dangerous environment that it is, and that this vision ultimately proves fatal to her. Still, the critic regards this vision as a static entity. As a result, he does not pursue an analysis of the environmental forces or the psychological mechanisms that lead Maggie to perceive her world in a dual manner.

To be sure, Fitelson's proposed model of Maggie's vision adds a new dimension to our understanding of the novel and brings to light important questions about Crane's work.   Yet, the absence of any interpersonal dynamics in Fitelson's model detracts somewhat from its interpretive value because Maggie's dream world, and the dual vision that this world generates, are not as static as Fitelson proposes. In order to understand the origin and makeup of this vision in greater detail, it will be useful to examine the nature of the protagonist's attitude vis-à-vis her environment. The first image of Maggie that Crane provides is one that reflects the girl's gentle soul in contrast with the world of filth and violence that surrounds her:

> Maggie blossomed in a mud puddle. She grew to be the most rare and wonderful production of a tenement district, a pretty girl. None of the dirt of Rum Alley seemed to be in her veins. The philosophers, upstairs, downstairs, and on the same floor, puzzled over it. When a child, playing and fighting with gamins in the street, dirt disgusted her.[21]

The above passage sheds light on a crucial aspect of the protagonist's behavior toward her environment. It is not the fact that other human beings like herself find themselves trapped in a world of destitution and violence that distresses Maggie, but rather that *she* has to live in such a world. She resents that by some cruel twist of fate she has been thrown together with people with whom she has very little in common. Even though she is in many respects a product of her environment, the world where she is condemned to live does not measure up to her expectations. It only inspires repugnance. Her disgust with the violence and dirt in her milieu stems not only from her idea of what is good and refined, but also from the demands imposed on her by family and society:

> About this period her brother remarked to her: "Mag, I'll tell yeh

dis! See? Yeh've eeder got t'go on d'toif er go t'work!" Where-
upon she went to work, having the feminine aversion to the alternative. By a chance, she got a position in an establishment where
they made collars and cuffs. She received a stool and a machine in
a room where sat twenty girls of various shades of yellow discontent (58).

Maggie can either "go on the turf," that is, earn a living as a
prostitute, or go to work, which she does but only "yellow with
discontent." It is not so much what she must do to earn her keep that
seems to bother Maggie. Rather, it is the inescapable fact that whatever
she may decide to do, she will have to carry it out in an environment that
she loathes. Her ideas of what constitutes refinement and her attitudes
toward her world are defined from the beginning of the novel. However,
Crane describes these negatively, mostly in terms of what she does *not*
like, *cannot* accept, or will do but *without* joy or dedication. Maggie's
perception of what she rejects is matched by her awareness of the things
that she lacks and yearns for. Even as a young girl, she already has a
clear picture of what a world of refinement is supposed to be like:

> She began to note with more interest the well-dressed women she
> met on the avenues. She envied elegance and soft palms. She
> craved those adornments of person she saw every day on the street,
> conceiving them to be allies of vast importance to women.
> Studying faces, she thought many of the women and girls she
> chanced to meet smiled with serenity as though forever cherished
> and watched over by those they loved (68-69).

Maggie reveres the smartly dressed women whom she meets in the
streets of New York in much the same way that the protagonist in
Flaubert's *Madame Bovary* looks up to the elegant world of Parisian
gentry. Like Emma Bovary, who longs for the sophistication of

cosmopolitan living, Maggie covets "elegance and soft palms" and "adornments of person." To Maggie, the life of refinement enjoyed by these women is a constant reminder of all the things that she never had or knew firsthand. She looks up to the real or imagined conventions of this other world and willingly allows her conception of it to play an important role in her life, especially in the way she regards and reacts to her real environment. Her vision of this finer world becomes the standard against which everything in her real environment is measured and judged. It becomes her epistemological yardstick.

Maggie's dream world serves as the "rose-tinted" glass through which she looks at reality. In the context of Girard's theory of mimetic desire, Maggie's fantasy world becomes her mediator. Just as Emma Bovary surrenders to the socialites of Paris her prerogative to choose, so does Maggie with regard to her dream world. Both women surrender to perfect strangers their freedom of choice, and do so willingly, because in their eyes these nameless men and women possess the spontaneity and autonomy that they want for themselves. In other words, they relinquish the privilege to determine for themselves the objects of their own desire. The people who make up these worlds now choose for them, and Emma Bovary and Maggie, accordingly, pursue only those objects that they believe to be favored by the mediator. In the case of Maggie, her desire involves a great deal more than the simple linear movement of a desiring subject toward a desired object. Before she takes the first step in the direction of something that may have caught her fancy, the mediator will have already been there:

> The mediator is there, above that line, radiating toward both the subject and the object. The spatial metaphor which expresses this triple relationship is obviously the triangle. The object changes with each adventure but the triangle remains.[22]

The mediator can be either a person, as in the case of the protagonist in *Don Quijote* (whose desire is mediated by the fictional hero Amadis of Gaul), a thing, or a whole microcosm, as in the case of Emma Bovary and Maggie. Whether it is an individual or a thing, the mediator occupies a privileged position with regard to the subject and largely determines the subject's likes and dislikes. The triangle made up by the mediator, the subject, and the object of desire is a dynamic structure that remains constant as the subject goes from one object to another, following the mediator's cues. It is this dynamic dimension to the protagonist's desire that Fitelson either fails to discern or chooses not to pursue in his otherwise elegant and insightful interpretation of *Maggie*. He correctly identifies the elements that determine the nature of Maggie's desire, but he never makes a connection between the influencing factors underlying the protagonist's vision of her dream world and the events in her real environment that lead to her death.

This is not to say that the static structure of Maggie's dual vision proposed by Fitelson is devoid of merit. There is, to be sure, a certain entity beyond the protagonist's real world that competes for her belief. This influencing element is played against Maggie's realistic vision of the world fashioned from the object lessons to which she is daily exposed. However, Fitelson fails to make clear the distinction between Maggie's dream world — one "in which there is love and in which people depend upon and assume responsibility for one another"[23] — and its influence on her. The protagonist regards these two entities (her world of make-believe and its influence on her) as inherently good, and Fitelson apparently shares her opinion because he assumes this view in his interpretation of the novel. The critic neglects to differentiate between Maggie's romantic conception of her dream world and his own interpretation of such a vision. Fitelson writes as though he, too, believes that Maggie's vision of a better world is the manifestation of something essentially benign. He does not consider the possibility that it may be the pleasant façade for something unwholesome and destructive.

The question that ought to be asked here is not whether the world of make-believe that Maggie dreams up is good or bad, but rather how the influence of this world on the protagonist contributes to her downfall and ultimately to her destruction. On the surface, it appears that she only wants to improve her lot. She elicits sympathy because she plays the role of the underdog. Even when faced with insurmountable obstacles, Maggie clings fast to her dreams, and tries her best to make them come true. However, it seems that her dreams, good and praiseworthy though they may be, actually conspire against her. By not being blatantly evil themselves, her dreams do not call attention to the harmful influence that they exert on the protagonist, and therefore are never renounced. On the contrary, they are embraced more forcefully, more desperately, as the protagonist's condition deteriorates. Consequently, they lead her, with her implicit consent, down the road to hell, to a realm of perpetual suffering whose gates are said to be always open. Maggie is taken and remains there of her own free will.

The implication in Fitelson's reading of *Maggie* is that the influence of the protagonist's romantic dreams must itself be a positive one, since it is derived from a world of inherent goodness. Fitelson puts forth this view even though in Crane's Darwinian universe it proves to be unprofitable, that is, not suited to the kind of environment where Maggie is condemned to fight for survival. Furthermore, Fitelson sees the persistence of the possibility of escape to the protagonist's dream world as something positive and good, and provides no indication of a possible darker side to Maggie's vision. These two factors — the origin of Maggie's vision in a world of inherent goodness and the positiveness associated with the concepts of change and progress — serve to discourage Fitelson from probing further into the nature of the influence exerted on the protagonist by her romantic ideals. Also, these elements prevent the critic from viewing this influence as something harmful. As a result, he construes Maggie's dependence on her vision of a world of "elegance and soft palms" to be superficial and benign. Certainly, Fitelson does not expose the virulence that an analysis of the kind proposed by Girard would reveal. Maggie's vision of her dreamland, and the way this fantasy affects her, can hardly be considered merely the innocuous awareness of the "vague possibility of escape to the other world." As I will show, these influences are stronger and more harmful than what Fitelson suggests.

The way Crane structures the interpersonal dynamics in *Maggie* and the manner in which the story concludes reflect something markedly different from what is implied in Fitelson's assessment of the novel. Far from being the product of a world of love and goodness, the influence that Maggie's dream world exerts on her is clearly destructive, as exemplified by the novel's tragic denouement. Moreover, we might ask how can an effort toward goodness (love, companionship) possibly lead to prostitution, abandonment, and death? The ghastly conclusion to Maggie's story suggests something unhealthy about her interaction with her dream world. In an idealized universe of romantic fiction, one might expect poetic justice and reason to prevail, and our deeds, good and bad, to bring about results that reflect the ideas and beliefs that generated them. Despite the fundamental differences between Romanticism and Naturalism, the same can be said about the universe of the naturalistic novel as well. In such a world, the continuous recurrence of wickedly tragic events may very well point to origins just as tragically wicked. A reading couched in Girard's model of mimetic desire should provide an adequate answer to this question and at the same time open a new avenue into the problem of misapprehension and destruction in *Maggie*.

Girard's model of mimetic desire lends itself particularly well to an explication of Maggie's dual vision and an examination of her fantasies vis-à-vis her suicide because it elucidates the epistemological and spiritual chaos at the heart of her predicament. According to Girard, the subject of desire is drawn to certain objects because he or she believes them to be desired by another whom the subject regards as superior. In the case of Maggie, this superior Other is the world of refinement for which she yearns but which seems to be hopelessly out of her reach. Her world of make-believe plays the role of mediator in much the same way that the elegant world of Parisian gentry functions as model to Madame Bovary, determining her likes and dislikes. Thus, the mediator is present in Maggie's life from the instant she starts craving the "culture of refinement" to the moment when she decides to commit suicide. With the subject's implicit consent, the mediator designates what will and will not be desirable to the subject. Maggie's brief liaison with her brother's friend illustrates this point. It is not so much Pete's innate qualities that make him attractive to Maggie, as a linear reading of their affair would imply, but rather certain attributes in him that she associates with her dream world. Maggie takes a liking to Pete because he reflects those traits present in this other world that she thinks are desirable. Note Crane's description of the way Maggie views Pete:

> Maggie observed Pete.
> He sat on a table in the Johnson home, and dangled his checked legs with an enticing nonchalance. His hair was curled down over his forehead in an oiled band. His pugged nose seemed to revolt from contact with a bristling moustache of short, wire-like hairs. His blue, double-breasted coat, edged with black braid, was buttoned close to a red puff tie, and his patent leather shoes looked like weapons. His mannerisms stamped him as a man who had a correct sense of his personal superiority. There were valour and contempt for circumstances in the glance of his eye. He waved his hand like a man of the world who dismisses religion and philosophy, and says "Rats!" He had certainly seen everything, and with each curl of his lip he declared that it amounted to nothing (59-60).

Maggie finds in Pete a number of attributes that she thinks exist in this other world of refinement: his "enticing nonchalance," his clean-cut look and good taste in clothes, his mannerisms, which supposedly gave him an air of respectability, and the fact that he had "contempt for circumstances." These imagined qualities make Pete desirable to Maggie not so much because he embodies them (he does not) but rather because they are the product of a vision determined for the protagonist by her mediator. The point of contact between the two lovers is not some idealized reciprocal love. Maggie's romantic attachment to Pete stems from her perception of him in two complementary ways. She sees him both as a man with desirable traits and as someone who can help her to escape her oppressive environment:

> Over the eternal collars and cuffs in the factory Maggie spent the most of three days in making imaginary sketches of Pete and his daily environment. She imagined some half-dozen women in love with him, and thought he must lean dangerously toward an indefinite one whom she pictured as endowed with great charms of person, but with an altogether contemptible disposition. She thought he must live in a blare of pleasure. He had friends and people who were afraid of him. She saw the golden glitter of the place where Pete was to take her. It would be an entertainment of many hues and many melodies (63-64).

Pete proves especially attractive to Maggie because she believes him to complement her in an essential way. He embodies the qualities required for survival in a violent environment — something that she lacks. In her eyes, he has the power and the strength to defeat and transcend their world of violence and destitution:

> She reflected upon the collar-and-cuff factory. It began to appear to her mind as a dreary place of endless grinding. . . . To her the

> earth was composed of hardships and insults. She felt instant
> admiration for a man who openly defied it. . . . With Jimmie in
> his company, Pete departed in a sort of blaze of glory from the
> Johnson home. Maggie, leaning from the window, watched him as
> he walked down the street. Here was a formidable man . . . whose
> knuckles could ring defiantly against the granite of law. He was a
> knight (62-63).

This description of Pete is pervasive throughout the first half of the
novel, up to the point when he leaves Maggie for another woman. Pete
disappoints Maggie not so much because he abandons her but rather
because, for the first time, she sees him for what he is. Pete is made to
remonstrate with his new lover, Nellie, an older and tougher woman who
wields more power than he. Maggie's image of him as a "supreme
warrior," "a knight," and "a golden sun" is shattered:

> Maggie was dazed. She could dimly perceive that something
> stupendous had happened. She wondered why Pete saw fit to
> remonstrate with the woman, pleading forgiveness with his eyes.
> She thought she noted an air of submission about her leonine Pete.
> She was astounded (93).

Maggie's rejection of the Bowery must occur before any distinction
between her real and dream worlds can be made. She perceives the two
worlds as fundamentally different and mutually exclusive. In her mind,
the acceptance of one is equated with the rejection of the other. Before
she can gain access into her idealized world of refinement, she must exit
permanently the world of the Bowery. In order for the former to prevail,
the latter must be vanquished and transcended. A major part of *Maggie*
is developed around the juxtaposition between Pete's prowess and
Maggie's hopes of entering her dream world. The contrapuntal interplay
between the two characters remains constant as the protagonist fashions

those views that will lead her along the tragic road to prostitution, abandonment, and death:

> As thoughts of Pete came to Maggie's mind, she began to have an intense dislike for all of her dresses. . . . She began to note with more interest the well-dressed women she met on the avenues. She envied elegance and soft palms. She craved those adornments of person which she saw every day on the street, conceiving them to be allies of vast importance to women. . . .
>
> The air in the collar-and-cuff establishment strangled her. She knew she was gradually and surely shrivelling in the hot, stuffy room. . . . She became lost in thought as she looked at some of the grizzled women in the room, mere mechanical contrivances sewing seams, [their] heads bent over their work. . . . She wondered how long her youth would endure. She began to see the bloom upon her cheeks as something of value. She imagined herself, in an exasperating future, as a scrawny woman with an eternal grievance. She thought Pete to be a very fastidious person concerning the appearance of women (68-69).
>
> As Jimmie and his friend [Pete] exchanged tales descriptive of their prowess, Maggie leaned back in the shadow. Her eyes dwelt wonderingly and rather wistfully upon Pete's face. The broken furniture, grimy walls, and general disorder and dirt of her home of a sudden appeared before her. . . . Pete's aristocratic person looked as if it might soil. She looked keenly at him, occasionally wondering if he was feeling contempt. . . . When he said, "Ah, what d'hell!" his voice was burdened with disdain for the inevitable and contempt for anything that fate might compel him to endure.
>
> Maggie perceived that here was the ideal man. Her dim thoughts were often searching for far-away lands where the little hills sing together in the morning. Under the trees of her dream-gardens there had always walked a lover (61).

One might refer to Maggie's initial view of Pete as the positive manifestation of the influence exerted by the mediator. This view reasserts the desirability of something determined by the model. Maggie finds Pete attractive because she believes him to be like the men from her dream world: strong, loving, and courageous. Her opinion of him at the end of the novel on the surface seems to invalidate what has been established about the mediator and his role in this kind of desire, but in effect it does not. On the contrary, Maggie's rejection of Pete actually reasserts the influence of the mediator because her action represents the spurning of something that the mediator has deemed undesirable.

Initially, Pete measures up to Maggie's expectations for two reasons. First, she sees reflected in him those qualities that she associates with the men from her dream world. Second, she believes that he has the strength and the determination to take on and subjugate the environment that stands between her and the world of refinement for which she yearns. Thus, the bond that exists between the two is determined, positively or negatively, by Maggie's dream world. Maggie looks up to Pete only to the extent that he reflects desirable attributes present in her dream world. Actually, Pete plays a minor role in Maggie's relationship to her mediator. He happens to be but one among many objects that the mediator has deemed desirable to the subject. It could well be someone or something else. Pete's privileged position in his relationship with Maggie does not stem from qualities that are inherent or unique to him. Rather, it is determined by the position that he occupies in the mimetic structure vis-à-vis subject and mediator.

Maggie's yearning for a dream world beyond her reach defines a desire according to another as opposed to a desire according to oneself. Maggie borrows her desires from that other world in a movement that is so fundamental and primitive that she completely confuses it with the will to be oneself. The relentless pursuit of this world of refinement may appear to be the manifestation of a form of unmediated desire, where the subject alone chooses for herself which objects to aspire to. This belief overwhelms Maggie in such a way as to erase in her mind the distinction between self and Other. This allows for a gross and fatal error in judgment on her part that ultimately leads to her death. These events are possible because in such a chaotic state of affairs, desire is able to project a dream world around the heroine from which she can escape only on her deathbed.

According to Girard, the mediator is enthroned in an inaccessible heaven and transmits to his faithful disciple a little of his serenity. From the moment that his influence is felt, the sense of reality is lost and judgment is paralyzed. That is what appears to happen to Maggie. As a result of this paralysis, she allows her vision of a world of elegance to shape the way she views and deals with her real environment. Now, Maggie sees through soft-colored lenses, and her goals and longings are almost exclusively determined by the mediator. In the context of external mediation, this dream world is perceived by the subject as being hopelessly removed from her. When Crane describes Maggie's view of her lover, he does so in such a way as to make Pete appear more detached and important than she:

> He walked to and fro in the small room, which seemed then to grow even smaller and unfit to hold his dignity, the attribute of a supreme warrior. That swing of the shoulders which had frozen the timid when he was but a lad had increased with his growth and education in the ration of ten to one. It, combined with the sneer upon his mouth, told mankind that there was nothing in space which could appall him. Maggie marvelled at him and surrounded him with greatness. She vaguely tried to calculate the altitude of the pinnacle from which he must look down upon her (61-61).
>
> Her heart warmed as she reflected upon his condescension (66).
>
> Maggie [felt] little and new (65).

> [She] was afraid she might appear small and mouse-colored
> (64).

As I have discussed in Chapter 4, according to Rougemont, desire thrives on obstructions. And distance, both physical and interpersonal, is one of the more common forms that such obstructions take. The subject of desire tends to be passionate about those objects that are difficult to attain, and will ignore those that prove too easy. It is no accident that in the great love stories in the West, the lover traditionally confers divine qualities on his beloved. He commonly refers to her as a goddess looking serenely down upon him from an inaccessible height. By placing the object of his desire on a pedestal beyond his reach, the lover ensures the presence of an insurmountable distance between the two. The farther removed the object is from the lover, the more passionately he will desire it. And the more he desires it, the greater his need to maintain his beloved in the rarefied sanctum where he has enshrined her. Maggie, too, puts Pete on a pedestal. She describes him as a man with god-like qualities, a "supreme warrior" unafraid of the world because "there was nothing in space which could appall him." Maggie's portrayal of her lover is most instructive when she refers to his condescension toward her, which has the effect of "warming her heart." Also, she delights in her inability to "calculate the altitude of the pinnacle from which he must look down upon her." By "marvelling at him" as one would a god and "surrounding him with greatness," Maggie makes Pete appear superior to herself. This superiority translates into distance and this distance into a stronger desire. Commenting on the problem of distance and obstruction in desire, Cesáreo Bandera observes:

> Desire [is] a madness that feeds upon its own negation, a desire of
> the obstacle as if only in the obstacle would this desire find a sign
> of eternal happiness. The lover, the subject of this desire, only

becomes passionate about that which is denied to him. The farther away is the object of this desire the more ardently he wants it. Ultimately he strives towards a goal infinitely removed from him, at an infinite distance, because only there can such a goal shine in its infinite splendor. But that infinite distance is at the same time an infinite obstacle, the only insurmountable obstacle that will put an end to his desire: eternal fulfillment and death all in one.[24]

By not being in direct contact with the world of refinement that mediates her desire, Maggie does not enter in competition with the men and women from this world over those objects that may be desirable to both. The possibility of rivalry and conflict is therefore nonexistent. Her desire, like that of Emma Bovary, is based on external mediation, where the harmony between subject and mediator is never seriously undermined. Expounding on this form of mediation as found in *Don Quijote* and *Madame Bovary*, Girard writes:

> This distance is greatest in Cervantes. There can be no contact whatsoever between Don Quixote and his legendary Amadis. Emma Bovary is already closer to her Parisian mediator. Travelers' tales, books, and the press bring the latest fashions of the capital to Yonville. Emma comes still closer to her mediator when she goes to the ball at the Vaubyessards'; she penetrates the holy of holies and gazes at the idol face to face. But this proximity is fleeting. Emma will never be able to desire that which the incarnations of her "ideal" desire; she will never be able to be their rival; she will never leave for Paris.[25]

The objectivity of the distance that Maggie puts between herself and the object of her desire — that is, the objectivity of the obstacle — is purely illusory. Pete, she realizes later, is no "supreme warrior" nor is there any distance separating the two. They are very similar products of the same environment. If anything, Maggie seems to have more dignity than he, and as such should be the one "looking down from a pinnacle" upon her "small and mouse-colored" beau. Thus, we can see that the distance that Maggie at first discerns between herself and her lover is generated by mimetic desire itself. The obstacle that appears to stand between Maggie and Pete, and the desire that keeps her fascinated by him, are one and the same thing. The intensity of the desire and the magnitude of the obstacle are directly proportional to the distance that the subject puts between herself and the object of her desire:

> [Maggie] contemplated Pete's man-subduing eyes and noted that wealth and prosperity were indicated by his clothes. She imagined a future rose-tinted because of its distance from all that she had experienced before (85).

A character may try to rationalize her way out of this double bind, where, in order to desire passionately, she must continuously be confronted with a formidable obstacle. Of course, devising self-satisfying but fallacious reasons for her behavior will hardly help her to do away with the triangular structure of mimetic desire. Even an earnest and detached rational interpretation of her predicament might not be of much help. The more a character attempts to conceal or deny the presence of mimetic desire, the greater the havoc this desire is able to play in his or her life. The reasons for creating from nothing an obstacle that instigates and at the same time thwarts passion are as numerous and varied as the characters in literature affected by desire. Maggie tries to account for the great distance that separates her from her dream world, but she never frames the question in terms of a desire that thrives on obstruction. Instead, she believes that this great distance exists because she has never had any prolonged contact with this other world. Still, the fact remains that although the reasons may change, the structure and dynamics of mimetic desire stay the same. The triangle is always already there. The obstacle will be called different things by different individuals, but its basic dual function, namely, to entice *and* forbid, does not change.

One can see this obstacle at work in *Maggie* as it affects both the way the protagonist views Pete and the way he views her. Even though Pete's plight is almost inconsequential when compared to Maggie's, his desire is structured basically along the same lines as his lover's. His sexual appetite grows more intense only after Maggie starts playing hard to get. Whether she realizes it or not, Maggie awakens and foments Pete's desire for her. She does this with a simple "no," by placing an obstacle between her boyfriend and the object of his desire, namely, her body:

> "Say, Mag," said Pete, "give us a kiss for takin' yeh t' d' show, will yer?"
>
> Maggie laughed, as if startled, and drew away from him. "Naw, Pete," she said, "dat wasn't in it."
>
> "Ah, why wasn't it?" urged Pete.
>
> The girl retreated nervously.
>
> "Ah, go ahn!" repeated he.
>
> Maggie darted into the hall and up the stairs. She turned and smiled at him, then disappeared.
>
> Pete walked slowly down the street. He had something of an astonished expression upon his features. He paused under a lamp-post and breathed a low breath of surprise. "Gee!" he said, " I wonner if I've been played for a duffer" (68).

On the surface, Maggie's behavior can be explained in one of two ways: either she is trying to protect her honor or she is playing hard to get. Honor does not seem to be her main concern here because she eventually gives in to Pete's amorous overtures, and becomes his lover. The other possibility is that perhaps Maggie is only teasing her boyfriend.

That may be the perception afforded by a casual analysis of her relationship with Pete. On another level, however, her behavior may point to something less simplistic. Pete resents Maggie's refusal to give in to his advances and bemoans the fact that he may have "been played for a duffer." Maggie's position is not unlike that of the coquette, whom Girard describes as someone who is not willing to surrender her precious self to the desire that she awakens and stirs up in others. However, the coquette would not feel so precious if she were not able to arouse such a passion in her admirers. The worth that she sees in herself is a direct function of the extent to which others regard her as something desirable. Thus, Maggie becomes both the object of Pete's desire and, by denying herself to him, its obstacle. This multifaceted gate-hurdle acquires an ambivalent dual function:

> The obstacle is an extremely shining obstacle: that is to say, its function is not only to obstruct but, by obstructing, to reveal something extremely desirable, something which would not be revealed if it were not for the presence of a formidable "No."[26]

Even if on the surface it appears that what is involved between Maggie and Pete is of an erotic nature, the origin of her desire for him is not entirely sexual. Like M. de Renal's desire for objects associated with power and prestige in Stendhal's *The Red and the Black*, Maggie's fascination with Pete is rooted not so much in sex but rather in social status and the prospect of a life of comfort in a world of refinement and elegance. Her fascination with Pete seems strong because it is the reflection of an even stronger fascination, namely, the one that she nurtures for her mediator.

Maggie is destroyed by a mechanism of desire that has attracted little critical attention, perhaps because it does not appear at all harmful. She is killed by this desire, even if in her troubled mind she believes that her suicide is an autonomous and spontaneous act. The author's use in the last chapters of descriptions in the active voice, and the interpretation of these passages as an assertion of independence suggest a measure of autonomy on the part of the protagonist. However, a closer reading of the text does not support such a view. The casual reader may see Maggie in her last moments as a troubled and disheartened woman. Realizing that she will have to leave her real environment in a forcible and permanent manner if she is ever to enter her dream world, Maggie equates death with escape, and kills herself in a final act of liberation and defiance.

Some critics of Crane have found merit in this view. Fitelson argues that Maggie is "thoroughly committed to her yearning for the other world," and that one of the causes of her death is that she "retains a fatal measure of her vision of the other world." He says, in effect, that Maggie *acted* as opposed to having been *acted upon*. By endowing the protagonist with a generous measure of self-control, Fitelson implies that she possesses the autonomy to act on her desire in a strictly linear fashion. The mediator, or any other entity acting behind the scenes, is missing from this picture. There is also the implication in Fitelson's reading that the influence of Maggie's vision of a dream world varies in intensity throughout the novel and that the protagonist could have escaped this influence. As the novel's denouement poignantly shows, Maggie never relinquishes her vision nor is she ever able to transcend it. She cannot. Once a mediator is allowed to play a role in her life, she surrenders her freedom of choice to him (or it), and, consequently, her prerogative to repudiate the agent that now chooses for her.

Confused and heartbroken, Maggie is unable to distinguish between her own desire and that mediated by the world of refinement that she yearns for. She is unable to differentiate between self and Other. She never repudiates her dream world because in her mind a rejection of this world would be equated with the denial of oneself, with conscious self-destruction. Of course, annihilation is precisely what she brings upon herself, but she does not do this as a result of her repudiation of the mediator of her desire. On the contrary, she kills herself by giving in to the mediator's influence. Unable to escape her real environment, Maggie decides that the only way she can enter her dream world is by means of a forcible exit from the actual one. In her troubled mind, suicide becomes not the denial and destruction of the individual self but the means by which she can go on living. Ironically, this is never achieved. The only victor, if there is one, is the mimetic mechanism that destroys Maggie in the end. The influence exerted by the mediator is carried through to its full extent, with the result being death, as Girard argues:

> The truth of metaphysical desire is death. This is the inevitable end of the contradiction on which that desire is based. Novels are full of signs announcing death. But the signs remain ambiguous so long as the prophecy is not fulfilled. As soon as death is present it lights up the path behind it; it enriches our interpretation of the mediated structure; it gives full meaning to many aspects of metaphysical desire.[27]

In *Maggie*, the interpretation of the mimetic structure behind the protagonist's ordeal is enriched by the final revelation of desire's ultimate truth. Maggie walks to her death with the apparent awareness of the inevitability of the whole tragic situation. She does not fight her fate on philosophical grounds, nor does she offer any physical resistance to it. Even if she never realizes that it is her dream vision itself that is about to destroy her, Maggie is aware of the extent to which she is now divorced from the simple pleasures and signs of life in her environment. Furthermore, the world that she is about to leave for good makes no effort to interfere in her final walk. The distant "street car bells [that] jingled with a sound of merriment" (103) highlight the atmosphere of cold indifference that now prevails all around Maggie:

> She went into the blackness of the final block. The shutters of the
> tall buildings were closed like grim lips. The structures seemed to
> have eyes that looked over them, beyond them, at other things.
> Afar off the lights of the avenues glittered as if from an impossible
> distance (102-103).

Socially and psychologically alienated from her real environment,
and too thoroughly committed to her vision of a dream world, with silent
resolve Maggie kills herself by jumping into the river. She commits
suicide in an eerie atmosphere of quiet desperation, not unlike the
archetypal heroine in classical Greek tragedy who has finally reached the
end of a long and painful process by which she comes to realize that
death is her only viable alternative:

> At the feet of the tall buildings appeared the deathly black hue
> of the river. Some hidden factory sent up a yellow glare, that lit
> for a moment the waters lapping oilily against timbers. The varied
> sounds of life, made joyous by distance and seeming unapproach-
> ableness, came faintly and died away to a silence (103).

Maggie's story ends tragically in death, a far cry from what she had
expected — love, happiness, and the fulfillment of her dreams in a world
of comfort and refinement. The conclusion of her ordeal is a sad one,
but given the circumstances, one could hardly expect a different ending.
Maggie can be read as the story of a young woman affected by mimetic
desire and as a result "too thoroughly committed to her yearning for
another world" to consider that this fascination might spell her doom. As
such, her fate is largely decided from the beginning. As Maggie's
tormented life and untimely death illustrate, the only truth about mimetic
desire is not revealed in any grandiose or romantic realization of its

goals. Rather, it is manifested in the way desire ultimately works itself out, namely, in rivalry, violence, and death.

Notes

[1] Robert Stallman, "Crane's *Maggie*: A Reassessment," *Modern Fiction Studies* 5 (1959): 251-259.

[2] Stallman, "Reassessment" 251-259.

[3] Stallman, "Reassessment" 258.

[4] Joseph Brennan, "Ironic and Symbolic Structure in Crane's *Maggie*," *Nineteenth-Century Fiction* 16 (1962): 303-315.

[5] Brennan, "Structure" 313-314.

[6] James Colvert, "Structure and Theme in Stephen Crane's Fiction," *Modern Fiction Studies* 5 (1959): 199-208.

[7] Colvert, "Structure" 203-204.

[8] Florence Leaver, "Isolation in the Work of Stephen Crane," *The South Atlantic Quarterly* 61 (1962): 521-532.

[9] Leaver, "Isolation" 522.

[10] Leaver, "Isolation" 527-528.

[11] Leaver, "Isolation" 527.

[12] William Stein, "Stephen Crane's *Homo Absurdus*," *Bucknell Review* 8 (1959): 168-188.

[13] Stein, "Crane" 175-176.

[14] Thomas Gullason, "Thematic Patterns in Stephen Crane's Early Novels," *Nineteenth-Century Fiction* 16 (1961): 59-67.

[15] Gullason, "Patterns" 61.

[16] Gullason, "Patterns" 61.

[17] Gullason, "Patterns" 61.

[18] David Fitelson, "Stephen Crane's *Maggie* and Darwinism," *American Quarterly* 16 (1964): 182-194.

[19] Fitelson, "Darwinism" 161.

[20] Fitelson, "Darwinism" 191-193.

[21] Stephen Crane, *Maggie: A Girl of the Streets*, in *Stephen Crane: An Omnibus*, ed. Robert Stallman (New York: Alfred Knopf, 1966) 58. All subsequent quotations from *Maggie* are from this edition. Citations by page number appear in parentheses in the text.

[22] René Girard, *Deceit, Desire, and the Novel: Self and Other in Literary Structure*, trans. Yvonne Freccero (Baltimore, Maryland: Johns Hopkins University Press, 1980) 2.

[23] Fitelson, "Darwinism" 191.

[24] Cesáreo Bandera, "Literature and Desire: Poetic Frenzy and the Love Potion," *Mosaic* 8 (1975): 37.

[25] Girard, *Deceit* 8.

[26] Bandera, "Literature" 50.

[27] Girard, *Deceit* 282.

Chapter 6

Violent Symmetries: Self and Other in *O cortiço*

The literary criticism of *O cortiço* produced before 1960 is largely digressive, and lacks clearly defined critical parameters.[1] It touches on many tangential aspects of the novel, but leaves out some fundamental technical considerations. In this type of analysis, the text is often used merely as a medium through which non-literary concerns are articulated. Azevedo's early critics seem more interested in history, biography, sociology, or politics than in literature. As a result, his fiction is made to appear to be of secondary importance, something that only illustrates background. Most of this criticism was written by Brazilians anxious to establish a distinct and recognizable critical literary tradition in their country. However, in their eagerness to demonstrate the relevance of Azevedo's contribution to Brazilian letters, they failed to devote sufficient time to the text itself. Because of the sociopathological themes that recur in naturalistic fiction, some of these critics read Azevedo's novels as sociological commentary. On that basis, they pronounced him a seer who did the motherland a great service by "prenunciando os problemas de nossa evolução social [predicting the problems of our social evolution]."[2] While this patriotic overoptimism may have added to national pride, it contributed little to our understanding of Azevedo's work *qua* literature.

Fortunately, this gap in Brazilian literary criticism is being filled by scholars such as Dorothy Loos, Antônio Cândido, Sônia Brayner, Affonso Romano de Sant'Anna, Flora Süssekind, and Rui Mourão.[3] The first of these critics to analyze the work of Azevedo on aesthetic grounds and with clearly defined critical tools was Loos. Her brief but informative survey of the naturalistic novel of Brazil draws some important parallels between the French *roman expérimental* and Azevedo's own adaptation and transformation of this model. Although the context of Loos's study does not allow for a detailed examination of *O cortiço*, she nonetheless offers an illuminating reading of some relevant aspects of the novel.

Other students of the naturalistic novel of Brazil who have since expanded on Loos's analysis of *O cortiço* include Cândido, Brayner, Sant'Anna, Süssekind, and Mourão. Recent developments in literary theory and criticism have enabled these critics to go beyond traditional questions of biography and literary history as they examine form and structure in the text, and, in the case of the post-structuralists, as they probe the grounds of language itself. Mourão exemplifies this critical stance with one of the most lucid readings of the novel to date. By concentrating exclusively on *O cortiço*, and by drawing on a rich tradition in textual criticism (e.g., New Criticism, Formalism, Structuralism, and Post-Structuralism), Mourão produces a cogent and elegant interpretation of *O cortiço*.[4] He develops his critique very closely to the text, always attentive to recurring structures and patterns. One of Mourão's most enabling insights is the formulation of *O cortiço* as a novel structured around binary oppositions:

> Nesse ir e vir, a narrativa acaba assumindo uma feição paralelística muito evidente, o que de saída deixa claro que Aluísio Azevedo encontrou a maneira correta de estruturação que deseja abordar o cortiço e o sobrado, a existência das camadas sociais mais inferiorizadas e das camadas burguesas com pretensões aristocratizantes. E, ao longo de todo o livro, vamos verificar que, além desses

amplos blocos conjugados, o relato vai se desdobrar em elementos rigorosamente binários.[5]

In this ebb and flow, the narrative ends up taking on a parallelism that is quite evident, which makes it clear at the outset that Aluísio Azevedo had found the right way to structure and probe the relationship between [João Romão's] tenement and [Miranda's] mansion, between the existence of the scorned lower class and the bourgeoisie with its aristocratic pretentiousness. And throughout the book, we observe that besides these major interlinking groups, the plot unfolds according to strictly binary elements.

Mourão argues that these oppositions play a major role in the structure of the novel. He sees them at work in the relationships between Miranda and João Romão, Miranda's mansion and João Romão's tenement, and Jerônimo and Firmo. However, the critic is quick to point out that the parallelism between opposing characters or entities does not imply that the conflicting elements "se isolem em planos eqüidistantes. Ao contrário, o que existe . . . é um estado de permanente tensão e mútua agressão"[6] [isolate themselves on equidistant planes. On the contrary, what exists . . . is a state of permanent tension and mutual aggression]. Even though Mourão's reading of *O cortiço* does not formalize the system that gives rise to these binary oppositions, it is nonetheless a valuable and welcome contribution to the study of the naturalistic novel of Brazil. It allows for the grouping of different forms and states of rivalry and adds a new dimension to our understanding of Azevedo's work. Note, for example, Mourão's observations regarding the tension between Miranda and João Romão:

> O palacete desejava se expandir com a incorporação de um quintal, enquanto a casa de cômodos sonhava poder se alastrar pelos fundos do primeiro. O muro que se levanta entre as propriedades, verifi-

cada a insuperabilidade do impasse, tem mais aparência de trinchei-
ra do que outra coisa. Encerrada a disputa em torno do terreno, a
competição continuará em outro plano. Despeitado com a prosperi-
dade de João Romão, Miranda se põe a lutar pelo título de barão,
buscando desta forma suplantar o rival; espicaçado pela vitória do
patrício . . . o rude proprietário do cortiço procura o caminho de
se requintar socialmente e parte para a conquista da filha do
adversário, o que alcança.[7]

The mansion wanted to expand by acquiring a backyard, while the
tenement house dreamed of widening its boundaries by invading its
neighbor from behind. The wall that was built between the two
properties, attesting to the insurmountability of the impasse, looked
more like a war trench than anything else. With the dispute over
the land concluded, the competition would continue in other areas.
Resentful of João Romão's prosperity, Miranda sets out to acquire
the title of baron, seeking this way to outdo his rival; taunted by his
neighbor's achievement . . . the boorish tenement owner strives to
refine himself socially and sets out to win over his rival's daughter,
which he eventually manages to do.

Mourão goes beyond the commonly held notion of lincar desire and
avarice as he probes the passions and obsessions at the heart of *O cortiço*.
He sees more at work than the simple movement of a subject toward a
desired object in the opposition between João Romão and Miranda or
between Jerônimo and Firmo. Mourão is able to perceive certain external
features of their harmful interaction and correctly foresees the conclusion
that awaits all players in these adversarial relationships:

E no desdobramento das vicissitudes dessa divergência, o que
prossegue se impondo é o mesmo esquema de oposições. Miranda
e a esposa são adversários dentro de casa; como adversários acabam

se revelando, na morada ao lado, João Romão e Bertoleza. Jerônimo e Firmo travam combate de morte. . . . Rita e Piedade
também chegam a se atracar físicamente. . . . Mas dessa luta
ninguém sairá vencedor ou vencido.[8]

As the sudden changes stemming from these differences unfold,
what eventually is established is the same scheme of oppositions.
Miranda and his wife are rivals at home, just as João Romão and
his common-law wife Bertoleza prove to be rivals in their home.
Jerônimo and Firmo engage in mortal combat. . . . Rita and
Piedade also come to blows. . . . But from these struggles no one
will come out victorious or defeated.

Still, Mourão never brings the origin and dynamics of this violent
"esquema de oposições" [scheme of oppositions] under close scrutiny.
No doubt, the critic is able to discern the overall picture of common
passions and thwarted desires that provide the structure around which the
action in *O cortiço* is developed. He translates this perception into an
engaging and persuasive reading of the novel. However, even though the
overall picture is there, the details of this vision remain blurred. On the
one hand, Mourão identifies a major structural aspect of Azevedo's novel
and correctly points out that the narrative in *O cortiço* is developed
around a scheme of oppositions based on the destructive rivalry of
contending elements. On the other hand, however, he detracts from this
insight by trying to accommodate a denouement that calls into question
the very oppositions that he seeks to disclose and formalize with his
analysis. To be sure, the oppositions discussed by Mourão are present
in Azevedo's work, and function as a major structural device in the
narrative of *O cortiço*. However, the critic dismisses perhaps the most
important and virulent of these oppositions because of a plot twist that
cannot be accounted for in his reading, namely, the peaceful and
uneventful reconciliation of the two rival neighbors, João Romão and

Miranda.   Consequently, Mourão suggests that the opposition João Romão-Miranda "se revela falsa" [proves false] in the end:

> Mas as aparências iludem e naquele mundo de equilíbrio instável, onde a vida se desencadeia tumultuária e as composições e recomposições não cessam de se fazer, só aos poucos vão se definindo as partes de fato em oposição. João Romão assume longamente todas as características de grande adversário de Miranda, para afinal com ele terminar identificado. . . . A oposição João Romão-Miranda se revela falsa.[9]

> But the appearances deceive, and in that world of unstable equilibrium, where life breaks out tumultuously and the arrangements and rearrangements never cease, only slowly do the parts in actual opposition become defined. Over time, João Romão [eventually] takes on all the characteristics of Miranda's great adversary, only to be identified with him in the end. . . . The opposition João Romão-Miranda proves false.

As I have noted, Mourão makes a significant contribution to our understanding of Azevedo's work. Yet, he fails to provide in his analysis of *O cortiço* textual evidence that might shed light on the network of opposing doubles that he discerns in the novel. In this chapter, I examine the origin and dynamics of this network and the role that it plays in Azevedo's work.

Written according to a prescriptive model of the Zolaesque *roman expérimental*, *O cortiço* is ostensibly a novel about the struggle for survival among members of the lower class. As such, it is expected to focus on the forces that rule the physical and social environment or on the plight of the individual as he battles these forces. Critics such as Olívio Montenegro, José Osório de Oliveira, and Sérgio Milliet have argued that as a *roman expérimental*, *O cortiço* does not — indeed, should not —

concern itself with the psychology of its characters.[10] However, much of the novel's appeal and structure is derived from the intrigues arising from the psychological dynamics of the many love triangles that pervade the work. These triangles figure prominently in *O cortiço*, and provide a medium through which the author articulates his particular conception of desire. Indeed, they are so pervasive that the novel could correctly be characterized — in the context of Girard's theory of mimetic desire — as an inferno replete with doubles absorbed in a potentially lethal game of imitation and rivalry.

There are several triangles of mimetic desire in *O cortiço* around which the action in the novel is structured. The most important of these is the one formed by the owner of the tenement house, his wealthy neighbor, and the objects that one deems desirable to the other. Like most forms of desire, the reciprocal mediation that affects João Romão and Miranda is set into motion by considerations that appear to be both mundane and innocuous: Miranda wants to purchase a piece of land that João Romão refuses to sell. On the surface, this situation does not appear problematic. However, this ostensible simplicity is challenged by the manner in which Azevedo structures and develops João Romão's relationship with his neighbor. Of the first encounter between the two, Azevedo writes:

> O Miranda comprou o prédio vizinho a João Romão. A casa era boa; seu único defeito estava na escassez do quintal; mas para isso havia remédio: com muito pouco compravam-se umas dez bra-ças daquele terreno do fundo. . . . Miranda foi logo entender-se com o Romão e propôs-lhe negócio. O taverneiro recusou formal-mente.
>
> Miranda insistiu.
>
> — O Senhor perde seu tempo e seu latim! retrucou João Romão. Nem só não cedo uma polegada, como ainda lhe compro,

se mo quiser vender, aquele pedaço que lhe fica ao fundo da casa!

— Isso é maldade de sua parte, sabe? . . . É que você é teimoso! . . . Creia que se arrepende de não me ceder o terreno! . . .

— Se me arrepender, paciência!

— Passe bem!

Travou-se então uma luta renhida e surda entre o português negociante de fazendas por atacado e o português negociante de secos e molhados.[11]

Miranda bought the residence next to João Romão's store. The house itself was good; the only drawback was its small backyard; but for this there was a remedy: with little money he could buy some twenty yards from that lot in the back. . . . Miranda went to talk business with João Romão at once, and proposed the deal to him. The innkeeper declined politely.

Miranda insisted.

— Sir, you are wasting your time and your words! replied João Romão. Not only will I not surrender one single inch [of my property], I will actually buy from you, if you are willing to sell, that piece of land in the back of your house.

— This is very mean of you, and you know it! . . . It's that you are stubborn! . . . Believe me, you will regret not having sold me the lot! . . .

— If I regret it, that's my problem.

— Good-bye!

After that, there ensued a vicious and silent struggle between the Portuguese fabric merchant and the Portuguese grocer.

There is obviously a good deal more at stake here than a mere plot of land. The object of desire over which João Romão and his neighbor contend is not made attractive because of its inherent attributes (it probably has none). It becomes prized and wanted in the eyes of

Miranda (the subject) because he believes it to be desired by someone else, namely, João Romão (the mediator). Thus, the main function of this apparently worthless piece of land is to link the two contending neighbors in a mimetic relationship. The uniqueness of this object is not to be found in the object proper, but it is rather a function of the position that it occupies in the mimetic triangle in relation to the subject and the mediator. As a result, both mediator and subject, especially as these are affected by double mediation, are able to shift their attention from one object to the other as they remain locked in a "luta renhida e surda" [vicious and silent struggle]. The objects change but the spatial metaphor of desire, the triangle, remains.

At this point in the novel, the roles of subject and mediator are played by Miranda and João Romão respectively. The triangle is maintained as the two neighbors go from squabbling over possession of the contested lot to wrangling over what the prospective buyer should do with his property. In the final stage of their strife, the two adversaries trade places, with João Romão on the offensive, trying to "comer-lhe [a Miranda] não duas braças, mas seis, oito, todo o quintal . . . até . . . entrar pelos fundos da casa" (19) [devour from Miranda's property not only four yards, but twelve, sixteen, the entire backyard . . . until . . . he could invade his neighbor's house from the rear].

The framework of triangular desire provides an enclosure in which subject and mediator are able to exchange places without causing any change in the structure itself. This is possible because of a state of affairs where the actions of one are mirrored and repeated in the moves of the other. The prospective buyer loses his attributes of pursuer to become a man on the defensive, liable to suffer a serious loss. His counterpart, meanwhile, quickly fills the vacated position and becomes the hunter. Miranda is obliged to retreat to his realm and build a wall, both real and imaginary, to protect his estate and himself from his neighbor. João Romão, on the other hand, becomes the consummate predator. His only

concern now is "aumentar os bens" [to increase his possessions] by giving
free reign to his greed, "apoderando-se, com os olhos, de tudo aquilo que
não pudesse apoderar-se logo com as unhas" [seizing with his eyes all that
which he could not immediately seize with his claws]. The roles have
been reversed. The pursued becomes the pursuer and vice-versa:

> [João Romão] resguardava [sua propriedade] soltando à noite
> um formidável cão de fila.
>
> Este cão era pretexto de eternas resingas com a gente do
> Miranda, a cujo quintal ninguém de casa podia descer à noite sem
> correr o risco de ser assaltado pela fera.
>
> — É fazer o muro! dizia João Romão . . .
>
> — Não faço! replicava o outro. Se é questão de capricho, eu
> também tenho capricho! . . .
>
> — Depois de tentar um derradeiro esforço para conseguir
> algumas braças do quintal do vizinho, João Romão resolveu princi-
> piar as obras da estalagem.
>
> — Deixa estar, conversava ele na cama com a Bertoleza;
> deixa estar que eu ainda lhe hei de entrar pelos fundos da casa, se
> é que não lhe entre pela frente! Mais cedo ou mais tarde como-lhe,
> não duas braças, mas seis, oito, todo o quintal e até o próprio
> sobrado talvez!
>
> E dizia isto com uma convicção de quem tudo pode e tudo
> espera de sua perseverança. . . .
>
> Desde que a febre de possuir se apoderou dele totalmente,
> todos os seus atos, todos, fosse o mais simples, visavam um
> interesse pecuniário. Só tinha uma preocupação: aumentar os
> bens. . . . Aquilo já não era ambição, era uma moléstia nervosa,
> uma loucura, um desespero de acumular. . . . E seu tipo
> baixote . . . ia e vinha da pedreira para a venda . . . olhando para
> todos os lados, com o seu eterno ar de cobiça, apoderando-se, com
> os olhos, de tudo aquilo que ele não podia apoderar-se com as
> unhas (19).

[João Romão] protected [his property] by unleashing at night a formidable guard dog. This dog was the cause of constant arguments with Miranda's family because no one in his household could go down to their backyard at night without running the risk of being attacked by the savage beast.

— You'd better build a wall! João Romão would repeat . . .

— That I'll not do! the other would reply. If it's a question of being stubborn, I can also be stubborn! . . .

— After making one last effort to acquire a portion of his neighbor's property, João Romão decided to start building his tenement house.

— Let it be, he would say to Bertoleza in bed; let it be, in the end I shall invade his house from the rear, or better yet, through the front door! Sooner or later I shall devour from Miranda's property not only four yards, but twelve, sixteen, the entire backyard and even the mansion itself!

And he would say that with the conviction of a man who believed he could do anything, and who expected everything from his perseverance. . . .

Ever since the feverish frenzy to acquire possessions took total control of him, all his actions, no matter how simple, were motivated by money and profit. He had but one concern: to increase his possessions. . . . That was no longer just greed, it was a nervous disorder, a madness, a furious rage to amass wealth. . . . And the stocky innkeeper . . . would come and go from the stone quarry to his store . . . looking everywhere, with a constant air of avarice about him, seizing with his eyes all that which he could not immediately seize with his claws.

Miranda starts out on his expansionist enterprise appearing to act upon genuine desire. However, an examination of his motives will show that this is not the case. The events that follow the above passage show that there is nothing spontaneous about Miranda's desire. His insistent though foiled attempts to buy his neighbor's property are determined by the imaginary desire that he attributes to his rival, the mediator. There is on the part of Miranda a faithful imitation of this imaginary desire. Indeed, his is a meticulous imitation, because everything about the desire that is copied, including its intensity, depends upon the desire that serves as model.[12] Thus, the more adamant João Romão remains in not wanting to sell his property, the more insistent Miranda becomes in wanting to buy it. In the rival's obstinacy not to sell, the subject sees a formidable obstacle that he believes to have been placed in his way on purpose. The obstacle makes the contested object all the more desirable to the subject but at the same time it serves to remind him of the malicious intent on the part of the mediator not to allow him to obtain what he wants. The subject reveres the model, and longs for what the model possesses or wants to possess. However, unable to fulfill his desire, the subject curses the mediator for standing in his way: "Voce é teimoso. . . . Isso é maldade de sua parte, sabe?" [You are stubborn. . . . This is very mean of you, and you know it!].

Although Miranda is more deeply affected than his neighbor, he is not the only one involved in the dance of mimetic desire outlined above. I purposefully use the term "dance" here to underscore the notion of a two-way interaction between the characters afflicted by internal mediation. The other partner in Miranda's tragic choreography is his neighbor and rival, João Romão. At this point in their relationship, João Romão serves as the mediator who helps to determine which objects Miranda ought to pursue. But as the mediator, João Romão is far from being immune to the effects of mimetic desire. He cannot remain detached because the situation is one in which the mediator himself desires the object. João Romão wants the contested property, and he wants it just as passionately as his neighbor. At the outset of their conflict, it was the mediator's desire (João Romão's) that made the contested object appear so desirable to the subject (Miranda). But the situation has changed, and a state of relative equilibrium has been reached. The subject's desire appears to affect the mediator just as profoundly as the mediator affected the subject before.

João Romão starts out as his neighbor's mediator without fully understanding the role he plays. Furthermore, his inability to generate spontaneous desire ultimately leads to his acceptance of Miranda as his mediator. This complicates matters further. As a subject, João Romão copies the desire for material possessions and social status that he associates with his wealthy neighbor. By copying the desire of the subject whom he mediates, he is actually copying a copy of his own desire. With each cycle in the enclosed confines of internal mediation, this desire redoubles, affecting even more intensely those individuals in the mimetic triangle. Realizing that their desire is no longer entirely their own, the two neighbors cling even more forcefully to the objects and positions that they held before. They end up turning simple likes and dislikes into blind obsessions. Thus, what was for João Romão only a whim in the beginning is transformed into a violent passion. His unwillingness to sell his property grows as his neighbor's insistence to buy it increases. Eventually, this unwillingness becomes a fixation of monstrous proportion. Now, not only does he refuse to sell Miranda his plot of land, he sets out to acquire his neighbor's estate and usurp his privileged position in Carioca society. We now have a subject-mediator and a mediator-subject, a model-disciple and a disciple-model. Each imitates the other and at the same time looks on their counterpart as a cruel rival. There is very little that we can say of João Romão that is not equally true of Miranda. They are different, to be sure, but their differences are limited to outward appearance alone. They complement each other in their desires, dreams, and, most of all, in what they despise. They publicly show disdain for those objects associated with the Other with as much passion as they secretly admire their rival. There is between them a sterile opposition of contraries that becomes gradually more tragic and empty as their desires intensify.[13]

Azevedo conveys this reciprocity between the two mediator-subjects by means of a common type of discourse that João Romão and Miranda share. In a moment of soul-searching, Miranda describes and praises João Romão's situation in life in much the same way that João Romão describes and praises Miranda's. They see themselves as hapless men and, not surprisingly, use the same words to refer to their respective positions in life: they had both been "uma besta!" (22, 82) [a fool]. By having João Romão and Miranda repeat the same moves — psychologically, as they wrestle with their respective shortcomings, and verbally, as they voice these shortcomings in the text — the author creates a *doppelgänger* [double] effect. Accordingly, the same thought, utterance, or action can be realized in two distinct yet complementary ways by two different characters. This allows the reader to view and experience any one given passage from more than one angle. As a literary device, the concept of the *doppelgänger* may prove very useful to novelists in the practice of their craft. However, in order for such a device to be effective, a concession of sorts is required. The novelist must allow the *doppelgänger* characters to relinquish their individual identity. These characters surrender their individuality and the prerogative to choose once they become the double of each other. Like the main character in Cervantes's *Don Quijote*, they allow someone else to choose for them. And like the tormented characters in Dostoyevsky's *Notes from the Underground*, they bitterly resent the fact that it is the Other before them, their double and nemesis, who does the choosing.

In *Maggie*, the protagonist's desire is based on external mediation. Maggie never gets close enough to her mediator to upset the harmony between the two. In *O cortiço*, the checks and balances guaranteed by distance are all but gone. The situation in Azevedo's novel is typical of internal mediation, where any impulse on the part of either subject or mediator toward a desired object is translated into an impulse toward the

Other. Any movement by either Miranda or João Romão is kept in check because these two individuals have a dual and mutually restraining effect on each other. They function both as the instigator of each other's desire and as the obstacle that prevents the fulfillment of this desire.

By getting closer to the subject, the mediator opens up the possibilities for contact and rivalry, and in this way ensures the magnitude of the obstacle that they set in each other's way. They are both caught in a double bind. On the one hand, they blame each other for their rivalry, and belittle everything that originates with the Other. On the other hand, however, they still desire in private the very objects that they deprecate in public. Miranda appears to have nothing but contempt for João Romão: "Aquele tipo! um miserável, um sujo, que não pusera nunca um paletó, e que vivia de cama e mesa com uma negra!" (22). [That good-for-nothing! a filthy wretch who had never worn a suit and tie in his entire life, and who lived, bed and board, with a black woman!]. But when Miranda is left alone to gather his thoughts, and has a chance to compare his neighbor's situation to his own, this acrimonious contempt turns to admiration and envy:

> Era ainda a prosperidade do vizinho o que lhe obsedava o espírito, enegrecendo-lhe a alma com um feio ressentimento de despeito.
>
> Tinha inveja do outro, daquele outro português que fizera fortuna sem precisar roer nenhum chifre; daquele outro que, para ser mais rico tres vezes do que ele, não teve de casar com a filha do patrão ou com a bastarda de algum fazendeiro freguês da casa!
>
> Mas então, ele, Miranda, que se supunha a última expressão da ladinagem e da esperteza . . . nao passava afinal de um pedaço de asno comparado com o seu vizinho! . . .
>
> — Fui uma besta! resumiu ele em voz alta. . . . A febre daquela inveja lhe estorricava os miolos.
>
> Feliz e esperto era o João Romão! esse, sim, senhor! Para

esse é que havia de ser a vida! . . . Filho da mãe, que estava hoje
tão livre e desembaraçado como no dia em que chegou da terra sem
um vintém de seu! esse, sim, que era moço e que podia ainda
gozar muito. . . .

Fui uma besta! repisava ele sem conseguir conformar-se com
a felicidade do vendeiro (22).

It was his neighbor's prosperity that tormented his spirit,
darkening his soul with an ugly and bitter resentment.

He was envious of the other, of that other Portuguese who
managed to get rich without having to kowtow to anyone; the other,
who, in order to be three times richer than he, did not have to
marry his boss's daughter or the bastard child of some rich
customer.

This meant that he, Miranda, who thought of himself as
exceptionally shrewd . . . was really no more than a bumbling fool
when compared to his neighbor.

— I was a fool! he said out loud. . . . His envy was like a
fever, burning and consuming his entire self.

João Romão was the one who was fortunate and smart! Yes,
sir! The best in life would be his. Remarkable! today he was as
free as when he first arrived from Portugal without any money! He
was still young and had his entire life ahead of him to enjoy.

I was a fool! Miranda would say repeatedly, unable to
stomach the innkeeper's happiness.

Finding himself consumed with envy and in the middle of a sterile
conflict from which he cannot voluntarily withdraw, Miranda tries to put
some distance between himself and his rival. This feat, he reasons, could
be accomplished by doing or acquiring something of preeminence.
Consequently, in an attempt to outdo and distinguish himself from his
neighbor, Miranda decides to acquire a title of nobility:

Foi da supuração fétida destas idéias que se formou no coração vazio do Miranda um novo ideal — o título. Faltando-lhe temperamento próprio para vícios fortes que enchem a vida de um homem; sem família a quem amar e sem imaginação para poder gozar com as prostitutas, o náufrago agarrou-se àquela tábua, como um agonizante, consciente da morte, que se apega a esperança de uma vida futura (23).

It was from the fetid suppuration of these ideas that a new objective took shape in Miranda's empty heart — a noble title. He lacked the character required by those strong vices that play such an important role in the lives of some men; without a family to love and lacking the imagination needed to enjoy the company of prostitutes, Miranda, like a drowning man, clung to that last hope, agonizing against an impending death and fighting for the possibility of a life in the future.

Trying to distinguish himself from his rival at all costs only makes Miranda more like João Romão. At this point in the novel, João Romão does not want to acquire a title of nobility. However, like his wealthy neighbor, he does want to distinguish himself from his rival by assimilating the illusion of his superior difference. In this respect, they are very much alike, and as long as they carry on with their attempts to be superior and different from one another, they will ensure their imprisonment in a violent and futile reciprocity.

By acquiring a noble title, Miranda upsets the equilibrium in his relationship with João Romão. He manages to tip the scale of influence and prestige in his favor by distancing himself from his neighbor. The title, along with the aristocratic preeminence that it suggests, elevates Miranda above his rival and places even farther out of João Romão's reach the objects of his desire. The distance and the obstacle keeping the two apart become even greater. Realizing that he has been left behind, the subject is bound to interpret this separation brought about by the mediator as evidence that the model considers himself too superior to have any dealings with him or to accept him as an equal. Therefore, it is not surprising that João Romão goes into a fit of rage over his neighbor's new exploit:

> No outro dia a casa do Miranda estava em . . . festa (77).
>
> O Barão, todo de branco . . . brilhantes no peito da camisa, chegava de vez em quando a uma das janelas . . . agradecendo para a rua . . . risonho, feliz, resplandecente (81).
>
> João Romão via tudo isto com o coração moído (82).
>
> Ele esse dia estava intolerante com tudo e com todos. . . . Nunca o tinham visto assim, tão fora de si, tão cheio de repelões; nem parecia aquele mesmo homem inalterável, sempre calmo e metódico.
>
> E ninguém seria capaz de acreditar que a causa de tudo isso era o fato de ter sido o Miranda agraciado com o título de Barão.
>
> Sim, senhor! Aquele taverneiro, na aparência tão humilde e tão miserável . . . invejava agora o Miranda, invejava-o deveras, com dobrada amargura do que sofrera o marido de Dona Estela, quando por sua vez o invejara a ele. . . .
>
> Quando o vendeiro leu no "Jornal do Comércio" que o vizinho estava barão — Barão! — sentiu tamanho calafrio em todo o corpo, que a vista por um instante se lhe apagou dos olhos (79-80).

> The other day Miranda's household threw . . . a party [to celebrate his new title].
>
> The baron, all dressed in white . . . with diamonds on his lapel, would periodically appear at one of the windows in his house . . . acknowledging [his admirers] in the street . . . smiling, contented, beaming with joy.
>
> João Romão watched the whole spectacle with a crushed heart.

That day João Romão was in a very foul mood, arguing with everyone and everything. . . . They had never see him like that, so irritable, so beside himself with anger; he didn't seem his former self, whom his tenants knew to be even-tempered, always calm and disciplined.

And nobody could suspect that the reason for João Romão's anger was the fact that Miranda had been granted the title of baron.

Yes, sir! That simple and scruffy-looking innkeeper . . . now was envious of Miranda, and very envious indeed, twice as envious as Dona Estela's husband had been of him in the past. . . .

When João Romão read in the "Jornal do Comércio" that his neighbor had been granted the title of baron — baron! — his entire body grew cold as he momentarily went blind [with resentment].

However, this virulent display of envy does not prevent the owner of the tenement from showing genuine appreciation for the kind of life that his neighbor leads. João Romão evaluates his situation vis-à-vis Miranda's without any of the bitterness found in the above passage. The innkeeper's reflections can aptly be described as the mirror image of Miranda's own contemplations. The reciprocity between the two men is such that both João Romão and Miranda choose essentially the same terms to describe themselves:

Fora uma besta! . . . pensou de si próprio, amargurado: uma grande besta! . . . Pois não! por que em tempo não tratara de habituar-se logo a certo modo de viver, como faziam tantos outros seus patrícios e colegas de profissão? . . . Por que, como eles, não aprendera a dançar? e não freqüentara sociedades carnavalescas? e não fora de vez em quando à Rua do Ouvidor e aos teatros e bailes, e corridas e a passeios? . . . Por que não se habituara com as roupas finas, e com o calçado justo, e com a bengala, e com o lenço, e com o charuto, e com o chapéu, e com a cerveja, e com tudo que os outros usavam naturalmente? (82)

> He had been a fool! . . . he thought of himself, embittered:
> a great fool! . . . Of course! why hadn't he tried to get used to a
> certain lifestyle, as all his fellow countrymen and business
> associates did? . . . Why hadn't he, like them, learned how to
> dance? frequented *carnaval* clubs? and gone on a regular basis to
> [the business district on] Ouvidor Street, and to the theater, and
> balls, to races, and social outings? . . . Why hadn't he purchased
> and enjoyed fine clothes, attractive shoes, a walking cane, a hand-
> kerchief, cigars, a hat, good beer, and everything else that other
> men used so naturally?

This secret admiration does not imply that the subject is willing to accept openly the judgment and influence of his mediator. On the contrary, even though João Romão yearns for the social status and respectability enjoyed by his wealthy neighbor, he sees in the mediator's desire for these things an obstacle that prevents him from attaining what Miranda already has. Accordingly, Miranda is unable to act out his role of model without also playing the role of obstacle. By possessing or coveting the objects that João Romão desires, Miranda shows his disciple the gates of paradise, and forbids him to enter with one and the same gesture. And João Romão, ever fascinated with his rival and the world that he represents, invariably sees in the mechanical obstacle put in his way proof of the ill will borne him. Far from declaring himself a faithful vassal, he thinks only of repudiating the bonds of mediation.[14] Consider his reaction to Miranda's invitation for tea:

> Quando João Romão entrou na venda . . . um caixeiro
> entregou-lhe um cartão do Miranda. Era um convite para ir lá à
> noite tomar . . . chá.
> O vendeiro, a princípio, ficou lisonjeado com o obséquio,

primeiro desse gênero que em sua vida recebia; mas logo depois voltou-lhe a cólera com mais ímpeto ainda. Aquele convite irritava-o como um ultraje, uma provocação. "Por que o pulha o convidara, devendo saber que ele decerto lá não ia? . . . Para que, se não para enfrenisiar ainda mais do que já estava?! . . . Seu Miranda que fosse à tábua com a sua festa e com os seus títulos!" — Não preciso dele para nada! . . . exclamou o vendeiro. Não preciso, nem dependo de nenhum safardana! (84-85)

When João Romão entered the store . . . one of his clerks handed him a letter from Miranda. It was an invitation for him to join them for . . . tea that evening.

Initially the grocer felt flattered because of Miranda's invitation, the very first such request he had ever received; but soon afterwards his anger took control of him again, this time even more violently. That invitation goaded him as would an insult or a provocation from an enemy. Why had that good-for-nothing invited him, knowing for sure that he wouldn't accept the invitation? . . . Why, if not only to taunt him even more than what he had already done?! . . . Miranda could go to hell with his parties and his titles!"

— I don't need him for anything! . . . shouted the grocer. I don't need nor depend on any scoundrel.

Yet, the bonds of mediation are stronger than ever, because the mediator's apparent hostility does not diminish his prestige but instead increases it.[15] The above display of contempt for the mediator does little to preclude the subject from imitating the rival, as we see in this passage:

Desde que o vizinho surgiu como o baronato, o vendeiro transformava-se por dentro e por fora a causar pasmo. Mandou fazer boas roupas e aos domingos refestelava-se de casaco branco e de meias, assentado defronte da venda, a ler jornais. Depois deu

para sair a passeio, vestido de casimira, calçado e de gravata. . . .
Já não era o mesmo lambuzão! E não parou aí: fez-se sócio de um
clube de dança . . . começou a usar relógio e cadeia de ouro . . .
principiou a comer com guardanapo . . . entrou a tomar vinho
[especial], passou a receber . . . romances franceses traduzidos,
que o ambicioso lia de cabo a rabo, com uma paciência de santo,
na doce convicção de que se instruia. . . . E em breve o seu tipo
começou a ser visto com freqüência na Rua Direita, na praça do
comércio e nos bancos, o chapéu alto derreado para a nuca e o
guarda-chuva debaixo do braço (103-104).

After his neighbor acquired the title of baron, the grocer
underwent an amazing transformation, inside and out. He custom-
ordered fine clothes for himself, and on Sundays he would relax,
wearing a white jacket and socks, sitting in front of his store and
reading the newspaper. Later, he started taking long walks, and he
would put on his best woolens, fine shoes and a tie. . . . He was
no longer the same scruffy and careless dresser! And his
transformation didn't stop there: he joined a dancing club . . .
began using a gold watch . . . took to eating with a napkin . . . and
drinking [premium] wine, and began receiving . . . French novels
translated into Portuguese, which he eagerly read from front to
cover, with the patience of a holy man, convinced that he was
educating himself. . . . And soon he started to be seen on a regular
basis on Direita Street, in the business centers and at the banks,
sporting a hat and with an umbrella under his arm.

Under the mediator's influence and following his cues, João Romão
undergoes a remarkable transformation. He becomes increasingly more
like his aristocratic neighbor, engaging in social practices and acquiring
habits that he believes to be evidence of refinement and good taste. With
João Romão's metamorphosis, there comes about between the two

neighbors a reconciliation of sorts. After the owner of the tenement has successfully bridged the gap that his neighbor's noble title had created, Miranda relinquishes his position as mediator to play the role of subject. Once again, he is mediated by his counterpart:

> O Miranda tratava-o já de outro modo, tirava-lhe o chapéu, parava risonho para lhe falar quando se encontravam na rua, e às vezes trocava com ele dois dedos de palestra à porta da venda. Acabou por oferecer-lhe a casa e convidá-lo para o dia de anos da mulher, que era daí a pouco tempo (104).

> Miranda began treating [João Romão] differently. He would greet him by taking off his hat, and would stop, smiling, to talk to him whenever they ran into each other on the street, and sometimes he would engage [his neighbor] in lively conversation at the door of João Romão's store. Finally, [Miranda] invited [João Romão] over to his house, and asked him to come to his wife's birthday party, which would take place in a few days.

The two have now traveled full circle, returning to the initial configuration of their mimetic relationship. Now, João Romão shines and decrees while Miranda accepts his influence, and obligingly makes the mediator's likes and dislikes manifest in his own life:

> O Miranda escutava [João Romão] calado, fitando-o com respeito.
> — Você é um homem dos diabos! disse afinal, batendo-lhe no ombro. . . .
> Trazia uma grande admiração pelo vizinho. O que ainda lhe restava da primitiva inveja transformou-se nesse instante num entusiasmo ilimitado e cego.
> — É um filho da mãe! resmungava ele pela rua, em caminho

do seu armazém. É de muita força! (131)

>   Miranda listened to [João Romão] without saying a word, only
>   gazing at him with great respect.
>   — You're a remarkable man! he said finally, tapping João
>   Romão on his shoulder. . . .
>   He had developed a great admiration for his neighbor. What
>   remained of his erstwhile envy had been transformed into blind and
>   boundless enthusiasm.
>   — He's an extraordinary man! he would mutter on his way to
>   João Romão's store. He has so much energy!

Given the new variables now at work in the game, the old setup
between the two neighbors will not likely remain as uneventful and
pleasant as Miranda seems to want. The preservation of the status quo,
where a balance of power and influence favorable to Miranda is
maintained, seems to be wishful thinking entertained by Miranda alone.
João Romão has different plans for both himself and his neighbor. He
views the rapprochement between the two in a completely different light
than Miranda does. As a mediator-subject still very much intent in
outdoing his rival, he has but one thing on his mind — he wants to be
better and to have more than Miranda:

>   Com lembrar-se da sua união com [a filha do Miranda] um
>   largo quadro de vitórias rasgava-se defronte da desensofrida avidez
>   da sua vaidade. . . . Fazia-se membro de uma família tradicional-
>   mente orgulhosa . . . aumentava consideravelmente os seus bens
>   com o dote da noiva, que era rica e . . . afinal, caber-lhe-ia mais
>   tarde tudo o que o Miranda possuia, realizando-se deste modo um
>   velho sonho que o vendeiro afagava desde o nascimento de sua
>   rivalidade com o vizinho.
>   E via-se já na brilhante posição que o esperava: uma vez de

dentro, associava-se logo com o sogro e iria pouco a pouco . . . o empurrando para o lado, até empolgar-lhe o lugar e fazer de si um verdadeiro chefe da colônia portuguesa no Brasil; depois . . . tome lá alguns pares de contos de réis e passe-me para cá o título de visconde. . . .

Ah! ele . . . sustentava de si para si nos últimos anos o firme propósito de fazer-se um titular mais graduado que o Miranda (145-146).

Reflecting on his union with [Miranda's daughter] and moved by greed and vanity, João Romão envisioned a vast sequence of accomplishments for himself. . . . He would join a family of traditional pride and social standing . . . he would substantially increase his possessions with the dowry of the bride, who was very rich, and . . . finally, he would later inherit everything that Miranda owned, realizing this way the old dream that the grocer had nurtured ever since his rivalry with his neighbor began.

And he could already picture himself in the magnificent position that awaited him: once inside [Miranda's family], he would become his father-in-law's business partner and little by little . . . he would shove him aside, until he could take his place, thus becoming the real leader of the Portuguese immigrant colony in Brazil; later . . . by bribing the right official, he would acquire the title of viscount.

In the last few years, João Romão had secretly and steadfastly sustained the objective of acquiring a title of higher ranking than Miranda's.

In his dual role as mediator and subject, João Romão continues to be mediated by Miranda. He desires to possess what his rival already has and he does not. He yearns for the social status, respectability, and aristocratic ranking that he associates with his nemesis. Clearly, one should not take the relatively uneventful denouement in *O cortiço* to be an indication of the absence of virulence in the relationship between the two neighbors. Neither should one view it as an implied assertion on the part of the author that everything will eventually end peacefully between the two rivals. Even if the ending in *O cortiço* is not as violent and final as that in *Maggie*, we are still allowed some revealing glimpses into the "febre" [feverish frenzy], the "loucura" [madness], and "desespero" [furious rage], that afflicts both neighbors. The way in which this "moléstia nervosa" [nervous disorder] works itself out in rivalry, conflict, and destruction suggests what kind of conclusion one might expect from this mimetic relationship. Their affair is left largely unresolved. It lacks anything resembling a clearly defined resolution. Miranda is happy with the status quo that he has managed to attain vis-à-vis his future son-in-law. João Romão, however, is already busy scheming new ways to outdo Miranda and usurp his privileged place in society, maybe even have him killed. Given the principles under which mimetic desire operates, and that the possibility of a violent denouement is clearly articulated in the text, one cannot expect the resolution between these two to be anything but disastrous. The likelihood of a mutually destructive conclusion is conveyed in the language that Azevedo uses to describe João Romão's intended usurpation of Miranda's place in society:

> Mais cedo ou mais tarde como-lhe . . . todo o quintal e até o próprio sobrado. [João Romão] dizia isto [possuido de] um desespero de acumular . . . com o seu eterno ar de cobiça, apoderando-se, com os olhos, de tudo aquilo que ele não podia apoderar-se logo com as unhas (19).
>
> Iria pouco a pouco . . . empurrando [o sogro] para o lado, até empolgar-lhe o lugar (145).

> Sooner or later I shall devour [Miranda's] entire backyard and even the mansion itself! [João Romão] said that repeatedly,

[possessed by] a furious rage to amass wealth . . . with a constant air of avarice about him, seizing with his eyes all that which he could not immediately seize with his claws.

He would gradually shove [his father-in-law] aside, until he could take his place.

Certain terms in the above passage convey in vivid detail the magnitude of the havoc that the two mediator-subjects are bound to wreak upon each other. "O sobrado" [Miranda's mansion] can be interpreted as a surrogate of the owner himself, thus revealing the anthropophagic dimension of the verb "comer" [to eat, devour]. "Apoderar-se com as unhas" [to seize with one's claws] suggests an act of usurpation in which the desired object is ravaged. "Empurrar" [to shove aside] implies the application of force against someone in order to move the individual away from a privileged position in life, possibly toward abandonment and death. "Empolgar-lhe o lugar" [to take one's place] denotes the forcible taking of one's position in society. This could be attained either by having the person killed or, as with cannibals, by physically consuming the individual, thereby appropriating, in a literal sense, the victim's strengths and qualities. Moreover, a brutal denouement is virtually ensured because João Romão's intended victim is bound to copy whatever schemes the mediator concocts and puts into action. In the violent reciprocity of internal mediation, any attempt on the part of one of the mediator-subjects to destroy the other will inevitably be realized as the destruction of both.

The dynamics at work in the mimetic opposition that pits João Romão against Miranda are projected and reproduced in the interaction between the *sobrado* (Miranda's mansion) and the *cortiço* (João Romão's tenement). The mansion and the tenement are depicted by Azevedo in much the same way that he portrays the men and women in his novel. The two dwellings are part of the environment, and as such they are supposed to have power over the other characters. However, as Massoud Moisés points out, "não se trata apenas do poder do 'meio' sobre as pessoas; é considerar esse 'meio' como *outra entidade* além da que as personagens compõem, interferindo na ação com sua presença forte e dominadora."[16] [It is not merely a question of the power of the "environment" over people; we must consider this "environment" as *another entity*, in addition to that which the characters make up, which shapes the action with its powerful and overwhelming presence].

Azevedo is particularly skilled at depicting the physical and social environment as if he were dealing with individual characters. By treating both the tenement and the mansion as characters subject to the same mimetic influence affecting the men and women in his novel, the author derives from their interaction an effect similar to that produced in the relationship between João Romão and Miranda. To be sure, the individuals who constitute the *sobrado* and the *cortiço* are not affected by mimetic desire to the degree that João Romão and Miranda are. Still, they follow the same basic moves that their landlords go through in their own game of internal mediation. Like Miranda, his family and the other residents of his mansion yearn for the freedom, excitement, and sensuousness that they associate with life in the tenement. Zulmirinha, Miranda's only daughter, embodies the least attractive qualities of the *sobrado*:

> [Ela] crescia muito pálida e precisava de largueza para enrijar e tomar corpo (16).
>
> Era o tipo acabado da fluminense; pálida, magrinha . . . respirava o tom úmido das flores noturnas, uma brancura fria de magnólia; cabelos castanho-claros, mãos quase transparentes (23).

> She looked anemic, and needed space and fresh air to grow healthy and strong.
>
> She was a frail and tired-looking native of Rio de Janeiro;

pale, skinny . . . like a fragile and clammy nocturnal flower, she had a whiteness as cold as that of a magnolia; her hair was light brown, and her hands were almost translucent.

The *cortiço*, by contrast, is described in lusty and vibrant terms:

As casinhas do cortiço, a proporção que se atamancavam, enchiam-se logo, sem mesmo dar tempo a que as tintas secassem. . . . E naquela terra encharcada e fumegante, naquela umidade quente e lodosa, começou a minhocar, a esfervilhar, a crescer, um mundo, uma coisa viva, uma geração, que parecia brotar espontânea, ali mesmo, daquele lameiro, e multiplicar-se como larvas no ester-co. . . . Durante dois anos o cortiço prosperou de dia para dia, ganhando forças, socando-se de gente. E ao lado o Miranda assus-tava-se inquieto com aquela exuberância brutal de vida, aterrado defronte daquela floresta implacável que lhe crescia junto da casa, por debaixo das janelas, e cujas raízes piores e mais grossas do que serpentes, minavam por toda a parte, ameaçando rebentar o chão em torno dela, rachando o solo e abalando tudo (20-21).

As soon as they finished building additional houses in the tenement, these were snatched up immediately, with the tenants hardly waiting for the paint to dry. . . . And in that wet and steamy soil, in that warm and humid mire, there began to stir, to teem, to grow forth, a world, something alive, a generation that seemed to sprout spontaneously, right then and there, from that swamp, and to multiply like maggots in manure. . . . In the space of two years, the tenement prospered from day to day, gaining strength, stuffing itself with people. And beside [João Romão's grocery store], Miranda grew frightened. That brutal exuberance of life troubled him. He was terrified by the forest that now thrived and expanded inexorably right next to his mansion, under the windows, and whose roots, more loathsome and thicker than serpents, spread everywhere, threatening to crack open the ground all around him, shattering the floor and disturbing everything.

When the residents of the *sobrado* find themselves face to face with the things that they desire, instead of being drawn to them, they pull back. They react this way because they cannot accept, at least not openly, an object designated or possessed by the rival. Consider, for instance, Miranda's reaction to the thriving "voluptuoso mundo" [voluptuous world] of João Romão's tenement.

> O Miranda rebentava de raiva.
> — Um cortiço! exclamava ele, possesso.   Um cortiço!
> Maldito seja aquele vendeiro de todos os diabos!   Fez-me um cortiço debaixo das janelas! . . . Estragou-me a casa, o malvado! (20)
> À noite e aos domingos ainda mais recrudescia o seu azedume, quando ele, recolhendo-se fatigado do serviço, deixava-se ficar estendido numa preguiçosa, junto à mesa da sala de jantar, e ouvia, a contragosto, o grosseiro rumor que vinha da estalagem numa exalação forte de animais cansados.   Não podia chegar à janela sem receber no rosto aquele bafo quente e sensual, que o embebedava com o seu fartum de besta no coito (22).

> Miranda became livid with anger.
> — A tenement! he would shout furiously.   A tenement! Damn that grocer!   He built a tenement right under my window! . . . He ruined my home, that scoundrel!
> At night and on Sundays his exasperation would intensify, when he, coming home fatigued from work, would lie down in a chaise longue next to the dinner table, and would be forced to listen to the crude sounds coming from João Romão's tenement, [sounds that resembled] the forceful panting of tired animals.   He could not

approach the window without being struck in the face with that steamy and sensual exhalation, a stench of animals in heat that intoxicated and overwhelmed him.

Even if the subject of desire (the mansion) does not publicly acknowledge the influence of the mediator (the tenement), it does not follow that the model's power is neutralized. The subject's overt disdain for the things associated with the mediator is the reverse reflection of a secret and equally passionate admiration for the rival. A tragic opposition of contraries is ensured as long as the subject continues to covet and reject, in one and the same move, those things deemed desirable by the mediator. In the condition of mediator-subject, the *cortiço*, like its proprietor, plays a dual role in its relationship with the *sobrado*. The tenement mediates and at the same time it is mediated by the mansion. The men and women in João Romão's tenement yearn for the social status and respectability that they lack. By taking cues from the model, the tenement ends up pursuing goals that put it on a collision course with the mediator. On the one hand, the *cortiço* becomes more like the *sobrado*:

> Mas o cortiço ja não era o mesmo; estava muito diferente; mal dava idéia do que fora (140).
> Já lá não se admitia assim qualquer pé-rapado: para entrar era preciso carta de fiança e uma recomendação especial. Os preços dos cômodos subiam, e muitos dos antigos hóspedes . . . iam, por economia, desertando . . . e sendo substitutidos por gente mais limpa. . . . O cortiço aristocratizava-se (153).

The tenement was no longer the same; it had changed a lot; it hardly resembled the way it was before.

Now, the poor tenants were not so easily admitted: in order to rent a house, they needed references and a deposit. The rent had

> gone up, and many of the former tenants . . . who had to leave in
> order to save money . . . were being replaced by people with more
> resources. . . . The tenement was moving up the social ladder.

On the other hand, however, the tenement never stops looking for
ways to outdo and supplant its model and adversary. As the two rivals
strive to realize their individual goals — keeping, as a result, each other
in check — the tension that has permeated the relationship from the outset
threatens to erupt in violence. Therefore, it does not come as a surprise
that Azevedo should choose to use terms of warfare such as "recuar" [to
retreat], "perseguir" [to pursue, hound], "batalhão" [battalion], and
"triunfante" [triumphant] to describe the situation into which the *sobrado*
is pushed by its less aristocratic counterpart:

> O prédio do Miranda parecia ter recuado alguns passos, perseguido
> pelo batalhão de casinhas da esquerda, e agora olhava a medo, por
> cima dos telhados, para a casa do vendeiro, que lá defronte erguia-
> se altiva, desassombrada, o ar sobranceiro e triunfante (141).

> It looked as though Miranda's mansion had retreated a few steps,
> hounded by the battalion of little tenement houses on the left, and
> now, frightened, it stared over the roofs at the grocer's home,
> which farther down the street loomed proud, undaunted, confidently
> flaunting its triumph.

However, as in the hostile exchange between Miranda and João
Romão, the same *sobrado* that now finds itself pulling back as it is
hounded by its rival will eventually trade places with its pursuer. The
distinguishing characteristic of internal mediation is its ability to create
situations in which the actions of one of the rivals are faithfully copied by
the other. Consequently, whatever one decides to do to the other, in the
end this action will invariably be realized as the common fate of both

partners. By alternating places and by pursuing a course of action where each of the mediator-subjects is "perseguido" [pursued, hounded] and has to "recuar a medo" [retreat in fear], the mansion and the tenement ensure a conclusion to their affair just as violent as that which the text suggests for João Romão and Miranda.

The grim denouement hinted at in the oppositions between João Romão and Miranda and between the *sobrado* and *cortiço* is fully realized in the mimetic relationship between Jerônimo, Firmo, and Rita Baiana. These three characters form another major triangle of mimetiç desire in *O cortiço*. Along with the two that I have already discussed, this love triangle serves as the focus of complication and intrigue around which a good part of the action in the novel is developed. Jerônimo functions as a double of Firmo in much the same way that João Romão enacts his role as Miranda's *doppelgänger*. In both cases, there is much more at work than the simple juxtaposition of opposing characters. The doubles share an organic reciprocity that goes beyond the mere weighing of shared similarities and differences. They complement each other physically and psychologically by sharing a mimetic desire that works itself out in conflict, rivalry, and death. From the day Jerônimo appears at João Romão's tenement, the fates of the Portuguese immigrant, Jerônimo, and the Brazilian *malandro* [rogue, con artist], Firmo, become entwined. On the physical level, they are depicted as having exact opposite traits. Note Azevedo's description of Jerônimo:

> um português de seus trinta e cinco a quarenta anos, alto, espadaúdo, barbas ásperas . . . pescoço de touro e cara de Hércules, na qual os olhos todavia, humildes como os olhos de um boi de canga, exprimiam tranqüila bondade (35).

> a Portuguese man of about thirty-five to forty years of age, tall, with broad shoulders, coarse beard . . . a very thick neck and the

face of a Hercules. His eyes, gentle like those of an ox, radiated tranquility and kindness.

In contrast, Firmo, because he embodies entirely different physical attributes, negates and at the same time complements those of his *doppelgänger*:

> Era um mulato pachola, delgado de corpo e ágil como um cabrito; capadócio de marca, pernóstico, só de maçadas, e todo ele se quebrando nos seus movimentos de capoeira. Teria seus trinta e tantos anos, mas não parecia ter mais de vinte e poucos. Pernas e braços finos, pescoço estreito . . . não tinha músculos, tinha nervos. A respeito de barba, nada mais que um bigodinho crespo, petulante (49).
>
> Pulou à arena o Firmo, ágil, de borracha, a fazer coisas fantásticas com as pernas, a derreter-se todo, a sumir-se no chão, a ressurgir inteiro com um pulo, os pés no espaço, batendo os calcanhares, os braços a querer fugir-lhe dos ombros, a cabeça a querer saltar-lhe [do corpo] (56-57).

He was a conceited mulatto, skinny and nimble as a goat; an incorrigible crook, arrogant, always making a nuisance of himself. He walked with a swagger, moving to the rhythms of *capoeira* [Afro-Brazilian martial art]. He was a little over thirty years of age, but he looked as though he was in his twenties. His legs and arms were very slender, he had a thin neck . . . and sinewy nerves instead of muscles. He had no beard, only a coarse, petulant little moustache.

Firmo joined in the dancing, agile and supple as if made of rubber, doing incredible things with his legs, melting and disappearing into the ground, then jumping back on his feet and reappearing whole again. He would kick into the air, click his heels, and swing his arms and head as if they were about to be torn [from his body].

Jerônimo and Firmo are opposites who form what Wilma Newberry calls a "complementary completive pair."[17] This synergetic opposition becomes apparent in the scene in which the two men fight over Rita Baiana. Here, the physical persona of each rival is defined negatively vis-à-vis the other. It is as though they are each other's reverse mirror image:

> E, no meio da grande roda, iluminados amplamente pelo capitoso luar de abril, os dois homens perfilados defronte um do outro, olhavam-se em desafio.
> Jerônimo era alto, espadaúdo, construção de touro, pescoço de Hércules, punho de quebrar um coco com um murro: era a força tranqüila, o pulso de chumbo. O outro, [Firmo], franzino, um palmo mais baixo que o português, pernas e braços secos, agilidade de maracajá: era a força nervosa; era o arrebatamento que tudo desbarata no sobressalto do primeiro instante. Um sólido e resistente; o outro, ligeiro e destemido, mas ambos corajosos (86).

And in the middle of that big circle, lit up by a bright and intoxicating April moon, the two men faced each other defiantly.
Jerônimo was tall, with broad shoulders, built like a bull, with the neck of a Hercules, and fists strong enough to crack open a coconut with a single blow: he represented calm, strength, and firm resolve. The other [Firmo], was thin and a little shorter than the Portuguese; he had slender arms and legs, and possessed the agility of a wildcat: he was high-strung, powerful, explosive, and in the habit of overcoming his enemies by surprise. One was robust and strong, the other was quick and bold, and both were equally courageous.

This conflictive complementarity on the physical level is reproduced on other levels as well. Jerônimo's industriousness and discipline — "Era tão metódico e tão bom trabalhador quanto o era como homem" (41) [He was as conscientious and diligent a worker as he was a man] — are highlighted and at the same time kept in check by his nemesis. The *malandro*'s indolence complements and negates Jerônimo's qualities: "[Firmo] era oficial de torneiro, oficial perito e vadio; [o que] ganhava [em] uma semana . . . gastava num dia." (49) [Firmo worked as a lathe operator. He was an expert in his trade and in the art of loafing; what he earned in one week . . . he spent in a day]. The object that brings Jerônimo and Firmo together is a woman, Rita Baiana, whose attractiveness may be construed by the casual reader as the major factor behind their rivalry. Rita is described by Azevedo as a sensual and desirable woman:

> Toda ela respirava o asseio das brasileiras e um odor sensual de trevos e plantas aromáticas. Irrequieta, saracoteando o atrevido e rijo quadril baiano, respondia para a direita e para a esquerda . . . com um realce fascinador (45).
>
> [Rita] saltou em meio da roda [de samba], com os braços na cintura, rebolando as ilhargas e bamboleando a cabeça . . . como numa sofreguidão de gozo carnal, num requebrado luxurioso que a punha ofegante . . . a tremer toda, como se fosse afundando num prazer grosso que nem azeite. . . . Depois [vergava] as pernas, descendo, subindo, sem nunca parar com os quadris, e em seguida sapateava, miúdo e cerrado freneticamente, erguendo e abaixando os braços, que dobrava . . . sobre a nuca, enquanto a carne lhe fervia toda, fibra por fibra, titilando (56).

Like other Brazilian women, she kept herself clean and well-groomed, and exuded a sensual odor of aromatic herbs. Restless, always swinging her firm and saucy hips, she would sway rhythmically to the left, then to the right . . . with fascinating charm.

[Rita] jumped into the circle of samba dancers, her hands at her waist, her head and hips moving wildly, as if she were in the throes of an orgasm. Her body convulsed so deliriously that she soon grew exhausted . . . trembling all over, absorbed in a carnal pleasure as sweet and thick as honey. . . . Then she would bend her legs, bringing them up and down, always swinging her hips, and afterwards she would tap-dance, fast and frantic, raising and lowering her arms around her neck while her entire body burned with desire.

In a linear reading of the affair between Jerônimo, Firmo, and Rita Baiana, one could argue that the source of desire is the object herself. However, such a reading would leave too many questions unanswered. Certain fundamental changes in the participants in this love triangle prove too relevant and pervasive to be explained in terms of a desire based on subject and object alone. Jerônimo undergoes a slow but profound transformation from a conscientious and hard-working newcomer into the consummate *malandro*. Firmo, on the other hand, develops a fierce jealousy about a woman whom the author describes as merely one among his many lovers and who apparently is not his favorite. The abnormal passion that consumes both Jerônimo and Firmo stems neither from Rita's attributes nor from the spontaneity that the subject (Jerônimo) is presumed to enjoy. This transfiguring desire is a function of the influence that the subject and the mediator have on each other.

As the subject of desire (Jerônimo) surrenders his freedom of choice, he allows the mediator to designate for him what objects should be pursued. Of course, the most conspicuous and attractive of all objects associated with the mediator (Firmo) is his lover, Rita Baiana. To Jerônimo, she embodies both the appeal of the new land and the negation of the old world that he left behind:

> Naquela mulata estava o grande mistério, a síntese das
> impressões que ele recebeu chegando aqui: ela era a luz ardente do
> meio-dia; ela era o calor vermelho da sestas da fazenda; era o
> aroma quente dos trevos e das baunilhas, que o atordoara nas matas
> brasileiras; era a palmeira virginal e esquiva que não se torce a
> nehuma outra planta; era o veneno e era o açúcar gostoso (57).

> That black woman held the answer to a great mystery. She
> was the synthesis of his first impressions as he arrived [in Brazil]:
> she was the blazing light of a midday sun; the red heat of an after-
> noon siesta in the countryside; the warm smell of clovers and
> vanilla trees, which had overwhelmed him in the local forests; she
> was the pristine and evasive palm tree that does not bend to any
> other tree; she was at once poisonous and deliciously sweet.

In order to fulfill his desire and enjoy Rita's favors, Jerônimo is
forced to undergo a profound transformation. This metamorphosis requires him to relinquish his erstwhile qualities before he can usurp those
of the mediator. He eventually accomplishes his goal, but only over an
extended period of time in which he gradually becomes more like Firmo
and less like his former self. The first changes occur in the domestic
sphere. He starts out by giving preference to the food, drinks, and music
favored by Firmo and Rita Baiana:

> Jerônimo já nunca pegava na guitarra senão para procurar
> acertar com as modinhas que a Rita cantava (69).
> Tomava agora, todas as manhãs, uma xícara de café bem
> grosso, à moda da Ritinha (66).

> Jerônimo now took up his guitar only to play melodies that

Rita liked to sing.

Every morning he drank a cup of thick espresso, having been introduced to it by his darling Rita.

Later, Jerônimo grows less industrious as he becomes more infatuated with Rita Baiana. His entire life eventually changes. At first, Jerônimo is physically and morally the superior opposite of Firmo. Now, the sole distinguishing feature between the two is their outward appearance. In character, they have become remarkably alike. The mediator's influence on Jerônimo is not immediately apparent at the outset of their relationship, but over time its effects prove to be significant and far-reaching:

> Uma transformação, lenta e profunda, operava-se nele, dia a dia, hora a hora, reviscerando-lhe o corpo e alando-lhe os sentidos, num trabalho misterioso e surdo de crisálida. . . .
>
> E assim, pouco a pouco, se foram reformando todos os seus hábitos singelos de aldeão português: Jerônimo abrasileirou-se. . . .
>
> E o curioso é que quanto mais ia ele caindo nos usos e costumes brasileiros, tanto mais os seus sentidos se apuravam, posto que em detrimento das suas forças físicas (66-67).

> He was undergoing a slow but profound transformation, gradually, imperceptibly, his body changing before his eyes, his senses growing sharper, in a mysterious and silent process, as with a chrysalis. . . .
>
> Thus were transformed, little by little, all the simple habits that this villager had brought with him from Portugal: Jerônimo had become Brazilian. . . .
>
> Curiously, the more he embraced the local customs and the Brazilian way of life, the sharper his senses became, even though he grew weaker physically.

Of course, this movement on the part of Jerônimo toward the object of desire (Rita Baiana) does not sit well with the mediator (Firmo). Like João Romão, Firmo never becomes fully aware of the role that he plays as model and rival. If he did, he might be able to stop the mimetic mechanism about to destroy him. He would not feel compelled to fight over the contested object and risk being maimed or killed. As the events in the novel make clear, no such awareness is ever attained. Firmo remains a prisoner of his desire, and is never able to transcend the confines of double mediation. Instead, he trades places with his nemesis and goes on to play the role of subject. Firmo's initial function in the mimetic relationship with Jerônimo is that of mediator, but over time their roles are eventually reversed. Firmo's liaison with Rita Baiana suddenly becomes important to him, just as Jerônimo starts courting Rita. The *malandro*'s desire for the voluptuous *mulata* [black woman] is awakened by the desire that he sees originating with his rival. He takes as a prototype the desire of the subject whom he has mediated until now. In other words, he elects to have as his model a copy of his own desire. Double mediation contributes to a state of affairs in which simple whims are easily transformed into violent passions:

> E um ciúme doido, um desespero feroz rebentou-lhe por dentro e cresceu logo como a sede de um ferido. "Oh! precisava vingar-se dela! dela e dele! O amaldiçoado resistiu à primeira, mas não lhe escaparia da segunda!" . . .
>
> Com o chapéu à ré, a gaforina mais assanhada que de costume, os olhos vermelhos, a boca espumando pelos cantos, todo ele respirava uma febre de vingança e de ódio (109).

And a maddening jealousy, a fierce rage took control of him, and grew as immense and frightful as the wrath of a man whose pride has been wounded. "Oh! he had to seek revenge on her! on both of them! That damned [Portuguese] escaped the first [murder attempt], but he wouldn't escape the second!" . . .

With his hat pushed to the back, his hair in disarray, he frothed in the mouth with anger, his bloodshot eyes and entire demeanor betraying a feverish and hateful frenzy to retaliate.

Since double mediation entails a faithful reciprocity between the two foes, Firmo's "desespero feroz [de] vingar-se" [fierce rage to seek revenge] is eventually realized as a common fate that befalls both men. He acts on his jealousy and comes very close to killing Jerônimo in a street fight. This situation is exacerbated when the Portuguese immigrant, after having recovered from the maiming inflicted by Firmo and his cohorts, copies the actions of his rival, and does to Firmo what Firmo tried to do to him. Jerônimo kills Firmo, and by doing so takes his place beside Rita Baiana:

> Estava completamente mudado. Rita apagara-lhe a última réstia das recordações da pátria. . . . O português abrasileirou-se para sempre; fez-se . . . amigo das extravagâncias e dos abusos, luxurioso e ciumento . . . e deu-se todo, todo por inteiro, a felicidade de possuir a mulata e ser possuido só por ela, só ela e mais ninguém.
>
> A morte do Firmo não vinha nunca a toldar-lhes o gozo da vida; quer ele, quer a amiga, achavam a coisa muito natural (135-136).

> He had changed completely. Rita had erased all memory of his home country. . . . The Portuguese had become Brazilian forever; he grew . . . extravagant and wasteful, lustful and jealous . . . and he gave all of himself in pursuit of his [greatest goal and] happiness, [which was] to love the black woman [Rita Baiana] and to be loved by her exclusively.
>
> Firmo's death never disturbed their pleasant married life; both lovers viewed it as something perfectly natural.

With the *malandro*'s death, Jerônimo is finally united with the contested object of his desire, and attains the *brasilidade* [distinctly Brazilian character] that he, as an immigrant, never possessed. He becomes more Brazilian, more like Firmo. With the demise of his former nemesis, Jerônimo's metamorphosis is complete.

Notes

[1] For examples of this kind of criticism, see Adherbal de Carvalho, *O naturalismo no Brasil* (São Luis do Maranhão: Júlio Ramos, 1894).

Valentim Magalhães, *A literatura brasileira* (Lisboa: A. M. Pereira, 1896).

Elísio Carvalho, *As modernas correntes estéticas na literatura brasileira* (Rio de Janeiro: Garnier, 1907).

José Veríssimo de Mattos, *História da literatura brasileira* (Rio de Janeiro: José Olympio, 1916).

Domingos Barboza, "Os despojos de Aluísio Azevedo," *Revista da Academia Maranhense de Letras* (1919): 80-95.

Alcides Maya, *Romantismo e naturalismo através da obra de Aluísio Azevedo* (Porto Alegre: Globo, 1926).

Agrippino Grieco, *Evolução da prosa brasileira* (Rio de Janeiro: Ariel, 1933).

A. M. Rodrigues Alves Filho, *O sociologismo e a imaginação no romance brasileiro* (Rio de Janeiro: José Olympio, 1938).

Álvaro Lins, "Dois naturalistas: Aluísio Azevedo e Júlio Ribeiro," *Revista do Brasil* maio 1941: 131-144.

José Bezerra de Freitas, *Forma e expressão no romance brasileiro* (Rio de Janeiro: Pongetti, 1947).

For an informative overview of Brazilian literary criticism before the 1960s, see "Critics and Criticism," in *Dictionary of Brazilian Literature*, ed. Irwin Stern (New York: Greenwood Press, 1988): 96-100. This article provides a synopsis of Brazilian literary criticism from the eighteenth century to the present, and argues that "Brazilians who dabbled in literary commentaries after independence were primarily concerned with identifying a nationalistic orientation and sentiment for their newly independent country. . . . With the exception of [José de] Alencar and [Machado de] Assis, these writers approached their tasks from an impressionistic viewpoint, which characterized most of Brazilian literary criticism until the mid-1950s.   Impressionistic criticism exists without any formal aesthetic philosophy of art behind it; rather, it is based on extremely personal, often emotional, beliefs or prejudices that are tangential to the artistic process" (96).

[2] Brito Broca, "O aparecimento de *O cortiço* em 1890," *Revista do livro* 2 (1957): 99.

[3] Dorothy Loos, "The Influence of Émile Zola on the Five Major Naturalistic Novels of Brazil," *Modern Language Journal* 39 (1955): 3-8.

Dorothy Loos, *The Naturalistic Novel of Brazil* (New York: Hispanic Institute, 1963).

Antônio Cândido, *Formação da literatura brasileira: Momentos decisivos* (São Paulo: Livraria Martins Editora, 1964).

Antônio Cândido, "El paso del dos al tres," *Escritura* 3 (1977): 21-34.

Sônia Brayner, *A metáfora do corpo no romance naturalista: Estudo sobre O cortiço* (Rio de Janeiro: Livraria São José, 1973).

Sônia Brayner, "Romance e modernidade," *Minas Gerais, suplemento literário* 17 de junho, 1978: 10.

Sônia Brayner, *Labirinto do espaço romanesco* (Rio de Janeiro: Civilização Brasileira, 1979).

Affonso Romano de Sant'Anna, *Análise estrutural de romances brasileiros* (Petrópolis, Brazil: Vozes, 1973).

Affonso Romano de Sant'Anna, "Curtição: *O cortiço* do Prof. Cândido e o meu," *Minas Gerais, suplemento literário* 16 de abril, 1977: 6-7 e 23 de abril, 1977: 8-9.

Affonso Romano de Sant'Anna, *Por um novo conceito de literatura brasileira* (Rio de Janeiro: Eldorado Tijuca, 1977).

Flora Süssekind, *Mímesis e modernidade: Formas das sombras* (Rio de

Janeiro: Graal, 1980).

Flora Süssekind, *Tal Brasil, qual romance?* (Rio de Janeiro: Achiamé, 1984).

Rui Mourão, introduction, *O cortiço*, by Aluísio Azevedo (São Paulo: Editora Ática, 1981) 5-9.

Other recent critics who have analyzed Azevedo's work include Raimundo de Menezes, *Aluísio Azevedo: Uma vida de romance* (São Paulo: Livraria Martins, 1958).

Josué Montello, *Aluísio Azevedo* (Rio de Janeiro: Agir, 1963).

Nélson Werneck Sodré, *O naturalismo no Brasil* (Rio de Janeiro: Editora Civilização Brasileira, 1965).

Sérgio Milliet, introduction, *O cortiço*, by Aluísio Azevedo (São Paulo: Livraria Martins Editora, 1967) 11-16.

Sigurt Schmidt, "A fragmentária teoria literária de Azevedo," *Philologica pragensia* 15 (1972): 213-219.

Herberto Sales, *Para conhecer melhor Aluísio Azevedo* (Rio de Janeiro: Bloch Editores, 1973).

Antônio Andrade, "A Gênese d'*O mulato* de Aluísio Azevedo," Ph.D. dissertation, Indiana University, 1975.

Jean-Yves Mérian, "Genre, signification et portée . de *O cortiço*," *Nouvelles études portugaises et brésiliennes* 9 (1975): 53-94.

Josué Montello, *Aluísio Azevedo e a polêmica d'O mulato* (Rio de Janeiro: José Olympio, 1975).

Gerald Moser, "The Persistence of Naturalism in the Brazilian 'Northeastern Fiction.'" *Studies in Honor of Lloyd A. Kasten* (Madison, Wisconsin: Hispanic Seminary of Medieval Studies, 1975): 199-208.

Antônio Dimas, *Aluísio Azevedo: Seleção de textos, notas, estudos biográfico, histórico e crítico e exercícios* (São Paulo: Abril Educação, 1980).

Juan Armando Epple, "Aluísio Azevedo y el naturalismo en Brasil," *Revista de crítica literaria latinoamericana* 6 (1980): 29-46.

Jean-Yves Mérian, "Les débuts du naturalisme au Brésil," *Recherches et études comparatistes ibéro-francophones de la Sorbonne Nouvelle* 3 (1981): 27-37.

Enrique Laguerre, "De Rita Baiana a Teresa Batista: personajes de la novela brasileña," *Sin nombre* 12 (1982): 25-37.

Ruth Brandão Lopes, "Loucura/repressão da mulher em *Encarnação, A doida do Candal,* e *O homem,*" *Minas Gerais, suplemento literário* 23 de janeiro, 1982: 4-5.

João Sedycias, "Crane, Azevedo, and Gamboa: A Comparative Study," Ph.D. dissertation, State University of New York at Buffalo, 1985.

João Sedycias, "Violent Symmetries: Self and Other in Aluísio Azevedo," in *Studies in Modern and Classical Languages and Literatures I,* ed. Fidel López Criado (Madrid: Orígenes, 1987): 83-90.

Luzia Navas Toríbio, "O entrave social ao mestiço em *O mulato* de Aluísio Azevedo e em *Portagem* de Orlando Mendes," *Estudos portugueses e africanos* 14 (1989): 49-56.

[4] Mourão, introduction, *O cortiço* 5-9.

[5] Mourão, introduction, *O cortiço* 5.

[6] Mourão, introduction, *O cortiço* 5.

[7] Mourão, introduction, *O cortiço* 6.

[8] Mourão, introduction, *O cortiço* 6-7.

[9] Mourão, introduction, *O cortiço* 6.

[10] Olívio Montenegro, *O romance brasileiro: As suas origens e tendências* (Rio de Janeiro: José Olympio, 1938) 63-64.

José Osório de Oliveira, *História breve da literatura brasileira* (Lisboa: Editorial Verbo, 1964) 93.

Milliet, introduction, *O cortiço* 14.

[11] Aluísio Azevedo, *O cortiço* (São Paulo: Editora Ática, 1981) 18. All

subsequent quotations from *O cortiço* are from this edition. Citations by page number appear in parentheses in the text.

[12] René Girard, *Deceit, Desire, and the Novel: Self and Other in Literary Structure*, trans. Yvonne Freccero (Baltimore, Maryland: Johns Hopkins University Press, 1980) 6.

[13] Girard, *Deceit* 100.

[14] Girard, *Deceit* 10.

[15] Girard, *Deceit* 10.

[16] Massoud Moisés, "Alguns Aspectos da Obra de Aluísio Azevedo," *Revista do livro* 4 (1959): 113.

[17] Wilma Newberry, "Ramón Pérez de Ayala's Concept of the *Doppelgänger* in *Belarmino y Apolonio*," *Symposium* 34 (1980): 59.

Chapter 7

Federico Gamboa as Geometrician of Desire

The early criticism of *Santa*, like the literary analyses of *O cortiço* produced before 1960, for the most part lacks the critical rigor required of a formal and detailed examination of the text.[1] As with Azevedo, Gamboa's first readers tend to emphasize the historical or biographical aspects of his work, often at the expense of fundamental thematic and structural considerations. Their critiques of *Santa* seldom address questions of language, structure, or themes of the work itself. Instead, they focus on the biography of the author or the history and politics of his times. The inevitable result is that the text is relegated to a position of secondary importance, one in which the novel serves merely to characterize specific anthropological, historical, or sociological paradigms.

However, a number of contemporary critics such as Seymour Menton, Joaquina Navarro, Alexander Hooker, Bartie Lee Lewis, Jr., Ana María Alvarado, and Alberto J. Carlos have helped to remedy this situation as they have addressed relevant aspects of the Mexican novel of the 19th century, paying special attention to the work of Federico Gamboa.[2] Besides these critics, several literary historians such as R. Anthony Castagnaro, Kessel Schwartz, and John Brushwood have formally analyzed Azevedo's work, although they often had to limit the length and depth of their critiques, since their readings encompass not only other novels by Gamboa but the works of other Spanish-American writers as well.[3] Consequently, they devote only a few pages to *Santa*. However limited these studies may be, some of them have made important contributions to our understanding of Gamboa's work.

In their respective studies of the novel in Spanish America, Castagnaro, Schwartz, and Brushwood observe that *Santa* is the tragic story of an innocent country girl who is seduced, deflowered, and subsequently abandoned by her lover, family, and society to live and ultimately to die as a prostitute. But *Santa* is also the portrayal of an adult woman caught in the sometimes violent dynamics of dysfunctional interpersonal relationships. It is the sad tale of an unfortunate human being seeking to find in an inhospitable environment some peace with herself just as it is the tragic saga of an individual striving for an objective that keeps eluding her.

Santa's journey from an expensive house of prostitution to Mexico City's most squalid brothels plays a dual role in the novel. It functions as the core of the story's plot, but it also serves to make more poignant the protagonist's attempts to regain an elusive paradise lost. At first, what Santa wants to regain is not so much her lost honor but rather the wholesomeness of "muchachas pobres que nacen en el campo y en el campo se crían al aire libre, entre brisas y flores; ignorantes, castas y fuertes"[4] [poor country girls who grow up free in the open air, among flowers and gentle breezes; innocent, chaste, and strong], a paradise that is robbed from her along with her virginity. When this objective proves unattainable, Santa seeks another goal that becomes a surrogate, namely, the forgiveness of her sins, redemption, and salvation. She attempts to realize this second objective with the help of her three lovers, El Jarameño, Rubio, and Hipólito. Of the many characters in the novel, these three exert the greatest influence on the protagonist.

Santa's search for forgiveness and relief from a life of suffering serves as an important structural element in the novel. It is the backdrop against which her fatal descent is juxtaposed and developed. In this juxtaposition, the following dynamic configuration can be discerned: the lower Santa descends, the farther she moves away from her first two lovers and the closer she finds herself, physically as well as spiritually, to Hipólito and to her goal. In her first attempt to return to the haven from which she has been expelled, Santa seeks to parlay the energy arising from her hatred of men into strength and power. Her longing and determination to regain her lost paradise originate in her anguish and sense of incompleteness. It is this sense of fragmentation and absence that prompts Santa to act. She looks back in anger and shame to a fateful moment in her recent past that marks the beginning of her life of misery as an uprooted and once "muchacha casta del campo" [chaste country girl]:

> — ¡Amarlos [a los hombres]! . . . ¿Y como había de amarlos, si el primer tunante con quien tropezó dejóla sin el menor deseo de que la aventura se repitiese? ¿Acaso los hombres merecen ser amados? (74)
>
> Excepcionalmente reñía con las mujeres ¿por qué, si las mujeres no le habían hecho nada? . . . Buscaba a los hombres, al Hombre para dañarlo, para herirlo, para marcarlo e infamarlo con sus uñas pulidas y tersas de cortesana, saciando en el que más cerca le quedase al alcance de su cuerpo prostituido, el alevoso golpe que le asestara aquel que le quedaba lejos, en sus borrosos recuerdos de virgen violada. Era su furia, cual secreto sedimento de dolor vengativo que arrolla ciegamente, que desgarra cruelmente, que destruye implacablemente por desquitar anejos rencores medio muertos que de improviso resucitaban (112-113).

> — Love men? . . . How could she? if the very first rogue that she came across left her without any desire whatever to go through the same ordeal again? Do men deserve to be loved at all?

> She rarely quarreled with the other women. Why should she? After all, the women hadn't done anything to her. . . . She was after the men, the Man. She wanted to harm and wound him, to brand and defile him with her sharp and smooth courtesan's claws. She wanted to satiate [her need for revenge] in any man who came within reach of her corrupted body, to strike back as treacherously as she had been struck by someone far away, according to the blurred memories of a raped virgin. That was her fury, like a secret residue of vengeance and pain that overwhelms blindly, that tears brutally, that destroys inexorably because it brings back concomitant and half-forgotten hatreds that come alive again suddenly.

Santa tries to obtain through the prowess of El Jarameño and the influence of Rubio what she finally manages to secure only through the selflessness of Hipólito. Through her blind friend, she is freed from vanity and pride, and is able to receive divine forgiveness and salvation. As we shall see, her liaisons with El Jarameño, Rubio, and Hipólito are largely based on mimetic desire, and give rise to the kind of triangles described in the previous chapters. From Santa's dealings with these three men, two different types of mimetic relationships emerge. The first type is one in which the protagonist plays the role of desiring subject while her three lovers function as mediators. In the second type of mimetic relationship, El Jarameño, Rubio, and Hipólito take turns as subjects, Santa's clientele functions as mediator, and the protagonist herself plays the role of desired object. The entwining of these mimetic triangles gives rise to much of the intrigue and tension in the novel, and constitute a major structure around which the action in *Santa* is developed. For example, early on in the novel, the protagonist hints at what may be expected in terms of triangular complications when, reflecting on the "hombres que le habían jurado amores" [men who had sworn their love for her], she singles out El Jarameño, Rubio, and

Hipólito. The players in the leading mimetic triangles in the novel are thus introduced:

> Y en rápida revista mental, consideró la legión de hombres que le habían jurado amores ¿por qué "El Jarameño" triunfaba si acababa de conocerlo; ¿por qué Rubio, "el caballero decente" que le prometía casa, también le atraía; ¿por qué Hipólito, que jamás le dijo sílaba que a achaques del querer se refiriera, interponíase entre ella y los pretendientes? (91)

> In her mind, she quickly examined the hordes of men who had sworn their love for her. Why did El Jarameño win over the others, even though she had just met him? Why was she also attracted to Rubio, the "decent gentleman" who had promised her a home of her own? Why did Hipólito — who had never spoken to her, even indirectly, about his lovesickness — keep coming in between Santa and her suitors?

When Santa first meets El Jarameño, her reaction to the haughty Andalusian bullfighter is one of profound antagonism:

> — ¿Diga usté, salecita del mundo —, le preguntó [El Jarameño] con exagerado cerrar andaluz —, usté no tiene cortejo? . . .
> ¿Y a usted qué le importa, hombre, que yo tenga lo que tenga? ¿qué es eso de cortejo? (85-86)

> — What do you say, pretty girl? — greeted [El Jarameño], exaggerating his peculiar Andalusian accent — don't you have a boyfriend to keep you company? . . .
> What is it to you? Is it any of your business if anyone keeps me company or not? And what do you exactly mean by "boyfriend"?

Santa's unexplained hostility toward El Jarameño is exacerbated as
the novel progresses:

> — ¿Qué noche dormirás conmigo, Santa? — le preguntó [El
> Jarameño].
> — ¿Contigo? . . . ¡Nunca! (88)
> [Y] le repetía "El Jarameño" su continua pregunta:
> — ¿Cuándo, Santa? . . .
> — ¡Nunca, nunca! — respondíale ella con la mayor resolución
> y entereza (119).

> — When will you sleep with me, Santa? — [El Jarameño]
> asked her.
> — With you? . . . Never!
> [El Jarameño] repeated his question constantly:
> — When, Santa?
> — Never, ever! — Santa would reply with the utmost resolve
> and forcefulness.

Realizing that she is trapped in a life of suffering, Santa marvels at
the bullfighter's prowess and ability to manipulate those forces that now
control and oppress her. El Jarameño is a man fully in charge of his life.
Like Pete in *Maggie*, the bullfighter in *Santa* embodies certain qualities
that the protagonist desires. To Maggie, power represents the means to
transcend her wretched environment in order to gain admission into her
dream world. To Santa, power is the tool that will help her to overcome
her present condition and regain her paradise lost. El Jarameño represents the strength and ability to deal with the violent world of the lower
class on its own terms. In the protagonist's eyes, he is a model to be
emulated. Yet, by being the possessor of something that Santa lacks, El
Jarameño takes on the dual role characteristic of the mediator. He
functions at once as model and as obstacle. He shows Santa the means

by which she can escape from her world of suffering and re-enter paradise. However, by being the sole possessor of these means, and apparently not willing to share them without getting something in return, his role as potential ally quickly changes to that of antagonist. This impasse is further exacerbated by Santa when she arrogantly spurns El Jarameño's amorous overtures, thereby ensuring that they remain locked in a conflict in which nobody wins. Later, she gives in to the bullfighter's advances, and moves in with him. On the surface, this action suggests that Santa and her lover eventually manage to overcome their unprofitable stalemate, thus making it possible for them to attain their respective goals: she, of surmounting the difficulties of her new home environment and lifestyle, and he, of making her his exclusive lover. However, the brute force to which Santa turns for help is actually used against her when her lover learns that she has been unfaithful to him. Their affair is abruptly brought to an end in a scene charged with tension in which Santa comes close to being killed by El Jarameño. In the violence of conflicting desires, this particular triangle is dissolved. The subject, however, simply moves on and takes her search elsewhere.

El Jarameño is subsequently replaced in his role of mediator by Santa's second live-in lover, Rubio. This time, Santa attempts to find fulfillment for a dream of liberation through the bourgeois preeminence of her new lover. Rubio represents another possible resolution to the same problem. Now, Santa tries to use social status instead of brute force and prowess as a tool with which to overcome her oppressive environment. Working from within the mechanism of desire, and aided by the authority derived from a higher social standing, Santa plans for the second time her escape from prostitution:

> Rubio . . . érale simpático al extremo, pues operábase en Santa . . .
> el naturalísimo deslumbramiento que ejerce en ánimo de plebeyo
> origen el calcularse igual al antiguo señor respetado y quimérico

que, a la larga, desgastado por los años y por los vicios, baja . . .
al nivel del antiguo vasallo (138).

Santa, afortunada renació a la vida en las mejores condi-
ciones: por segunda vez abandonó el burdel y sus antihigiénicas
esclavitudes . . . convencida de que Rubio la quería de veras y la
mimaría a pedir de boca; convirtiéndose de la noche a la mañana,
en dueña y señora de una casita suya (268).

Rubio . . . proved extremely attractive to Santa. . . . She was
under the same spell that mesmerizes the common man, compelling
him to put himself on an equal footing with his respectable and
capricious former master, who, in the end, worn out by the years
and his vices . . . decides to come down to the level of the servant.

Santa was fortunate to begin her new existence in the best of
conditions: for the second time she left the brothel and the filthy
captivity that it entailed . . . convinced that Rubio truly loved her,
that he would pamper her as one pampers a child, and that
overnight she would become the lady and ruler of her own home.

Both with Rubio and El Jarameño, Santa's attempts to transcend her
environment prove unsuccessful. In her dealings with Rubio, the "caballero decente" [decent gentleman], whom she thought would rescue her
to a haven of middle-class comfort and respectability, her life is less
physically violent though definitely more painful than during her affair
with the bullfighter. At times her second lover seems to take pleasure in
pointing out to Santa that the "tierra de promisión" [promised land], her
lost paradise, is hopelessly off limits to her:

A cada paso de la prostituta hacia la quimérica e inasible Tierra de
Promisión, — a cuyos lindes creía ir llegando —, cada vez que las
alas entumecidas y torpes de su alma convaleciente pero en vía de
alivio, intentaban volar a la altura, Rubio encargábase de desen-

gañarla en términos rudos, con saña de amante:
— "Las meretrices no arriban a las tierras de promisión ¡no
faltaba más! las almas de las mujeres perdidas no vuelan porque no
poseen alas, son almas ápteras. . . ." (274)

Each time the prostitute took a step toward the fabled and
inaccessible promised land, which she believed to be increasingly
closer to her grasp, each time the stiff and ungainly wings of her
convalescent soul, which was finally about to rest, attempted to fly
to the heavens, Rubio took upon himself, like an angry lover, to
dash her hopes with the harshest of words:
— "Prostitutes cannot ascend to the promised land. It's
absurd! The souls of fallen women cannot fly because they do not
have wings, they are wingless creatures. . . ."

This sadistic streak in Rubio reflects a serious psychological disorder
that only slowly becomes apparent to Santa. The pain that Santa feels
increases significantly when she sees in the disease that affects Rubio
something of the malady that afflicts her. Rubio is consumed by a search
for something that on the surface appears to be love and understanding.
This search takes him to all sorts of people and places but leads nowhere,
thus making his frustration all the more acute. In Rubio, Santa is able to
discern the futility of the kind of life that she has been leading. She
recognizes and thus repudiates the lie that they have both been pursuing.
In place of a bourgeois morality from which she thought to derive self-
respect and social respectability, she is left with "la hipócrita y falsa
moral burguesa practicada por Rubio desde niño" (276) [the hypocritical
and false bourgeois morality practiced by Rubio from childhood].

After her two disastrous affairs, Santa recognizes the destructive and
self-defeating nature of her desire. In order to free herself from its
harmful influence, she renounces both her pride and the means by which
she sought earlier to bring that desire to fruition. With El Jarameño and

Rubio, Santa lives and pursues a false dream. She uses her lovers and they in turn use her in a mimetic relationship of internal mediation. She attempts to subdue and transcend the forces that control her life by trying to deal with the world of prostitution and vice on its own terms. She hopes to accomplish her objective either by force or with the power of a privileged social position. During her first two affairs, Santa attempts to defeat mimetic desire by confronting it head on. She may think that she is fighting it when actually she is only conforming to it. The path that she chooses in her liaisons with El Jarameño and Rubio is merely a *via negativa*, a fact exemplified by the disastrous manner in which both affairs conclude. As a result, her first two attempts to liberate herself from the forces that ultimately destroy her are doomed from the start. Like Maggie, Santa turns to religion for help when her attempts to confront her oppressive milieu prove unsuccessful. In Maggie's case, her pleas go ignored. The priest to whom she turns in her hour of need seems more intent on steering clear of street people like Maggie than on saving souls. Crane describes him thus:

> A stout gentleman in a silk hat and a chaste black coat, whose decorous row of buttons reached from his chin to his knees. The girl had heard of the grace of God and she decided to approach this man. His beaming, chubby face was a picture of benevolence and kindheartedness. His eyes shone with good will.
>
> But as the girl timidly accosted him, he made a convulsive movement and saved his respectability by a vigorous side step. He did not risk it to save a soul.[5]

In *Santa*, the protagonist suffers a similar rejection. First, we see her after the failure of her two painful affairs, as she turns to divine clemency and forgiveness, seeking respite from her ordeal:

Recatadamente, gacha la cabeza y entornados los párpados, reali-
zando un supremo esfuerzo, penetró en el templo. . . . Por su
gusto habría penetrado de rodillas. Arrodillóse en su medio escon-
drijo, aturdida de la emoción. . . . Acometiéronla entonces
mayores ansias de orar, por eso, por desgraciada y vil. . . . Con
el objeto de alcanzar el Cristo del altar mayor, abrió sus ojos, a par
que escuchaba con deleite como el órgano ahora le reiteraba las
promesas de un perdón excelso. . . . Santa, en éxtasis, pidió
mentalmente la muerte, olvidada de su vida y de sus manchas.
Morir ahí, en aquel instante, frente por frente del Dios de las
bondades infinitas, y de los misericordiosos perdones (131-132).

Bashfully, with her head down and her eyes half closed, making a
supreme effort, she went into the church. . . . If she could, she
would have entered on her knees. She knelt down in a secluded
corner of the temple, as if she were hiding, overwhelmed with
emotion. . . . Subsequently, a strong desire to pray for her
wretched and disgusting life came over her. . . . In an attempt to
reach the Christ figure in the largest altar, she opened her eyes, as
she listened with pleasure to the way the organ echoed the promise
of divine forgiveness. In ecstasy, Santa mentally asked to die,
forgetting her life and her blemishes. To die right there, in that
very instant, face to face with the god of infinite goodness and of
compassionate mercy.

However, Santa resorts to institutionalized religion in her hour of
need only to be forced out of a place of worship. After she is recognized
as the popular young courtesan from Elvira's brothel, the chaplain of the
church where she has sought refuge is pressured by some "damas princi-
palísimas" [most respectable ladies] to have her thrown out. A sexton is
then instructed to remove Santa from the premises, which he does with
conspicuous zeal:

Contra [Santa] se disparó el sacristán:

— Se va usted a salir de aquí al momento — dijo brutalmente a Santa, que lo vio sin comprender lo que decía, perturbada en su oración y en su ensueño místico.

— ¿Que me vaya yo? . . . ¿y por qué he de irme? Usted no es el dueño de esta iglesia y en la iglesia cabemos todos, más los que somos malos.

— No me obligue usted a echarla a la fuerza — declaró el sacristán. . . .

Santa salió del templo y se arrimó a una de las columnas del atrio.

— No, aquí tampoco, — decretó el celoso sacristán —, ¡a la calle, a la calle!

A la calle se dirigió Santa, obediente y muda. Y en la calle, la examinaban con extrañeza las personas ayunas de lo acaecido (133-134).

The sexton charged toward [Santa]:

— You must leave this place at once — the sexton said harshly. Santa looked back at him, unable to understand what he was trying to say, still lost in her prayers and mystical reverie.

— Are you are telling me to leave? . . . Why should I? You don't own this church, and we are all welcome here, especially those of us who have sinned.

— Then, I may have to throw you out by force — said the sexton. . . .

Santa left the church and walked up to one of the columns in the courtyard.

— You can't stay there either — declared the overzealous sexton — leave at once! Go back to the streets!

Obedient and silent, Santa started walking toward the street, and once there some passers-by who did not know what had just happened looked at her with surprise and cold indifference.

It is only through Hipólito that Santa is able to escape the mechanism of mimetic desire. Of her three lovers, he is the only one who consciously refuses to use Santa. In order to allow for the deliverance of his beloved, Hipólito renounces his pride, and waits patiently for Santa to finish her descent, when she is finally free from the desire and violence that affect her lovers and herself. At first, the protagonist is not attracted to Hipólito. But there is a certain quality to the blind piano player, human kindness perhaps, that makes him endearing to Santa. Her regard for Hipólito is as spontaneous and complex as her antagonistic reaction to El Jarameño. On the one hand, she finds Hipólito physically repulsive:

> Ni asomos de amor nutría por él, ni pizca. Moralmente nutría estimación amasada con su poquito de piedad, sin interés carnal y su bastante de gratitud; físicamente casi repugnancia, con más, miedo a sus ojos sin iris, de estatua de bronce sin pátina (137).
>
> Hipo era un monstruo. . . . Era un pianista de burdel, mugriento y mal trajeado, sin tener en que caerse muerto; un individuo quizás más desdichado que ella misma (231-232).

> She did not love him, not even a little. Morally she felt a mixture of esteem and pity for him, with plenty of gratitude but no carnal desire; physically she found him almost repulsive, and his eyes without irises, staring blankly into space like a bronze statue without patina, frightened her.
>
> Hipo looked like a monster. . . . He played the piano at a brothel. He was dirty and poorly dressed, without a penny to his name; a man perhaps more wretched than [Santa] herself.

Yet, on the other hand, she relishes his care for her: "— Hipo ¿viene usted por mirarme? ¡la verdad! me daría tantísimo placer que alguien me cuidara así" (114). [— Hipo, did you come to see me? Tell me the truth! I would be so happy if someone cared about me like this]. In the end, her dual vision of Hipólito fuses into one as Santa is drawn further away from her other lovers toward the one individual who can help her to overcome the harmful effects of mimetic desire:

> Por la primera vez, antojósele que Hipólito sin ser un Adonis tampoco era un monstruo, no, era un hombre feo, feísimo por su exterior, mas, si en realidad por dentro difiriese de los que a diario la poseían, junto a quienes Santa reconocíase inferior y degradada . . . ¿si en efecto Hipólito la estimase mujer perfecta y superior a él? . . . ¿si resultáramos con que la haría feliz? (231)

> For the first time, she realized that Hipólito, while not being an Adonis, was not a monster either. To be sure, he was ugly, very ugly on the outside, but inside he seemed different from the men who had sex with her daily, beside whom Santa felt inferior and degraded. . . . Didn't Hipólito in fact look up to her as a perfect woman superior to him? . . . As a result, wouldn't he be able to make her happy?

As Santa approaches death, she is finally freed from suffering. The connection between her liberation from mimetic desire and Hipólito's selfless intervention in her life becomes apparent. She turns to death as the only way out of her misery after she has been disgraced and shunned by lovers and society alike. She yearns for the peace to be found only in the permanent cessation of her ordeal. Without fully realizing it, she turns to Hipólito for help as she tries to escape the destructive mechanism of mimetic desire:

> " . . . dicen que los muertos, reposan en calma,
> que no hay sufrimientos en la otra mansión. . . ."

Al llegar a estas palabras últimas, por asociación natural de
ideas, como por ensalmo aparecíasele Hipólito, el ciego, mirándola
sin verla con sus horribles ojos blanquizcos de estatua de bronce sin
pátina (307-308).

" . . . it is said that the dead rest peacefully,
that there is no suffering in the other world. . . ."
When she came upon these last words, because of a natural
association of ideas, as if by magic, she would think of Hipólito,
looking at her though unable to see anything, with his horrible
whitish eyes, like those of a bronze statue without patina.

Hipólito represents hope to Santa because he is the only one of her
lovers willing to go through the ordeal of renouncing his pride on her
behalf. By doing so, he neutralizes the mechanism of mimetic desire,
and is able to render it powerless. Of his steadfast love for Santa,
Hipólito declares:

— Yo mismo no sé cuánto te quiero, ¡hay cosas que no se
saben! . . . si tú, en medio de un desierto, mil veces más enferma
y más pobre y más depreciada y más fea, ¡vaya, que asustaras a las
fieras!, si tú un día me llamabas como me has llamado hoy . . .
volé a tu lado y a tu lado me tienes y a tu lado me tendrás hasta
que no nos muramos . . . habría ido hasta ti, a bendecirte y
adorarte, como en este momento te adoro y te bendigo (315).

— I myself don't know how much I love you. There are
things we just don't know! . . . If you were in the middle of a
desert, if you were a thousand times sicker, and poorer, and uglier,
and more wretched, to the point that wild beasts would be afraid of
you, if you were to call me as you have done today . . . I'd fly to
your side and would stay with you so that neither one of us would
die, and I would bless and love you as I love and bless you now.

In order for Santa to be able to step out of the mimetic whirlwind about to destroy her, Hipólito makes a superhuman effort to refrain from using her the way her other lovers have. Santa is freed in the end, but only at Hipólito's expense and at the threshold of death. To the blind man, his unfulfilled physical desire for Santa represents one more chapter of suffering and deprivation in his long life of misery: "tú no sabes lo que es vivir sin amor toda una vida" (316). [You have no idea what it is like to go through life without any love at all].

According to Girard, the ultimate meaning of desire is death, but death is not the novel's ultimate meaning.[6] Physically and spiritually Santa is a very sick woman who is healed just before death and whom death finally sets free. Before she sinks to the lowest of hovels and dies, she allows herself to be engulfed by the life of vice, excess, and intrigue that rules the brothel. Her enjoyment of her "reign" as the most sought-after prostitute in Mexico City and the manner in which she tries to overcome the forces that oppress her have their roots in the ontological disorder brought about by mimetic desire. Her departure from her oppressive environment as she sinks lower in the underworld does not represent a descent in the strict and negative sense of the word. Rather, it symbolizes death and the return to the "cuidado de la tierra, nuestra eterna madre cariñosa" (39) [nurturing care of the Earth, our eternal and loving mother]. Santa's roaming finally takes her to the "risueño cementerio de Chimalistac" [cheerful cemetery of Chimalistac] where her friend Hipólito marks with a "plegaria sencilla" [simple prayer] the beginning of her peace.

The closer Santa comes to death, the more she withdraws from self-delusion and lying. The greater the distance she puts between herself and Elvira's brothel, the closer she gets to Hipólito and to salvation. To be sure, this progression inspires fear in the protagonist as well as in the reader, but it also suggests hope and redemption. As such, the novel purges the reader of this fear, and allows for the possibility of a tragic though distinctly positive denouement. The apocalypse would not be complete without an optimistic and redeeming resolution. Shortly before her death, Santa is restored to life with the help of Hipólito: "inauguróse una existencia de ensueño, no vivían, no, ni el uno ni el otro, ¡resucitaban!" (324). [They began a dream-like existence. They no longer lived, they resuscitated!]. Subsequently, Santa dies, but something of the happy "muchacha casta del campo" [chaste country girl] is redeemed and kept alive through the selfless love of the blind piano player.

Hipólito is touched, and his life is changed for the better by the contrite harlot. In his successful attempt to curb his desire in order to help his beloved, Hipólito becomes the noblest of all characters in the novel. Having transcended the world of mimetic intrigue of the brothel, he is also restored to life. The conclusion of Santa's story can thus be viewed as a fresh beginning — a new life commences both for Santa and Hipólito, for her in eternity and for him in a transformed world.[7]

The mimetic triangles examined thus far represent those in which Santa plays the role of desiring subject. The first two triangles, the ones in which El Jarameño and Rubio function as mediator, illustrate in vivid detail a particularly virulent form of internal mediation. The last triangle (Hipólito's), on the other hand, represents a departure from this violent *modus operandi*, and culminates in the neutralization and transcendence of mimetic desire itself. The spiritual problems at the heart of *Santa* center around these structures. In these triangles, the protagonist's objective is to overcome oppressive environmental forces. Santa plays the role of subject and her three lovers that of mediator or, in the case of Hipólito, negator of mimetic desire. In the group of mimetic triangles that I will examine next, the object of desire is an attractive and lustful prostitute. Due mostly to their racy and sensationalistic nature, these love triangles have attracted more attention than the ones analyzed earlier. They constitute the heart of the intrigue and action in Gamboa's novel.

The first triangle is made up by El Jarameño, Santa, and Santa's clientele. The author describes the protagonist as an attractive and desirable young woman who, "por ser aún carne fresca, joven y dura, disputábansela día a día los viejos parroquianos y los nuevos que iban aprendiendo la existencia de tesoro semejante" (73). [Because she was still fresh meat, young and firm, the old customers of the brothel constantly fought over her, just as did the new ones, as they learned of the existence of such a treasure]. A linear or one-dimensional interpretation of Santa's affair with the bullfighter strictly in terms of a subject's unmediated desire for an object may posit the origin of this desire in the object herself. However, Gamboa's text suggests otherwise. As a prostitute, Santa is available to anyone willing to pay for her services. Because of this unrestricted availability, she cannot really be possessed by any one man. She can be anybody's for a limited time, but this accessibility precludes any one individual from having her favors exclusively. Hipólito is one of the few characters in the novel to realize this fact, and he seeks to capitalize on this knowledge:

> Empinado en su asiento, Jenaro exploraba el salón y agachábase al oído alerta del ciego que reclamaba informaciones. No parecía "El Jarameño"; había diversos toreros . . . pero de "El Jarameño" ni luz. . . .
>
> — ¡Busca bien, Jenarillo, busca bien! . . . ¿Tampoco ves a Santita? . . .
>
> No, tampoco . . . aunque sí, un momento, que la mirara de frente para poder cerciorarse...
>
> — Sí la veo, patrón, ya la vide . . . está en la platea de los *catrines* del *clú* . . . todititos se le amontonan, amo, como si ella juera panal y los "rotos" moscas. . . .
>
> — Sobra, Jenaro, ya no mires más y vámonos, que al menos con *esos* se halla segura y no corro el riesgo de que vuelvan a robármela (228).

Standing on tiptoes on his seat, Jenaro carefully scanned the hall and then he bent down to tell the blind man what he had seen. El Jarameño hadn't appeared yet; there were several bullfighters . . . but no hide nor hair of El Jarameño. . . .

— Search well, little Jenaro, search well! . . . Can't you see my dear Santa either?

No, he couldn't see her either . . . although he would look again, this time straight ahead, to make sure.

— Yes, I see her, master, I see her . . . she is on the main floor of the club, surrounded by her admirers, who are falling all over her, like flies on honey.

— Enough, Jenaro, you can stop looking now. Let's go. At least with *these* men she will be safe, and I don't run the risk of losing her again.

To Hipólito, Santa is safer in the brothel. There, she can be approached by anybody, but no one will be able to lay total claim to her. This impasse gives rise to an uncommonly difficult obstacle: in the very act of having sex with the prostitute, one's inability to possess her is inscribed. In each move of a customer, the moves of all the other customers are reflected. The sexual act between customer and courtesan takes on a special meaning, one that goes beyond the mere exchange of money and services. The transaction acquires a dual role. It discloses a formidable desire by allowing the subject to possess briefly a desired object, while at the same time it prevents the ultimate fulfillment of this desire: the permanent possession of the object. The Other is always already there, behind whatever anyone may choose to do with regard to the prostitute. Thus, in his desire for Santa, El Jarameño recognizes the role played by the mediator and goes so far as to identify the Other who determines the objects that he finds desirable: "'El Jarameño' fijóse desde luego en Santa, porque no sólo valía la pena sino porque era la solicitada de los niños finos; un relámpago de deseo, que hizo hervir su sangre árabe de vencedor de hembras" (85). [El Jarameño took notice of Santa at once not only because she was attractive but also because she was the favorite of the refined young men; a bolt of passion, that set fire to his Arab womanizing blood]. The desire for Santa on the part of El Jarameño intensifies as a result of the protagonist's rejection:

> Impulsada por repentina antipatía [por El Jarameño], esmeróse [Santa] en prodigar a los señoritos que se la disputaban, halagos y mimos; se sentó encima de éste, bebió en la copa de aquél, consintió en que la descalzara el de más allá . . . y haciendo mil visajes, le pegó dos chupadas al puro de otro. La "juerga" subía de punto (86).

> Moved by a sudden dislike [for El Jarameño], [Santa] went out of her way to please and pamper the young men who competed for her attention. She sat in one's lap, drank from the glass of another, allowed a third to remove her shoes . . . and all the while making faces, took a few puffs from the cigar of another. The "good times" rolled uninterrupted.

Santa expects her indifference toward El Jarameño and her sexually provocative behavior with her other customers, especially the "niños finos" [refined young men], to excite the bullfighter's desire for her. Even if a mediator can be identified in Santa's liaison with El Jarameño, in sexual desire the presence of a rival is not needed for the desire to be triangular. According to Girard, the beloved is often divided into both subject and object in the lover's eyes. This division produces a triangle occupied by the lover, the beloved, and the body of the beloved. Sexual desire, like other forms of mimetic desire, is contagious. To speak of contagion, Girard argues, is to speak unavoidably of a second desire that is fixed on the same object as the original desire. To imitate the desire of one's lover is to desire *oneself*, thanks to the lover's desire.[8] This particular form of double mediation is called coquetry. Girard explains further:

> The coquette does not wish to surrender her precious self to the desire which she arouses, but were she not to provoke it, she would not feel so precious. The favour she finds in her own eyes is based exclusively on the favor with which she is regarded by others. For this reason the coquette is constantly looking for proofs of this favor; she encourages and stirs up her lover's desires, not in order to give herself to him but to enable her the better to refuse him.
>
> The coquette's indifference toward her lover's sufferings is not feigned but it has nothing to do with ordinary indifference. It is not an absence of desire; it is the other side of desire of oneself. The lover is fascinated by it. He even believes he sees in his mistress' indifference that divine autonomy he burns to acquire. This is why desire is stimulated by coquetry, and in its turn feeds coquetry.[9]

It is not surprising, therefore, that in this vicious cycle of double mediation, El Jarameño copies Santa's actions and seeks to do to her what she intends to do to him. The similarity in their behavior is what keeps the two together, and is what contributes to the violent resolution of their ill-fated relationship:

> Por lo que al Jarameño respecta . . . el problema continuaba insoluto, negándose Santa y enardecido él. Ya no suplicaba ni preguntaba *cuándo*, había variado de táctica; ahora trataba de hallarse junto a Santa lo más posible, y acicateado por anhelos casi animales, por apetitos insaciados, diose a frecuentar el burdel a todas horas, a cortejar a las guapas de la casa, con quienes hasta dormía sin tocarlas, para ver despertar en Santa un conato de despecho (138).

> With respect to the affair with El Jarameño . . . the stalemate continued: Santa saying no on the one hand, and on the other El Jarameño, still hurt, angry, and fired with passion. He no longer begged her to sleep with him, nor asked her "when?" He changed his tactics. Now, he tried to be around Santa as much as possible, and spurred by an almost animalistic desire, by cravings yet to be fulfilled, he began to frequent [Elvira's] brothel at all times, courting the most attractive women there, with whom he would sleep, though without having sex. [He did this] to see if he could awaken in Santa some sign of jealousy.

In El Jarameño's actions, we see something of the metaphysical disorder and desperate behavior caused by double mediation. Girard points out that the lover's despair and the beloved's coquetry increase step by step together, because the two sentiments are copied from each other. It is the same desire, growing ever more intense, that circulates between the two partners. If the lovers are never in accord, it is not because they are too different, as common sense and sentimental novels assert, but because they are too alike, because each is a copy of the other. However, the more they grow alike, the more different they imagine themselves to be. The *sameness* by which they are obsessed appears to them as an absolute *otherness*. Double mediation ensures an opposition as fierce as it is meaningless, a confrontation at once symmetrical and vicious in which the contending elements fuel each other's desires while at the same time keeping each other in check.[10] Girard continues further:

> In this case, as in others, it is nearness which brings about the conflict. A fundamental law is involved which has much control over "cerebral" love as it has over social evolution. This proximity, never known but always felt, is the cause of the lover's despair; he cannot despise the loved one without despising himself; he cannot desire her without her desiring herself. . . .

In the universe of internal mediation indifference is never simply neutral; it is never pure absence of desire. To the observer it always appears as the exterior aspect of a desire of oneself. And it is this supposed desire which is imitated. Far from contradicting the laws of metaphysical desire, the dialectic of indifference confirms them.[11]

In the world of internal mediation, every desire can produce other rival desires. Thus, yet another triangle is generated from the above mimetic structure. This time the mediator is not Santa's unidentified clientele, but El Jarameño himself. When the bullfighter brings Santa out of Elvira's brothel, he takes her to a boarding house where they share quarters with six other tenants. Among them is an eccentric "ingeniero inventor" [inventor engineer] named Ripoll. This idiosyncratic scientist enjoys the respect and attention of the other residents for his "sabiduría y españolidad" [wisdom and Spanishness] until the day El Jarameño and Santa decide to take residence there. Before their arrival, Ripoll basks in the contentment of his privileged position, acknowledging in his cavalier demeanor the deference that the other residents pay him:

> "hablábale [la dueña de la pensión] igual que a los demás, sin que registrara tuteo o preferencia en la repartición de manjares. Él sí la tuteaba, como tuteaba al resto de los inquilinos" (177).

> "[the owner of the boarding house] addressed him the same way she addressed everybody else, without any intimacy or playing favorites when it came time to pass the food around at dinner time. He, on the other hand, would address her informally, the same way he addressed the other tenants.

Ripoll's nonchalant use of the informal "tú" with the residents of the boarding house, especially when no one there practices such an intimate form of address, is an indication of his special status. The only exception occurs in his dealings with the priest and later, not surprisingly, with El Jarameño. When the bullfighter moves in, a great deal changes:

> El reinado de Ripoll . . . duró bastante menos de lo que él necesitaba que durase. Con el arribo de "El Jarameño," que se entró una mañanita con carta de recomendación; pesos y billetes a porrillo; copia de baúles y valijas, y un mozo de espadas . . . se relegó a Ripoll a la indiferencia y el "Aragonés" al olvido. Atávicamente, étnicamente volviéronse en masa al torero; impulsados por secreta fuerza irresistible se desvivieron por mirarlo y agasajarlo, cual si con él hubiera entrado en la "Guipuzcoana" milagrosa bendición, años y años codiciada (187-188).

> Ripoll's reign [and period of influence] . . . lasted much less than he had hoped. With the arrival of El Jarameño . . . Ripoll and his friend from Aragón were ignored and eventually forgotten. El Jarameño arrived early one morning with a letter of reference, money in abundance, an endless number of trunks and suitcases, and an assistant in tow. . . . Atavistically, ethnically, they all gravitated to the bullfighter; driven by a secret and irresistible power, they yearned to welcome and marvel at him, as if he were a miraculous blessing that the "Guipuzcoana" boarding house had been anxiously expecting for a long time.

Ripoll's reaction for having been outstaged by the bullfighter is decidedly virulent. El Jarameño's "secreta fuerza irresistible" [secret and irresistible power] proves inexorable as it draws Ripoll's erstwhile followers away from him and toward the bullfighter. Understandably, this change increases Ripoll's hatred of El Jarameño:

> Ripoll almorzó en la calle (188).

Tornóse agrio el genio y amarilla la piel. Mal encarado, sentábase a la mesa sin cortejar a "El Jarameño," y, a manera de desesperado, convirtióse en blasfemo y de pésimas pulgas; irascible, gruñón, agresivo; soltando palabrotas que a los otros les resultaban geroglíficos y charadas amenazantes (189).

> [That day] Ripoll ate lunch in town.
> He grew bitter and his skin took on a yellowish hue. Always in a bad mood, he would sit at the table but would not make small talk with El Jarameño. Like a desperate man, his language became increasingly more disrespectful and violent. Cantankerous, grumpy, and aggressive, he would let fly all kinds of curses that sounded to the other tenants like hieroglyphics and threatening riddles [in some foreign tongue].

The pain of being eclipsed by someone better able to command the attention and respect of those around him is aggravated when Ripoll's former admirers start heaping upon the bullfighter the kind of praise that Ripoll himself never received:

> "El Jarameño" se entronizó; era el cuerno de la abundancia, fuente inagotable de gracejo y la alegría de la casa. Don Praxedes confesó francamente "que era mucho hombre"; el empeñero [dijo] "que lo adornaban magníficas prendas"; Gallegos nombróse a sí mismo perito catador de sus cigarros y puros; doña Nicasia sólo "hijo" lo llamaba, y todos, a una, adoptaron para tratarlo, el honroso título que le prodigaban Bruno y los banderilleros y picadores de su cuadrilla, sus visitantes perennes: *maestro* denominábanlo y *maestro* denomináronlo la patrona y los huéspedes (188-189).

El Jarameño took possession of his throne; he was like the horn of plenty, [an] inexhaustible source of charm and the joy of the boarding house. Don Praxedes confessed openly "that he was a hell of a man;" the pawnbroker [said] "that he was endowed with amazing talents;" Gallegos appointed himself expert sampler of his cigars and cigarettes; the bullfighter was the only one to be addressed by Doña Nicasia as "son," and all of them, one by one, adopted the lofty title that Bruno and the banderilleros and picadors of his bullfighting team, his constant visitors, used when addressing him: they called him *master*, and *master* was what the owner of the boarding house and her tenants started to call him from then on.

Thus, the rivalry between Ripoll and El Jarameño is established. However, the animosity that exists between the two arises mostly from Ripoll. El Jarameño is actually oblivious to the profound changes that he is causing in his fellow tenant, and he goes so far as to try to be kind to Ripoll:

> Inopinadamente, "El Jarameño" diose a protegerlo [a Ripoll], atraído y deslumbrado por aquel su guirigay pseudocientífico, por su fisionomía barbada y viril, casi hermosa y por su decidida fortuna pésima. Apaciguó el chubasco, pagó a doña Nicasia un mes de su pupilaje y, monarca absoluto . . . levantósele el entredicho, se le devolvieron unas miajas de su reputación de antaño.
>
> — ¡Es un tío que sabe! — proclamó "El Jarameño." . . . Yo lo defiendo porque me nace defenderlo . . . y una tarde he de brindarle un toro (190-191).

> Unexpectedly, El Jarameño took to protecting [Ripoll], attracted and dazzled by that pseudoscientific gibberish of his, by his virile and almost handsome bearded features, and by his decidedly rotten luck. After clearing the air and restoring calm, [El Jarameño] paid Doña Nicasia one month's rent on [Ripoll's] behalf, and now in total control [of the boarding house] . . . he lifted the ban [on the engineer]. Ripoll eventually got back a few crumbs of

what once had been his fame and prestige.

— That is one smart fellow! — declared El Jarameño. . . . I defend him because I feel like doing it . . . and one of these afternoons I will dedicate a bull to him.

This show of friendship on the part of El Jarameño only exacerbates an already tense situation. Contrary to the bullfighter's intentions, his attentions have an adverse effect on Ripoll. Instead of taking El Jarameño's act of good will for what it is, Ripoll, angered and at the same time fascinated by the mediator's "secreta fuerza irresistible" [secret and irresistible power], cannot help but view the rival's actions as proof of the ill will borne him. In his mind, the bullfighter pretends to act friendly only to spite him and to make his life even more miserable than what it already is. Consequently, Ripoll responds to El Jarameño's friendly overtures as one would react to the insult from an enemy: "No llegó hasta allí la gratitud del defendido, que, deponiendo enconos y antipatías, a cada paso se la manifestaba a su benefactor" (191). [Ungratefully, Ripoll never took El Jarameño up on his generous offer, although by putting aside his animosity and resentment, he began begrudgingly to express his gratitude to his benefactor].

Unable to vent his hatred of the bullfighter as he would have liked, Ripoll directs his anger and frustration toward bullfighting: "Odio a los toros y a los toreros, permítame que continúe queriéndolo mucho como hombre y como amigo" (191). [I hate bulls and bullfighters, but allow me to continue being good friends with you]. This statement borders on the preposterous, for what Ripoll is in effect saying is: "I hate who you are and what you do — that is, I hate you — but I still like you as a friend." Nevertheless, the rivalry between the two does not preclude the subject (Ripoll) from secretly admiring the mediator (El Jarameño) and those objects that the mediator deems desirable. At first, Ripoll tries to compensate for the mediator's influence on his life by overstating his feigned indifference toward those things associated with the bullfighter:

> — ¡Caracoles! — murmuró Gallegos, plantado a la mitad del
> pasillo —, ¡qué hembra se ha recetado el "maestro"! (192)
> La noticia circuló entre los huéspedes. . . . Hubo un
> encogimiento de hombros universal ¿qué les podia importar que
> hubiese una mujer de más en la casa? . . . Ripoll encogióse de
> hombros más que los otros al ser notificado del arribo de Santa . . .
> No se entusiasmaba Ripoll, de narices sobre sus números.
> ¿Las mujeres? . . . ¡puah! iguales, todas iguales, por mucho que
> cada enamorado sostenga lo contrario y para su dama exija una
> excepcionalidad que es subjetiva, meramente subjetiva (194-195).

> — Good heavens! — muttered Gallegos, standing in the
> middle of the hallway — what a woman the "master" has caught!
> The news quickly spread among the tenants. . . . Everybody
> shrugged their shoulders. What did they care if there was one more
> woman in the house? . . . Ripoll shrugged more than any of the
> other tenants when he was notified of Santa's arrival.
> Ripoll did not get excited, and kept his nose buried in his
> calculations. Women? . . . rubbish! they were all the same, despite
> what men smitten with love might say to the contrary, claiming that
> their beloved is different and superior [to all the others], a
> distinction that is subjective and totally open to question.

Later, Ripoll stops feigning indifference, and gives in to the
influence of the mediator. The significance of this change is not lost on
Santa, who now finds herself attracted to Ripoll but is unable to describe
why: "Ripoll la interesaba sin saber por qué" (208). [Ripoll appealed to
her, but she did not know why]. Even though El Jarameño "infudíale un
miedo atroz [a Santa]" [terrified Santa] — he had sworn he would kill her
if she should ever cheat on him — and Ripoll does his best to appear

unattracted to her, the two come together nonetheless, and end up having sexual relations. In the beginning, Santa and Ripoll actually go to great lengths to ignore each other and to deny their mutual attraction. She does this for fear of what El Jarameño might do to her should he find out. Ripoll has a different reason to ignore Santa. He wants to belittle and flaunt his indifference toward the stranger who usurped his privileged place in the boarding house. Ripoll is intent on ignoring those people and things identified with his rival, especially El Jarameño's lover, Santa. Yet, his and Santa's attempts at acting out their indifference prove unsuccessful. In the end, their thwarted efforts serve to underscore the fact that they are both affected by mimetic desire. Thus, Santa gives in to the "voluptuosa atracción que el peligro ejerce en los temperamentos femeninos" (210) [the voluptuous attraction that danger exerts on women], and Ripoll, "enardecido por la tentadora" (211) [aroused by the temptress], takes advantage of the opportunity that is presented to him: "Un domingo traicionero, Santa traicionó a "El Jarameño" entregándose cínicamente a Ripoll" (211). [On a fateful Sunday, Santa cheated on El Jarameño by cynically agreeing to have sex with Ripoll].

In Santa's affair with Rubio, we are led to believe that his desire for her is of the unmediated kind: "Es claro que Rubio no la amaba con vehemencia" (274). [It is obvious that Rubio did not love her with passion]. But later it becomes clear that Rubio shares a great deal more with El Jarameño than just the same lover. The mediator for both Rubio and El Jarameño is the unidentified Other — Santa's many customers — who precedes both men in their sexual encounters with Santa, and who promptly takes their place once the two rivals are gone. Of the two lovers, Rubio seems more cognizant of the mediator's presence. As a result, he is the one who fights the Other's influence more forcefully:

> Y en tanto se familiarizaba con la idea de que Santa únicamente a
> él pertenecía; en tanto apresurábase a raspar con sus besos los

vestigios indelebles de los miles y miles que . . . habían flagelado sin agotarla la planta deliciosa de su cuerpo trigueño, voluptuoso y duro, el amasiato fue llevadero, hasta con cierto picor, que en más apetitoso convertíalo, de besos de otros, de muchos; de caricias ajenas que persistían y le daban a la carne comprada y dócil, perfecta semejanza con esas monedas que han rodado por mercados y ferias y lucen la huella del sinnúmero de dedos toscos que las oprimieron (275).

Meanwhile [Rubio] persisted in his belief that Santa would be his alone. He hastened to wipe out with his kisses the indelible traces of thousands [of other men] who . . . had ravaged though not exhausted the allure of Santa's swarthy, voluptuous, and firm body. His illicit union [with Santa] was tolerable, it even had some of the sting from the kisses left over by other males, countless other males, a fact that only made their affair more appealing. [Also, there were] traces of other men's touches that lingered on Santa's docile flesh for hire, making her body bear a striking resemblance to these coins that circulate in all kinds of markets, displaying the traces of the countless rough hands that have clutched them.

To the subject, there is something even more desirable than taking possession of the object of desire itself, and that is to be able to erase completely the trace left by the Other on the object. The subject pursues this goal as he attempts to reclaim the autonomy of his desire, which he sees with resentment and shame as dependent on the Other. However, it is precisely this "vestigio indeleble" [indelible trace] of the mediator on the object that makes Santa appear attractive and desirable, glowing and calling attention to herself like the coins that grow shinier as they are handled by more and more people. Rubio fools himself into thinking that he can remove the Other's conspicuous mark from his lover's life — or from his psyche — but as long as he pursues the object, the mediator's trace will always be already there:

> Pero se percató pronto de que los remedios que vende el burdel son ineficaces, y de que a Santa ni con labios de bronce que en toda una vida se cansaran, le rasparía las entalladuras acumuladas y hondas de las ajenas caricias y de los besos de otros. Los horrendos celos retrospectivos, unidos a la perenne y humana presunción de que nosotros nada más seamos los preferidos y los primeros, desoldó el quebradizo vínculo que los engañaba y los mecía juntos (275).

> However, Rubio soon realized that the remedies available at the brothel were useless and that not even with his powerful bronze lips, trying frantically over a lifetime, would he be able to wipe out completely the countless deep traces left by other men's touches and kisses on Santa's body. The monstrous jealousy of past lovers, together with our enduring presumption that we are unique, that we are loved above all others, broke the fragile link that kept [the two lovers] bound together in their common deception.

The acknowledgment on the part of Rubio of his dependence on and hatred toward the Other in his affair with Santa carries into his dealings with his wife. The repercussions there are most serious. If his desire for Santa is determined by the presence or absence of the Other, that is, by the vestiges of "ajenas caricias y besos de otros" [other men's touches and kisses], so must be his desire for his wife. Even if she is not available to any man, the kind of desire of which Rubio is capable cannot exist independently of the mediator's trace. The "entalladuras" [traces] left by the "otros" [others] are always there. Like the deranged *hidalgo* in Cervantes's *Don Quijote*, Rubio has given up his prerogative to choose, and as such he looks to the Other for clues as to what should be desired. And like the wretched characters in Dostoyevsky's *The Possessed* and

Notes From the Underground, he curses his fate and his condition. Through the eyes of the Other, Santa's many customers, Rubio sees a cruel world where his desires are forever thwarted. His obsession with the complete erasure of the Other's trace in either wife or mistress takes him on a futile and tragic journey:

> Exasperado Rubio con su esposa, acababa de exasperarse con su manceba; iba de la una a la otra con la certeza de que ya habrían cambiado y alguna de las dos satisfaría lo que el venía persiguiendo, y frente al doble desengaño, con distintos modales y lenguaje distinto increpaba a las dos, sin hallar consuelo (276).

> Exasperated with his wife, Rubio ended up just as tormented by [the impasse with] his mistress. He ran from one to the other, certain that they would change and that one of them could give him what he had been pursuing. Faced with failure on both fronts, he would lash out at the two women, behaving differently toward each, yet unable to find any consolation in either.

The fourth triangle of mimetic desire in this second group is made up by Hipólito (the subject), Santa's clients, especially El Jarameño and Rubio (the mediator), and Santa (the object of desire). Even if the blind piano player manages to transcend the destructive mechanism of mimetic desire by resigning his pride and repudiating the mediator, at the beginning of his relationship with Santa, his behavior is similar to that of her first two lovers. With the intervention of the mediator, the "simpatía inconfesada y tímida" (72) [unspoken and timid attraction] on the part of Hipólito suddenly grows to gargantuan proportions. When confronted with the real possibility of losing his beloved, the mild desire that the mediator had awakened in the subject suddenly turns into a violent passion:

— Hipo, — le dijo Santa —, Rubio me ofrece ponerme casa si yo me "comprometo" con él ¿qué me aconseja usted?

¡Caramba, y el temblor nervioso que a duras penas pudo dominar el filarmónico al oír el secreto! (83)

— Hipo, Santa told him, Rubio has offered to move in with me if I agree to be only his. What do you advise me to do?

Good heavens! It was only with great difficulty that the piano player regained his composure after the shock of learning about Santa's secret.

When asked for his opinion on Santa's liaison with Rubio, Hipólito tries his best to lessen the influence that the mediator has over the object. He does this by painting the worst possible scenario that in his opinion would await Santa if she should move in with Rubio:

el burdel es como el aguardiente [y] la cárcel . . . el trabajo está en probarlos, [pero] después de probados . . . ¡la atracción que en sus devotos ejercen! . . . Usted regresará a esta casa, Santita, o a otra peor. . . . ¿Por qué no aguarda usted unos meses más? Lejos de perder, quizá gane, y si el señor Rubio desespera y vuelve las espaldas, probará que únicamente nutría un capricho por usted. ¡El que de veras ama nunca se cansa de aguardar! Además, hoy por hoy, ¿qué necesita usted? Salud le sobra, le sobran marchantes, buenos modos de Elvira y de Pepa, aprovéchese usted, hágase pagar a peso de oro, y siga la rueda.

Lo que siguió, por lo pronto, fue la cátedra del pervertido de Hipo, que . . . predicaba las peores atrocidades con una inverecundia mayúscula (84).

the brothel is like alcohol and prison. . . . The difficult part is trying them out for the first time, but once we do . . . we fall under their spell and become addicted. . . . You will end up returning to this house, Santa, or even to a worse one. . . . Why don't you wait for a few months? Instead of losing, you may actually come out ahead, and if Mr. Rubio loses hope, and turns his back on you, that will prove that his interest in you was only a passing fancy. The real lover never tires of waiting! Besides, what do you need right now? You're in the pink of health, you have plenty of customers, and Elvira and Pepa are very kind to you. You should enjoy [your good fortune], get as much money as you can [for your services], and let life take its course.

Meanwhile what followed was Hipo's disingenuous and perverted lecture [on the evils of the world], in which he shamelessly predicted the worst of atrocities [for Santa].

To be sure, Rubio's overtures toward Santa prove menacing enough to the blind piano player. After all, Rubio represents a very real danger. Yet, it is El Jarameño whom Hipólito admires and fears the most. The bullfighter poses a far greater threat to him than any of Santa's other customers, Rubio included. As a result, when Santa turns for a second time to Hipólito to ask him for advice on whether or not she should move in with another of her customers, this time with the much-feared El Jarameño, the blind man tries to deflect the imminent danger by choosing the lesser of two evils:

Intentó, por remediar un mal máximo con uno bastante menor, . . . fomentar la simpatía por [Rubio] inspirada:

— [Santa], ¿en qué ha parado su proyecto de "comprometerse" con aquel señor rubio? . . . Piénselo usted, Santita. [Rubio] es un caballero y si le afirma que la quiere, por algo ha de afirmárselo. [Hipólito] se azoraba de que Santa . . . no reparara en el dolor inmenso que a él representábale encomiar a un rival de segundo término, de preferencia al torero triunfante, y por ello, el más odiado. Los otros . . . no le inspiraban celos extraordinarios. . . . Eran distintos; provocábanle un malestar meramente físico, mientras los calculaba adueñados de su dama . . . pero "El Jarameño" le provocaba fenómenos mucho más intensos e interiores, hasta crispaturas en el mismísimo corazón, que le entrecortaban el respiro y le inventaban a la mente ideas criminales, de crímenes imprecisos o incomprensibles (148-149).

Trying to substitute a greater evil with a lesser one, [Hipólito] sought to encourage Santa's liaison with [Rubio]:
— [Santa], how is your project to move in with that blonde gentleman coming along? . . . Think about it, Santa. [Rubio] is a real gentleman and if he says he loves you, it's because he means it. [Hipólito] was astounded that Santa . . . never noticed how painful it was for him to have to praise and give preference to a second-rate rival over the successful bullfighter, whom he hated above all others. [Hipólito] was not overly jealous of . . . the other men. . . . They were different; they just made him feel a little queasy when he pictured them in the intimate company of his beloved. In contrast, El Jarameño, provoked in him a more profound and intense reaction. So much so that it made him choke, causing his heart to beat erratically and his breath to be cut short, and it produced in his fertile imagination wicked schemes for undefined or outrageous crimes.

Hipólito finally comes face to face with his rival. This happens when he literally has to hand Santa over to the bullfighter:

[Hipólito] había de llevar al rival detestado . . . él había de servir de instrumento para que el torero se adueñara de Santa. . . . Retrocedió unos pasos, cual si perdiese el equilibrio; rechazó con las manos tendidas peligros invisibles para los que veían, pero que él, ciego, veía y ahuyentaba con ese ademán de conjuro. . . .
Fue una lucha brevísima, de segundos, que a él le resultaron

interminables, como siglos. [Su] pasión [por Santa] . . . le difundía
por venas y arterias . . . haciéndose pedazos un mundo de entrañas
que no se sospechaba tan sensibles, y que ahora . . . se le quejaban,
cada cual en sus dominios: en la boca, hiel; en las piernas, temblo-
res; en los riñones, dolor de verdad, y en el corazón . . . una
tormenta desencadenada: latíale enloquecido, con punzadas que le
obligaban a llevarse las manos al sitio adolorido, disimulando,
fingiendo que buscaba algo en el pequeño bolsillo alto de su
chaleco. . . .

    Ni él ni "El Jarameño" hablaron palabra dentro del vehículo
que los conducía lado a lado. Se codeaban a causa de los tumbos
y se alejaban a causa de la voluntad, pues quizás el torero presentía
en su acompañante intenciones sobre Santa y por eso manifestábale
antipático y hostil (161-162).

    [Hipólito] had to take his hated Rival to Santa. He was
supposed to serve as a go-between so that she could be handed over
to the bullfighter. . . . [Hipólito] took a few steps back, as if he
had lost his balance, and with his arms stretched out, he tried to
repel dangers invisible to everyone else, but which he, although
blind, could see [only too well], and which he sought to drive
away.

    It was a very brief fight, lasting only a few seconds, which to
Hipólito seemed more like centuries. His passion for Santa . . .
had spread out through his veins and arteries . . . tearing to pieces
his insides, which he never suspected to be so sensitive, and which
now . . . bothered him, each [organ] with its own affliction: his
mouth tasted as bitter as bile; his legs trembled; his kidneys ached;
and inside of him a storm raged: his heart throbbed wildly, with
such an excruciating pain that he was forced to take his hands to his
chest, trying to conceal his discomfort by pretending he was looking
for something in his vest pocket.

    Seated side by side inside the coach, neither he nor El

Jarameño spoke a single word. They would elbow each other because of the bumps, but subsequently they would willingly move away. Perhaps the bullfighter suspected that his fellow traveler had designs on Santa, and because of that he behaved in a hostile and unpleasant manner toward him.

Even though Hipólito considers Santa's other lovers "de segundo término" [second rate] compared to El Jarameño, this does not mean that the blind man is willing to accept another rival just because he does not pose as great a threat as the bullfighter. Whether he is dealing with El Jarameño or Rubio, Hipólito's main goal is always to lessen or neutralize as best he can the influence of the mediator over Santa:

> — Santita, replicó el músico —, no sé yo si será tan caballero como parece. . . . ¿Sabe usted lo que me produce este Rubio y los [otros hombres] que gozan de usted? . . . me producen lástima . . . ¡majaderos! ¿qué más quieren [de usted]? (251)

> — Santa, replied the musician, I'm not so sure that [Rubio] really is the gentleman that he purports to be. . . . Do you know what impression I get from this Rubio character and [the other men] who exploit you? . . . They seem pitiful to me! . . . Idiots! What else do they want [from you]?

The praise that the patrons of the brothel heap on Santa and the favors that they enjoy in return may give her some pleasure or amusement, but serve only to exasperate Hipólito. The idea of his beloved constantly being pursued by a sex-hungry rival is too much for the blind man to take. Conversely, he is delighted to overhear the conversation between Santa and El Jarameño in which she flatly rejects the bullfighter's invitation to spend the night with her:

— ¿Qué noche dormirás conmigo, Santa? — le preguntó [El Jarameño].

— ¿Contigo? . . . ¡Nunca! . . .

El ciego Hipólito, que salía detrás y escuchó la declaración de Santa, no pudo reprimirse:

— La felicito a usted por su conquista, Santita. . . . No vale hombre ninguno lo que el último de estos individuos de trenza. . . . (88)

— When will you sleep with me, Santa? — [El Jarameño] asked her.

— With you? . . . Never!

The blind man, who happened to pass by at that moment, heard Santa's refusal, and could not contain himself:

— I congratulate you on your victory Santa. . . . [It's wise of you not to get involved with] a shady character with a pony tail — even if he were the last man on Earth!

Hipólito is tormented by a conflict similar to the one that afflicts Rubio. He cannot reconcile his almost religious affection for Santa with the fact that she is a prostitute, and, as such, is available to anyone willing to pay for her services:

En definitiva Santa no era manjar de dioses ni monja clarisa ¿por qué no había de probar fortuna presentándose al igual de los favorecidos, con sus dineros contantes y sonantes, a comprar una mercancía que se hallaba de venta y a la disposición del mejor postor? No digo yo el precio de una tarifa, el de mil tarifas le daría . . . con tal de curarse de aquel desasosiego que lo traía a maltraer y sin trazas de disminuírsele (141).

Santa was definitely no goddess. Neither was she some demure nun. Why shouldn't he have her, like any of her customers, [who would come to the brothel] with their cash, seeking to buy a product that was available to the highest bidder? I am not implying that he would pay [Santa] her regular price. He would give her a thousand times that much . . . as long as he could rid himself of that restlessness that tormented him relentlessly, without any indication of letting up.

It is through the Other that Hipólito and Rubio are able to desire at all. In the case of Hipólito, this predicament becomes apparent when Gamboa poignantly illustrates the blind man's inability to see or desire on his own. In a literal sense, Hipólito can see Santa only through the eyes of another, his *lazarillo* [blind man's guide] in this case, just as he initially can desire her only through the mediator:

"Jenarillo, te vas allá a la ['Guipuzcoana'] y mírala por mí" (207).

Por la millonésima vez . . . sujetó a Jenaro a un interrogatorio que formulaba a diario.

— Jenarillo, hijo, vas a explicarme como es Santita ¿eh? . . .

— ¿Otra vez don Hipólito? — exclamó Jenaro. . . . Pues Santita es preciosa. . . . (142)

— Su pelo es . . . negro, negrísimo. . . . Cuando lo *tray* suelto . . . le da más abajo de la cintura. . . . Su cara es muy linda cuando está seria. . . . Cuando se ríe, se le hacen hoyos en los cachetes y en la barba . . . y de los ojos yo creo que le sale luz igualita a la del sol (143-144).

— Cuando se viste de *catrina* . . . la veo más alta . . . la cintura se le achica y el seno se le levanta . . . las caderas le engordan y se le ven llenotas. . . . Las piernas, que cruza y campanea, son muy bonitas . . . delgadas al comenzar . . . y luego yendo pa arriba, gordas, haciéndole una onda donde todos tenemos la carne, atrás.

"My dear Jenaro, please go to the ['Guipuzcoana' boarding house] and look at Santa for me."

— For the thousandth time . . . Hipólito subjected Jenaro to his daily interrogation [about Santa].

— Jenaro, my dear boy, you are going to tell me what Santa looks like, aren't you?

— Again, don Hipólito? replied Jenaro. . . . Well, Santa is beautiful. . . .

— Her hair is . . . black, jet black. . . . When she wears it loose . . . it reaches all the way down past her waist. . . . Her face is very pretty when she is serious. . . . When she smiles, dimples appear on her cheeks and chin . . . and I swear that the glow from her eyes is as [brilliant as] the light of the sun itself.

When she dresses up . . . she looks taller . . . her waist becomes smaller and her chest is raised . . . her hips take on a more rounded shape and look fuller. . . . Her legs, which she crosses and swings rhythmically, are very attractive. . . . [They are] thin near her ankles . . . becoming thicker as you go up, and her behind is as full and round as a well-formed wave.

In the above passage, Hipólito instructs his guide to look at Santa carefully so that in turn he can describe her to him. His request exemplifies his position vis-à-vis a kind of desire in which the enjoyment of the desired object can only be accomplished through someone else's perception or possession of that object. Such a behavior comes close to being an accepted form of cuckoldry. Here, any pleasure on the part of the subject depends on another person's enjoyment of those things or individuals dear to the subject. After the *lazarillo*'s long and titillating description of Santa, a change of sorts takes place in Hipólito. For the first time in the novel, the mechanism of desire is neutralized. By refusing to ask his lazarillo for more information concerning Santa, Hipólito in effect eliminates the only means by which he can "see" and enjoy the physical attributes of his beloved. He renounces the Other. He repudiates the mediator who enables him to "see" the object of his desire, and who at the same time serves as a reminder that he cannot have it. As one would expect, the effects of this double bind on Hipólito are devastating:

> A partir de esta noche, no volvió el músico a pedirle a Jenaro amplificaciones o retoques en el retrato de Santa; en cambio, tampoco volvió a reír cual solía, faunescamente, al escuchar cuando tocaba sus danzas en casa de Elvira, como los parroquianos, excitados, palpaban los encantos de las mujerzuelas. Ahora permanecía inmoble, pegado a su piano y pensando en sus amores maldecidos (148).

> From that night on, the musician never again asked Jenaro to elaborate on or retouch Santa's portrait. On the other hand, neither did he ever laugh again the way he used to, like a mischievous faun, when he played the piano at Elvira's brothel, and listened as her customers excitedly fondled the prostitutes' feminine charms. Now, he remained motionless, glued to his piano, lost in thought about his star-crossed love.

Yet, it is precisely this change that enables Hipólito to transcend the destructive mechanism of mimetic desire and to play his role as liberator, rescuing Santa from the same whirlwind from which he has extricated himself. Free from the sphere of influence of the Other, Hipólito is capable of love-passion, and selflessly declares it to Santa:

> Conque la quiera a usted un hombre, uno nada más, pero hondo, hasta los huesos, hasta después de la muerte, un hombre que no le eche a usted en cara lo que es usted, y por usted viva; un hombre que la adore y que la abrace y la defienda y la sostenga; que se

enorgullezca de que usted le paga con un poquito de cariño, un poquito, una miseria, su idolatría tan grande; que la ponga por encima de las estrellas y se la incruste en el alma, le vele el sueño, le adivine el pensamiento . . . ¡ay, Santita, entonces sí que conocería usted la gloria en vida y no volvería a saber para qué sirven lágrimas ni lo que son las penas, las tristezas, las vergüenzas y los arrepentimientos! (153)

And so if a man should love you, just one man, yet love you from the bottom of his heart, even after death, a man who will not embarrass you by reminding you who you are; someone who will live only for you, a man who will adore you and [be by your side in your hour of need] to hold, defend, and support you; a man who will be more than happy to receive whatever little affection from you in return for his undying love; someone who will put you above everyone and everything else, and who will forever treasure your memory, a man who will watch over you as you sleep, and who will anticipate your every thought and feeling. . . . Only then, my dear Santa, will you know what true happiness is, and never again will you cry, feel guilt or shame, or be hurt or sad!

In the end, Santa is redeemed by Hipólito's true love. His selfless intervention on her behalf is prompted by what Girard refers to as love-passion. Hipólito's love for Santa is the opposite of pride or vanity. Before he extricates himself from the talons of mimetic desire, he behaves like the other players in the game of internal mediation. However, once free, he is set apart from former rivals like Rubio and El Jarameño by his emotional autonomy, by the spontaneity of his desire, and by his indifference to the opinion of others. He draws the strength of his desire from within himself and not from others. His true love does not in any way transfigure Santa. His is not a romantic love. He accepts the prostitute as she is. The qualities that his love discovers in its object and the happiness that he expects from it are not illusory. Hipólito's love-passion is accompanied by true esteem. It is based on a perfect agreement between reason, will, and sensibility.[12]

The denouement of Santa's story is certainly not a happy one. One could regard it as the poignant illustration of a basic tenet of internal mediation. The only truth of desire, Girard observes, is death. Still, however tragic the conclusion in *Santa* may appear, it also carries a positive message because at the time of death the subject is at last set free from the desire that imprisoned and destroyed her. Girard argues:

> Repudiation of the mediator implies renunciation of divinity, and this means renouncing pride. The physical diminution of the hero both expresses and conceals the defeat of pride. . . . In renouncing divinity the hero renounces slavery. Every level of his existence is inverted, all the effects of metaphysical desire are replaced by contrary effects. Deception gives way to truth, anguish to remembrance, agitation to repose, hatred to love, humiliation to humility, mediated desire to autonomy, deviated transcendency to vertical transcendency.[13]

Santa finally triumphs in her apparent defeat. She succeeds because she is at the end of her resources, and for the first time since leaving her countryside haven, she need not live a lie. She is forced to confront and acknowledge the true nature of mimetic desire and her own dependence on it. But this confrontation, which is the death of pride as well as her physical demise, is also her salvation.

Notes

[1] For examples of this kind of criticism, see Luis G. Urbina, "Federico Gamboa," in *Hombres y libros* (México: El Libro Francés, 1923): 151-160.

J. O. Theobald, "Naturalism in the Works of Federico Gamboa," M.A. thesis, University of Arizona, 1933.

S. Rosenberg, "El Naturalismo en Méjico y don Federico Gamboa," *Bulletin Hispanique* 36 (1934): 472-487.

Alberto María Carreño, "Federico Gamboa," *Abside 2* 12 (1938): 18-38.

Carlos González Peña, "Las bodas de oro de un novelista," *Letras de México* 2 (1939): 6-7.

Julio Jiménez Rueda, "Federico Gamboa," *Revista Iberoamericana* 1 (1939): 361-363.

Génaro Fernández MacGregor, "Federico Gamboa como diplomático," *Revista de literatura mexicana* 1 (1940): 30-53.

E. R. Moore, "Federico Gamboa: Diplomat and Novelist," *Books Abroad* 14 (1940): 364-367.

Robert Niess, "Federico Gamboa: the Novelist as Autobiographer," *Hispanic Review* 13 (1945): 346-351.

Robert J. Niess, "Zola's *L'Oeuvre* and *Reconquista* of Gamboa," *PMLA* 61 (1946): 577-583.

A. W. Woolsey, "Some of the Social Problems Considered by Federico Gamboa," *Modern Language Journal* 34 (1950): 294-297.

[2] Seymour Menton, "The Life and Works of Federico Gamboa," Ph.D. dissertation, New York University, 1952.

Seymour Menton, "Revalorización de Federico Gamboa," in *Memoria del*

Sexto Congreso del Instituto Internacional de Literatura Iberoamericana (México: Dirección General de Publicaciones de la Universidad Nacional Autónoma de México, 1954): 205-211.

Seymour Menton, "Influencias extranjeras en las obras de Federico Gamboa," *Armas y letras* 1 (1958): 35-50.

Seymour Menton, "Federico Gamboa: Un análisis estilístico," *Humanitas* 4 (1963): 311-342.

Seymour Menton, "Federico Gamboa," in *Latin American Writers*, vol. 1, ed. Carlos A. Solé and Maria Isabel Abreu (New York: Charles Scribner's Sons, 1989): 371-375.

Joaquina Navarro, *La novela realista mexicana* (México: Compañía General de Ediciones, 1955).

Alexander Hooker, *La novela de Federico Gamboa* (Madrid: Editorial Playor, 1971).

Bartie Lee Lewis, Jr., "The Myth of the Moment: A Reappraisal of the Novels of Federico Gamboa," Ph.D. dissertation, University of New Mexico, 1973.

Bartie Lee Lewis, Jr., "Myth in Federico Gamboa's *Santa,*" *Mester* 6 (1976): 32-37.

Ana María Alvarado, "Función del prostíbulo en *Santa* y *Juntacadáveres,*" *Hispanic Journal* 2 (1980): 57-68.

Alberto J. Carlos, "*Nacha Regules* y *Santa*: Problemas de intertextualidad," *Symposium* 36 (1982-1983): 301-307.

Other recent critics who have analyzed Gamboa's work include Ricardo Latcham, "En el centenario de Federico Gamboa," *Revista nacional* 9 (1964): 594-596.

Guillermo Ara, *La novela naturalista hispanoamericana* (Buenos Aires: Eudeba, 1965).

Jorge Campos, "El naturalismo mejicano: Federico Gamboa," *Ínsula* 20 (1965): 21.

Francisco Monterde, "Federico Gamboa y el modernismo," *Revista hispánica moderna* 31 (1965): 329-330.

María García Barragán, "Memorias de Federico Gamboa," *Abside* 36

(1972): 16-36.

Manuel Serna Maytorena, "Santa: México, Federico Gamboa y la realidad histórica del porfiriato," *Cuadernos americanos* 182 (1972): 168-183.

María García Barragán, "*Santa*, la novela olvidada que vuelve: Sus simbolismos e influencias sobre la literatura actual," *Proceedings of the Pacific Northwest Conference on Foreign Languages* (Corvalis: Oregon State University, 1974): 184-188.

María García Barragán, "Federico Gamboa," *Quaderni ibero-americani* 47-48 (1975-1976): 378-385.

Francisco Mena, "Federico Gamboa y el naturalismo como expresión ideológica y social," *Explicación de textos literarios* 2 (1976): 207-214.

María García Barragán, "*Santa*, de Federico Gamboa," in *Actas del sexto congreso internacional de hispanistas* (Toronto: University of Toronto Press, 1980): 290-292.

Amado Manuel Lay, "Visión del porfiriato en cuatro narradores mexicanos: Rafael Delgado, Federico Gamboa, José López Portillo y Rojas y Emilio Rabasa," Ph.D. dissertation, University of Arizona, 1981.

Silvana Serafin, "La città in *Santa* di Federico Gamboa," *Studi di letteratura ispano-americana* 15-16 (1983): 159-166.

João Sedycias, "Crane, Azevedo, and Gamboa: A Comparative Study," Ph.D. dissertation, State University of New York at Buffalo, 1985.

José Emilio Pacheco, *La novela mexicana: Federico Gamboa* (México: Coordinación de Difusión Cultural, Universidad Nacional Autónoma de México, 1988).

Rosa Levin, "El autor y el personaje femenino en dos novelas del siglo XX: *Santa* de Federico Gamboa y *La gloria de don Ramiro* de Enrique Larreta," Ph.D. dissertation, University of Colorado, 1989.

[3] R. Anthony Castagnaro, *The Early Spanish-American Novel* (New York: Las Américas, 1971) 61.

Kessel Schwartz, *A New History of Spanish-American Fiction* (Coral Gables, Florida: University of Mami Press, 1972) 115.

John Brushwood, *The Spanish-American Novel* (Austin: University of

Texas Press, 1975) 153.

[4] Federico Gamboa, *Santa* (México: Ediciones Botas, 1960) 39. All subsequent quotations from *Santa* are from this edition. Citations by page number appear in parentheses in the text.

[5] Stephen Crane, *Maggie: A Girl of the Streets*, in *Stephen Crane: An Omnibus*, ed. Robert Stallman (New York: Alfred Knopf, 1966) 100.

[6] René Girard, *Deceit, Desire, and the Novel: Self and Other in Literary Structure*, trans. Yvonne Freccero (Baltimore, Maryland: Johns Hopkins University Press, 1980) 290.

[7] Girard, *Deceit* 291.

[8] Girard, *Deceit* 105.

[9] Girard, *Deceit* 106.

[10] Girard, *Deceit* 106.

[11] Girard, *Deceit* 106-107.

[12] Girard, *Deceit* 19.

[13] Girard, *Deceit* 294.

Part Three

Conclusions

Chapter 8

Cultural Perspectives in New World Naturalistic Fiction

In his article on the history of literary Naturalism in American fiction, Malcolm Cowley observes that the naturalistic school in this country can be defined in two words: as pessimistic and deterministic.[1] Even though Cowley deals almost exclusively with the naturalistic novel of the United States, his definition can be expanded to include the movement in Europe and in other countries of the New World such as Mexico and Brazil. Other literary historians such as George Becker, Lars Ahnebrink, and Richard Chase concur with Cowley, and have accepted the traditional view of Naturalism as essentially an outgrowth of Realism infused with a pessimistic determinism.[2] In Chase's words, Naturalism is merely Realism with a "necessitarian ideology."[3] Becker views the school as "no more than an emphatic and explicit philosophical position taken by some realists," the position being a "pessimistic materialistic determinism."[4] Ahnebrink elaborates further, arguing that "the [naturalistic] author portrays life as it is in accordance with the philosophical theory of determinism . . . a natural belief that man is fundamentally an animal without free will."[5] Today, critics such as Antônio Cândido, Jean Franco, Sônia Brayner, Gordon Brotherston, John Conder, and Lee Clark Mitchell continue to view naturalistic authors as deterministic because in their view these writers believed in the overwhelming power of environmental and social forces.[6] Naturalists are pessimistic, Cowley contends, because they conceive of men and women as helpless "pawns on a chessboard . . . incapable of shaping their own destinies."[7] Williams James is said to have divided writers into two groups: the tough and the tender-minded.[8] Cowley takes James's classification one step further, and suggests that most of the naturalists belong in the last group. Cowley writes:

> They [the naturalists] write shocking books because they [themselves] had been shocked. . . . More than other writers they are wounded by ugliness and injustice, but they will not close their eyes to either; indeed, they often give the impression of seeking out ugliness and injustice in order to be wounded again and again. . . . They build up new illusions simply to enjoy the pain of stripping them away. It is their feeling of fascinated revulsion towards their subject matter that makes some of the Naturalists hard to read; they seem to be flogging themselves and their audience like a band of *penitentes*.[9]

Naturalists have also been blamed for holding a view of the world in which individuals are little more than "human insects," completely at the mercy of potentially destructive social and physical forces which they can neither understand nor control. The individual's actions and destiny are determined by drives that threaten to destroy him if he tries to resist. His struggle, instead of being grandiose and tragic, becomes a pitiful and meaningless exercise in irony.[10]

One may find the above definition of Naturalism appropriate to describe the work of writers such as Stephen Crane or Aluísio Azevedo. However, this approach proves less than adequate when applied to Federico Gamboa. In Gamboa's *Santa*, one finds neither the moralistic tone of Crane nor the consistently grim concept of the world typical of naturalistic fiction, as found in Azevedo. To be sure, Santa's story has a distinctly tragic ending, but it is not imbued in the gloom, violence, or despair found in *Maggie*. In order to interpret a novel like *Santa* adequately, the criteria by which New World Naturalism is defined above will have to be reconsidered. As I have noted, Naturalism has been closely identified with the widely accepted definition that characterizes the movement as primarily an extension of the realist school with a particular deterministic philosophical orientation.[11] In his study of nineteenth-century American Naturalism, Donald Pizer notes that "the common belief is that naturalists were like the realists in their fidelity to the details of contemporary life but that they depicted everyday life with a greater sense of the role of such causal forces as heredity and environment in determining behavior and belief."[12]

Pizer acknowledges that the historical and philosophical connection linking Naturalism to Realism has served a useful purpose for students of literature in their endeavor to define and analyze the two movements. On the other hand, he cautions about the inherent danger of making too much of this connection. One is bound to run into problems if one tries to define either of these literary schools solely in terms of the other, as critics such as Richard Chase and George Becker have sought to do.[13] Unfortunately, the approach to Naturalism through Realism and philosophical determinism has not proven very successful either in producing close readings of naturalistic writers or in fomenting a genuine appreciation of their work:

> It [the above approach] has resulted in much condescension toward those writers who are supposed to be naturalists yet whose fictional sensationalism (an aspect of Romanticism) and moral ambiguity (a quality inconsistent with the absolutes of determinism) appear to make their work flawed specimens of the mode.[14]

Federico Gamboa is a case in point. A novel of the caliber and complexity of *Santa* requires us to make some fundamental changes in the deterministic-pessimistic definition of Naturalism, lest we fall into the trap of trying to explicate the work by straightjacketing it into a pre-established set of literary tenets. The modified concept of nineteenth-century New World Naturalism used in the following analysis of *Santa* is derived in part from a definition first proposed by Charles Walcutt in 1947 and later elaborated on by Donald Pizer in 1965.[15] Pizer points out that the naturalist populates his novels primarily with individuals from the lower class, as is the case with all three novels examined in this study. As far as Gamboa's work is concerned, his characters are society's wretched. They are destitute, illiterate, disenfranchised. The world in which Santa's story unfolds is "that of the commonplace and unheroic in which life [seems] to be chiefly the dull round of everyday existence." As a naturalistic novel, *Santa* could be viewed as "an extension of Realism, but only in the sense that both modes often deal with the local and contemporary." Gamboa, unlike Crane or Azevedo, "discovers in this world those [human] qualities . . . usually associated with the heroic or adventurous, such as acts of violence and passion." The Mexican author goes further than his fellow realists as he tries to "discover in his material the extraordinary and excessive in human nature."[16]

Naturalistic writers such as Crane and Azevedo tend to portray their characters as individuals caught in the grip of deadly forces, whose lives are defined and controlled by their physical and social environments. To a certain extent, Gamboa does that too, but he compensates for the negative effect of such a somber view by suggesting a "humanistic value in his characters or in their fates, which affirms the significance of the individual and of his life." This is especially true of Santa and Hipólito. On the one hand, the author strives to depict in his fiction the crude and "discomforting truths which he has found in [his] world," but on the other hand, he also wants to discover "some meaning in experience that reasserts the validity of the human enterprise." Both Crane and Azevedo come across as deterministic and pessimistic, although their attitudes toward their protagonists are radically different. Azevedo not only allows Pombinha to adapt to the demands of her amoral and sex-hungry milieu, but also grants her a generous measure of success. Crane, on the other hand, has Maggie commit suicide after she has apparently overcome her scruples, and has become a successful prostitute. Gamboa differs markedly from Crane and Azevedo. To be sure, the Mexican author realizes that the individual may indeed be only a "pawn on a chessboard." Still, as Pizer suggests, even in an amoral and ominous world where man has forfeited responsibility for his destiny, "the imagination refuses to accept this formula as the total meaning of life and so seeks a new basis for man's sense of his own dignity and importance."[17]

Viewed in this light, naturalistic novels such as Gamboa's *Santa* are therefore not "so superficial or reductive as [they] implicitly appear to be in [their] conventional definition." One of the main themes in *Santa* is that "life at its lowest levels is not as simple as it seems to be from higher levels." With his poignant tale of seduction and *hamartia*, Gamboa submits to his readers that "even the least significant human being can feel and strive powerfully and can suffer the extraordinary consequences of his emotions." Santa and Hipólito are prime examples of characters who lack those qualities traditionally associated with the hero, and yet they are able to illustrate through their courageous struggle with society and themselves that "no range of human experience is free of . . . moral complexities and ambiguities."[18]

Santa is representative of the kind of naturalistic fiction that "reflects an affirmative ethical conception of life [because] it asserts the value of all life." The novel does this by endowing even the lowliest or most contemptible of characters "with emotion and defeat and with moral ambiguity, no matter how poor or ignoble [they] may seem." In the portrayal of his characters' plights and in the description of the environment in which they must fight for survival, Gamboa brings to life an intricate and moving drama. As we have seen, the author derives much of the novel's aesthetic effect from certain juxtapositions and contrasts. He involves his readers in the "experience of a life both commonplace and extraordinary, both familiar and strange, both simple and complex." In short, *Santa* presents the reader with what Frank Norris refers to as the "romance of the commonplace," the story of a prostitute and a blind man who sink together to the bowels of society, and somehow manage to maintain their dignity, respect, and love for each other.[19]

When one compares *Santa* to *Maggie*, one notes that whereas Crane often creates human figures that are universal in nature, Gamboa tends to develop highly individualized characters. These are men and women who embody distinctly personal qualities. In *Santa*, one finds many naturalistic traits, but more importantly, one also finds a unique sense of individuality that has come to characterize Hispanic peoples as a whole. Although named after its main character, Crane's novel does not concentrate on the psychology or individuality of the protagonist to the same extent that *Santa* does. Drawing on a tradition that goes back to the Spanish mystics — who manifest in their lives perhaps more poignantly than any other single group the characteristic traits of Hispanic individuality — Santa becomes a distinctly individualized woman as her story unfolds. She develops into a solitary soul, and through suffering and the purging of her sins, she gains awareness of the liberating force that drives her away from prostitution and toward her friend Hipólito. In *Maggie*, we find neither this individualism nor the portrayal of an individual's predicament as a uniquely personal affair, as opposed to being representative of the plight of a whole social group.

The sense of justice in each of the three novels is another cultural element that sets Crane, Azevedo, and Gamboa apart. Here, the notion of right and wrong can either originate in naturalistic ideology, that is, it can be merely the consequence of environmental forces and therefore essentially amoral, or it can stem from an ethical tradition. In *Santa*, the feeling of compassion and the willingness to forgive a weary soul who has suffered and repented stand in stark contrast to the rigid, puritanical sense of justice and righteousness in *Maggie*. In *Santa*, Catholic salvation triumphs over naturalistic justice. In *Maggie*, a strict sense of morality compels the protagonist's social environment to turn a deaf ear to her pleas for help.

The cultural traits that distinguish *Santa* from other works of the same genre — a strong sense of individuality, a relativistic conception of justice, and a profoundly religious philosophy of life — also represent the distinctive qualities that by and large characterize the Hispanic soul. These are essentially the same distinguishing features that the Spanish historian and social critic Salvador de Madariaga examines in his study of British, French, and Spanish civilizations. Madariaga focuses on the "distinctive attitude" in each of these cultures that in his view "determines their natural and spontaneous reactions towards life." According to Madariaga, "these reactions spring in each case from a characteristic impulse, manifesting itself in a complex psychological entity, an idea-sentiment-force peculiar to each of the three peoples."[20] He argues that the psychological center of the British is "fair play" [rule and action], of the French, "le droit" [intellect and reason], and of the Spanish, "el honor" [subjectivity and passion]. Madariaga contends further that "in Spain religion is above all an individual passion, just like love, jealousy, hatred, or ambition," and that the most important concern of the Spaniard is to save his or her soul, either in a religious or psychological sense.[21] Viewed in this light, *Santa* appears not so much as the product of an orthodox model of the *roman expérimental*, but rather as a culture-specific story with clear religious and moral overtones, a work of fiction conceived and developed in and for a very specific cultural milieu.

Certainly not every Hispanic or Catholic cultural trait outlined above is present in all Spanish-American countries. Nevertheless, I believe that one must turn to Spain when seeking the origins of the forces that have helped to define Spanish-American culture, such as religion and the ethical tradition that governs social life in this part of the world. The social historian James Bryce contends that all Spanish-American countries remain in a sense Spanish, exhibiting the broad features of Spanish character and temperament. According to Bryce, Spain lives on in the New World, in its culture, in its language, and especially in its intensely religious soul. Of course, this is not to say that Spanish America is a mere replica of Spain, because the process of differentiation between mother country and daughter colonies started immediately after the first conquistadors set foot on the American continent and found themselves in an alien environment that would change them irrevocably from *españoles peninsulares* [peninsular Spanish] into *criollos* [native to the New World].[22]

One of the more significant and pervasive cultural legacies that Spanish America has inherited from Spain is its profound sense of spirituality. To this day, this integral element of the Spanish *Weltanschauung* still largely defines and gives meaning to the individual and communal self in most Spanish-speaking countries. The inherently ethical psychological makeup of a character like Santa or Hipólito exemplifies this important facet of the Spanish-American psyche. This trait characterizes Gamboa's work both as Hispanic and Catholic, as well as Mexican, and at the same time sets it apart from other novels in the general corpus of naturalistic fiction.

As we have seen, Crane, Azevedo, and Gamboa reflect in their fiction a conception of life that draws as much on European naturalistic ideology as from their respective cultures. Crane is inherently puritanical in his treatment of prostitution in *Maggie*, although he would like his readers to believe otherwise. Gamboa, on the other hand, reflects a more benign attitude toward the fallen woman, and Azevedo articulates in his work a number of ideas unique to the Brazilian intelligentsia of his time.

Foremost among these ideas is the belief that Brazil was a country free of the moral or religious influences that have shaped the cultures of the United States and Spanish-America. In his 1967 study of immorality in Brazil, Abelardo Romero sums up this position thus:

O pior mal do Brasil é a desordem moral. A que atribuí-la? Para os colonialistas, que procuram justificar a escravidão, o clima indispunha o homem para o trabalho, ao mesmo tempo que o predispunha e até o excitava para a prática de atos libidinosos. . . . Se os colonizadores eram dessa espécie, os nativos, por sua vez, encontravam-se, e de há muito, em extrema decadência moral. Quanto aos negros, basta que se diga que chegavam aqui como peças, e não como seres humanos. . . . O Brasil foi . . . colonizado, numa infeliz coincidência histórica, por uma nação que se encontrava pràticamente falida, sem condições materiais, culturais [ou] morais para formar, nesta parte do mundo, uma sociedade de homens livres. Que se poderia, pois, esperar de uma sociedade fundada na aventura, e não no trabalho, na caça ao índio, na escravidão do negro, na degradação da mulher, na mancebia geral, na prostituição, na ignorância, e na superstição? . . .
Tendo o Brasil se formado à imagem de seu descubridor e colonizador e, tendo, como agravante, o fato de encontrar-se sua população autóctone na maior degradação, e tendo, ainda, na escravidão e no latifúndio o alicerce de sua economia, em que base moral, pois, poderia apoiar-se a nação? De nada valiam as missões catequistas, as lavagens espirituais de cérebros, a repetição constante, no lar, no leito e na escola, de preceitos e axiomas morais, o rigor dos feitores e o paternalismo dos governantes, se tudo não passava, afinal, de palavras e gestos vãos. . . . Se encontra . . . no clima [e] na raça a causa dos nossos males. . . . Está também nessa estrutura econômica quase inalterada em mais de quatro séculos. Somos, como povo, a expressão moral, a manifestação espiritual [desses fatores e] dessa estrutura.[23]

Moral disorder is Brazil's biggest problem. What should we attribute it to? To the colonialists, who seek to justify slavery, the climate indisposed the individual to work at the same time that it predisposed and even excited him to the practice of libidinous acts. . . . If the colonists were this way, the natives had been for a long time in a state of extreme moral decadence. As far as the blacks were concerned, suffice it to say that they arrived here [in Brazil] as articles of merchandise and not as human beings. . . . Brazil was . . . settled, in an unfortunate historical coincidence, by a nation that was already practically bankrupt, without the material, cultural, or moral means to create a society of free men in this part of the world. What, then, could be expected from a society founded on adventure, and not on work, on the oppression of the Indian, on the slavery of the black man, on the degradation of women, on the widespread concubinage, on prostitution, on ignorance and superstition?

The fact that Brazil was shaped in the image of its discoverer and settler, that the native population was already in a state of extreme degeneration [by the time the Portuguese arrived], and that the latifundium and slavery constituted the country's economic base, on what moral grounds, then, could the nation be founded? The religious missions, the intensive spiritual indoctrination, the constant repetition at home and at school of moral precepts and axioms, the strictness of the administrators, and the paternalism of the ruling class were of absolutely no value. After all, they were but empty words and actions. . . . One will find . . . the cause of our problems in our climate, our race . . . and in a [feudal] economic structure that has gone unchanged for over four centuries. As a people, we are the moral expression and the spiritual manifestation of these factors and of this structure.

Romero's low opinion of Brazil and its people finds a parallel in the decadent view of Brazilian society that Azevedo presents in *O cortiço*.

The depraved microcosm of Azevedo's novel — which he disingenuously puts forth as objective reality — represents much more than merely the complex and colorful fictional creation of a gifted writer. In his grim portrayal of his country and its people as essentially degenerate, Azevedo betrays a typical prejudice of the Brazilian intellectual elite that has survived into our own time, namely, the belief that the lower class in Brazil, most of which is nonwhite, is intellectually inferior and morally corrupt. Therefore, *O cortiço* moves on two distinct levels: it speaks as much to universal naturalistic concerns — the poor, heredity, prostitution — as to a uniquely Brazilian view of class and race deeply embedded in the cultural consciousness of the country. In his study of Brazilian literature and *Weltanschauung*, David Haberly observes that the white elite in Brazil has historically sought to rationalize the country's underdevelopment in terms of race, often blaming Brazil's problems on the nonwhite segment of the population. Whether or not they were aware of their role, naturalistic writers such as Azevedo, Adolfo Caminha, Júlio Ribeiro, and Raul Pompéia helped to perpetuate this racist view of Brazilian society. As Haberly notes:

> Brazilian Naturalism offers concrete evidence of the elite's disquiet about the nonwhite population. . . . Although the theory of Naturalism — as interpreted in Brazil — drew heavily upon such foreign models as Zola, in practice the movement represented a fusion of European biological and social determinism with the stereotypes of the national abolitionist tradition. Almost all of the characters in the major novels of Brazilian Naturalism can be seen as victims of the past — a past that very frequently revolves around the institution of slavery — and of the predetermined defects or *taras* that perpetuate the past in the present. Nonwhites, whether slave or free, retain both the biological *taras* of racial inferiority and the social *taras* engendered in an environment marked by subservience, poverty, and hunger.[24]

In the light of Haberly's argument, Azevedo's portrayal of depravity and corruption in *O cortiço* and Romero's indictment of Brazilian society appear not so much as dispassionate portrayals of the country but rather as the reflection of a specific social ideology unique to the Brazilian intelligentsia. To be sure, in *O cortiço* Azevedo writes as a naturalist. However, as a Brazilian and, more importantly, as a member of Brazil's intellectual elite, the naturalistic universe that he describes is conceived according to the value system prevalent in his time and in his social class. The Brazilian author reacts to his cultural and social milieu in much the same way that Crane and Gamboa respond, despite their efforts to do otherwise, to the religious forces that have influenced and shaped their respective cultures.   The attitudes about class and race that Haberly outlines above were too pervasive for Azevedo to have ignored them completely. Thus, these prejudicial ideas form an integral part of the *Weltanschauung* and theme of *O cortiço*, and support Haberly's account of the social dichotomy present in Brazilian society to this day:

> Even the elite, very sure of its own whiteness, has tended to view the national population as a whole as nonwhite and, therefore, inferior.
>
> This conviction of national inferiority does not depend upon statistics . . . but upon perception and, ironically, upon the elite's need to justify its own privileged position. If one group within Brazil is to define itself as genetically, somatically, and culturally superior, it must believe implicitly in the inferiority — that is, the nonwhiteness — of most of the rest of the population. And yet this justification of superior status, however comforting in personal terms, has had profoundly negative effects upon the Brazilian elite's vision of the nation and its future possibilities, a vision clouded by feelings of pessimism, of frustration, of alienation. For the elite, [Guilherme de] Almeida . . . expressed the reality of this vision: The Indians and Africans have been tortured by whites, but are also

crucified by their own inferiority; and the whites themselves are tormented by the knowledge that they are condemned to share their land with beings viewed as hopelessly and permanently inferior.[25]

There is little question that Haberly's description of the specious racial dialectic by which the white elite in Brazil defines itself coincides with Romero's position, which is likewise racist. Azevedo's vision of the lower class in *O cortiço* is couched in many of the same beliefs about class and race in Brazilian society as Romero's. Azevedo's literary imagination is stirred by a good deal more than just naturalistic literary ideology. His response to Zola, and his subsequent creation of a uniquely Brazilian naturalistic universe, is deeply entwined with the broader beliefs and prejudices of the Brazilian intelligentsia of his time. Thus, tacitly or overtly, both Azevedo and Romero blame the Other — the degenerate, nonwhite poor — for the ills of their country, and frantically search in their population for signs that might affirm the significance and worth of their culture. Romero finds none, and grows at once indignant and anguished over Brazil's future: "What could be expected from such a society? [Only] moral disorder." Although Azevedo does not despair as easily as Romero, his attitude toward the nonwhite majority in Brazil is in many ways similar to his fellow countryman's. They differ only in their choice of medium to express their views on class and race: Romero produces a vitriolic and utterly pessimistic essay; Azevedo writes a naturalistic novel.[26]

The pervading ethical sense and moral thrust in *Maggie* stand in vivid contrast to the amoral ambience of *O cortiço*. Crane's novel has none of the rampant licentiousness that characterizes Azevedo's work; on the contrary, the American author is careful to avoid any direct reference to the very lifestyle (prostitution) that he purports to describe in *Maggie*. Ironically, even though they are both products of the same naturalistic school, in many ways *Maggie* appears as the antithesis of *O cortiço*. This becomes clear when one considers Crane's cultural and religious background. The son of staunchly religious parents, Crane rebelled against the Christianity of his time, but he was never able to escape all of its effects. This influence was inherently moralistic, and is part of the cultural legacy that American society inherited from the Puritans of the seventeenth century. More than any other group, the Puritans deeply affected the national character. In their study on the backgrounds of American literary thought, Rod Horton and Herbert Edwards observe:

> The moral attitudes of the Puritans persisted in New England long after its sustaining religious conviction was gone. [Later immigrants] carried the Calvinist view of life solidly into the settlement of the great Mississippi valley. The religious conservatism that exists to this day in much of the Midwest, South, and Southwest attests to the tremendous moral force exerted by [the Puritans].[27]

The puritanical strain present in Crane's fiction is exemplified by the factors that lead to the moral confusion of a character like Maggie. She is apparently successful, yet she suffers. She is eager for the pleasures of this life, for "elegance and soft palms" and "adornments of person." She wants to survive and enjoy the fruits of her labor, but she is "unable to give [herself] over to complete enjoyment of them because of vague scruples of conscience."[28] Ultimately, because of her confusion and moral dilemma, she commits suicide, choosing the only alternative that could put a definitive end to her ordeal.

Of the three novels analyzed in this study, *O cortiço* comes the closest to a Zolaesque model of the *roman expérimental*. The other two deviate from this model because of influences that are essentially religious. *Santa* is characterized by a pronounced sense of compassion and forgiveness whereas *Maggie* can best be described as a stern sermon against the evils of prostitution, indeed against any excesses of the flesh. The elements that set these three novels apart, all of which clearly belong to the same naturalistic literary tradition, are the same factors that characterize and differentiate the cultures of the authors. The gap between theory and practice, the discontinuity between what Azevedo, Crane, and Gamboa received from European naturalists and what they actually produced can best be accounted for by their respective cultural backgrounds, and more specifically by the ethical and religious heritages on which they draw.

Notes

[1] Malcolm Cowley, "'Not Men': A Natural History of American Naturalism," *The Kenyon Review* 9 (1947): 414.

[2] Cowley "'Not Men'" 414.
See also Donald Pizer, "Nineteenth-Century American Naturalism: An Essay in Definition," *Bucknell Review* 13 (December 1965): 1. While acknowledging that the traditional approach to Naturalism through Realism and philosophical determinism may be historically justifiable, Pizer argues that, taken too far, such a rigid definition may have an adverse effect because it could make it difficult "thinking about the movement as a whole and about individual works within the movement" (2).

[3] Richard Chase, *The American Novel and Its Tradition* (Garden City: Doubleday, 1957) 186.

[4] George Becker, "Modern Realism as a Literary Movement," in *Documents of Modern Literary Realism*, ed. George Becker (Princeton, New Jersey: Princeton University Press, 1963) 35.

[5] Lars Ahnebrink, *The Beginnings of Naturalism in American Fiction: A Study of the Works of Hamlin Garland, Stephen Crane, and Frank Norris with Special Reference to Some European Influences* (New York: Russell and Russell, 1961) vi-vii.

[6] Antônio Cândido, *Formação da literatura brasileira: Momentos*

decisivos, vol. 2 (São Paulo: Livraria Martins Editora, 1964) 240.

Jean Franco, *An Introduction to Spanish-American Literature* (London: Cambridge University Press, 1969). Commenting on the *roman expérimental* of Argentina, Franco observes that the portrayal of the naturalistic hero is at once deterministic and pessimistic. The individual is seen merely as a "victim of forces over which he feels he has no control" (117).

Sônia Brayner, *A Metáfora do Corpo no Romance Naturalista: Estudo sobre O cortiço* (Rio de Janeiro: Livraria São José, 1973). See especially the Introduction and Chapter 1, "A argumentação naturalista" (7-29).

Gordon Brotherston, *The Emergence of the Latin-American Novel* (London: Cambridge University Press, 1977) 11.

Antônio Cândido, "El paso del dos al tres," *Escritura* 3 (1977): 21-34.

John Conder, *Naturalism in American Fiction: The Classic Phase* (Lexington: The University Press of Kentucky, 1984). See especially chapter 1, "American Literary Naturalism" (1-21), chapter 3, "Norris and Hard Determinism" (69-85), and chapter 4, "Dreiser's Trilogy and the Dilemma of Determinism" (86-117).

Lee Clark Mitchell, "Naturalism and the Languages of Determinism," in *Columbia Literary History of the United States*, ed. Emory Elliott (New York: Columbia University Press, 1988): 525-545.

Lee Clark Mitchell, *Determined Fictions: American Literary Naturalism* (New York: Columbia University Press, 1989). See especially the preface, "Taking Determinism Seriously" (vii-xvii). All critics mentioned here subscribe in varying degrees to the idea that naturalistic fiction is essentially deterministic, and that naturalistic writers such as Crane, Azevedo, and Gamboa believed in the omnipotence and destructive power of natural and social forces. However, it should be noted that the interpretations of determinism that these critics provide sometimes differ substantially from earlier definitions. Mitchell, for instance, acknowledges the deterministic character of naturalistic fiction but does so for reasons altogether different from those advanced by earlier critics. He claims that the almost fatalistic narratives of the naturalists "subvert our most basic assumptions about the self by exposing morality as irrelevant and by presenting consciousness fragmented through language itself" (editorial commentary on front flap of book jacket).

See also Rod Horton and Herbert Edwards, *Backgrounds of American Literary Thought* (New York: Appleton-Century-Crofts, 1952) 246-261.

Dorothy Scott Loos, *The Naturalistic Novel of Brazil* (New York: Hispanic Institute, 1963) 43.

R. Anthony Castagnaro, *The Early Spanish-American Novel* (New York: Las Américas, 1971) 60-61.

João Pacheco, *O realismo*, vol. 3 of *A literatura brasileira* (São Paulo: Editora Cultrix, 1971) 128-131.

Claude Hulet, *Brazilian Literature*, vol. 2 (Washington, DC: Georgetown University Press, 1974) 2-3.

John Brushwood, *The Spanish-American Novel* (Austin: University of Texas Press, 1975) 3-11.

Toni H. Oliviero, "'People as They Seem to Me': Determinism and Morality as Literary Devices in Three Novels of Stephen Crane," *Annales du Centre de Recherches sur l'Amérique Anglophone* 2 (1976-1977) 167.

Antônio Soares Amora, *História da literatura brasileira* (São Paulo: Edição Saraiva, 1977) 109-140.

Ronald Martin, *American Literature and the Universe of Force* (Durham, North Carolina: Duke University Press, 1981) 6-31.

Alfredo Bosi, *História concisa da literatura brasileira* (São Paulo: Editora Cultrix, 1982) 181-291.

Marcus Cunliffe, *The Literature of the United States* (New York: Penguin Books, 1986) 215-249.

Norwood Andrews, Jr., "Naturalism," in *Dictionary of Brazilian Literature*, ed. Irwin Stern (New York: Greenwood Press, 1988): 218-220.

[7] Cowley, "'Not Men'" 414.

[8] Cowley, "'Not Men'" 427.

[9] Cowley, "'Not Men'" 427.

[10] Cowley, "'Not Men'" 433.

[11] Cowley, "'Not Men'" 144.
See also Afrânio Coutinho, *A literatura no Brazil*, vol. 2 (Rio de Janeiro: Editorial Sul Americana, 1955) 13-34.
Chase, *Novel* 186.
Ahnebrink, *Beginnings* vi-vii.
Becker, "Realism" 35.
Afrânio Coutinho, *Introdução à Literatura no Brasil* (Rio de Janeiro: Livraria São José, 1964) 188-190.
Pizer, "Naturalism" 1.
Nélson Werneck Sodré, *História da literatura brasileira: Seus fundamentos econômicos* (Rio de Janeiro: Editora Civilização brasileira, 1969) 381-402.
Castagnaro, *Novel* 60-61.
Hulet, *Literature* 2-3.
Brushwood, *Novel* 3-11.
Fernando Alegría, *Nueva historia de la novela hispanoamericana* (Hanover, New Hampshire: Ediciones del Norte, 1986) 79-82.
Cunliffe, *Literature* 215-249.
Andrews, "Naturalism" 218-220.

[12] Pizer, "Naturalism" 1-2.

[13] Chase, *Novel* 186.
Becker, "Realism" 35.

[14] Pizer, "Naturalism" 2.

[15] Charles Walcutt, *American Literary Naturalism: A Divided Stream* (Minneapolis: University of Minnesota Press, 1956) 3-29.
Pizer, "Naturalism" 2. The views that Walcutt and Pizer present in their respective studies of American literary Naturalism have a good deal in

common. Both critics focus on the philosophical and literary ambivalences at the heart of the movement. They differ mostly in emphasis and conclusion. Walcutt is "concerned with the historical background and social effect of [Naturalism], and believes that the ambivalences of the naturalistic novel are often the source of its weaknesses." Pizer, on the other hand, is "more interested in the shape that these ambivalences take in the novel, and [tends to] see them more positively than [Walcutt]" (2).

[16] Pizer, "Naturalism" 2-3.

[17] Pizer, "Naturalism" 3.

[18] Pizer, "Naturalism" 3.

[19] Pizer, "Naturalism" 3.

[20] Salvador de Madariaga, *Englishmen, Frenchmen, Spaniards: An Essay in Comparative Psychology* (London: Oxford University Press, 1929) 3. See especially Introduction to Part I (3-12).

[21] Madariaga, *Englishmen* 233.
    See also W. Stanley Rycroft, *Religion and Faith in Latin America* (Philadelphia: The Westminster Press, 1958) 44.

[22] James Bryce, *South America: Observations and Impressions* (New York: Macmillan, 1912) 484-522.
    See also Lucas Ayarragaray, *La iglesia en América y la dominación española: Estudio de la época colonial* (Buenos Aires: L. J. Rosso, 1935).
    Pedro Henríquez Ureña, *Historia de la cultura en la América hispana* (México: Fondo de Cultura Económica, 1947).
    Mariano Picón-Salas, *A Cultural History of Spanish-America: From Conquest to Independence* (New York: Greenwood Press, 1962).
    John J. Considine, ed., *The Religious Dimensions in the New Latin*

America (Notre Dame, Indiana: Fides Publishers, 1966).

Américo Castro, *Iberoamérica: Su historia y su cultura* (New York: Holt, Rinehart, and Winston, 1971).

Raymond Dehainaut, *Faith and Ideology in Latin-American Perspective* (Cuernavaca, Mexico: Centro Intercultural de Documentación, 1972).

Benjamin Keen, *Latin-American Civilization* (Boston: Houghton Mifflin, 1974).

Eugene A. Nida, *Understanding Latin Americans, With Special Reference to the Religious Values and Movements* (South Pasadena, California: William Carey Library, 1974).

Seymour B. Liebman, *Exploring the Latin-American Mind* (Chicago: Nelson-Hall, 1976).

Bartolomé Bennassar, *The Spanish Character: Attitudes and Mentalities from the Sixteenth to the Nineteenth Century*, trans. Benjamin Keen (Berkeley: University of California Press, 1979).

Lyle C. Brown and William F. Cooper, eds., *Religion in Latin-America Life and Literature* (Waco, Texas: Markham Press, 1980).

Carlos Flores, *Antecendentes históricos de lo religioso en Latinoamérica* (Bogotá: Universidad de Santo Tomás, 1984).

Birgitta Leander, ed., *Cultural Identity in Latin-America* (Paris: Unesco, 1986).

Benjamin Keen, *A History of Latin America* (Boston: Houghton Mifflin, 1991).

Benjamin Keen, ed., *Latin-American Civilization: History and Society, 1492 to the Present* (Boulder, Colorado: Westview, 1991).

[23] Abelardo Romero, *Origem da Imoralidade no Brasil* (Rio de Janeiro: Editora Conquista, 1967) 225-227.

[24] David T. Haberly, *Three Sad Races: Racial Identity and National Consciousness in Brazilian Literature* (New York: Cambridge University Press, 1983) 124.

[25] Harberly, *Races* 4.

In his study of Brazil's sexual culture, Richard Parker also notes the connection that Brazilians, especially the white elite, have historically made between the concepts of *miscigenação* [miscegenation] and *degeneração social* [social degeneration], and the pivotal role that this prejudice has played in their definition of themselves and their culture. See Richard G. Parker, *Bodies Pleasures, and Passions: Sexual Culture in Contemporary Brazil* (Boston: Beacon Press, 1992) 7-29. According to Parker, "the questions of sexual interaction and racial mixture are constant themes in Brazilian letters. They have been the key issues around which the relatively small [white] intellectual elite has sought to explore its own identity, both in relation to the outside world of the foreigner and in relation to the wider [nonwhite] Brazilian population. Given the continued presence of the Judeo-Christian moral order, along with the . . . kind of scientific racism that so marked the thought of the nineteenth century . . . it is hardly surprising that [this] perceived . . . uninhibited sexual activity and unrestricted racial mixture should have been viewed by [the] elite with more than a little ambivalence. Indeed throughout much of the nineteenth and early twentieth centuries, the tragic consequences of such unbridled sensuality dominated Brazilian letters" (15). Commenting on Paulo Prado's *Retrato do Brasil* (1928), Parker elaborates further on this particular interpretation of Brazilian society by observing that "if the mythic dimensions of such a powerful self interpretation seem clear in Prado's text, so too is the profound ambivalence with which the Brazilian elite has often approached its own past. Indeed, placed within a historical context, the *Retrato do Brasil* summarizes a long line of late nineteenth and early twentieth-century Brazilian thought — a line of thought in which recognition of Brazil's multiracial formation is colored by the fear that the mixture of Brazil's races has somehow indelibly marked the character of the Brazilian people and doomed them to a degeneration at once moral and physical" (20).

See also Carl N. Degler, *Neither Black nor White* (New York: Macmillan, 1971).

Charles Wagley, *Introduction to Brazil* (New York: Columbia University Press, 1971).

Hemílio Borba Filho, *Sobrados e mocambos* (Rio de Janeiro: Civilização Brasileira, 1972).

Thomas E. Skidmore, *Black into White: Race and Nationality in Brazilian Thought* (New York: Oxford University Press, 1974).

Roger Bastide, *Brasil: Terra de Contrastes* (Rio de Janeiro: Difel, 1978).

Roberto da Matta, *Carnavais, malandros e heróis: Para uma sociologia do dilema brasileiro* (Rio de Janeiro: Zahar Editores, 1978).

E. Bradford Burns, *A History of Brazil* (New York: Columbia University Press, 1980).

Roberto da Matta, *Universo do carnaval: Imagens e reflexões* (Rio de Janeiro: Edições Pinakotheke, 1981).

Robert B. Toplin, *Freedom and Prejudice: The Legacy of Slavery in the United States and Brazil* (New York: Greenwood Press, 1981)

José Pastore, *Inequality and Social Mobility in Brazil* (Madison: University of Wisconsin Press, 1982).

Renato Ortiz, *Cultura brasileira e identidade nacional* (São Paulo: Editora Brasiliense, 1985).

David Brookshaw, *Race and Color in Brazilian Literature* (Metuchen, New Jersey: The Scarecrow Press, 1986).

Octavio Ianni, *Raças e classes sociais no Brasil* (São Paulo: Editora Brasiliense, 1987).

Clóvis Moura, *Sociologia do negro brasileiro* (São Paulo: Editora Ática, 1988).

Jeffrey D. Needell, *A Tropical Belle Époque: Elite Culture and Society in Turn-of-the-Century Rio de Janeiro* (New York: Cambridge University Press, 1988).

Clóvis Moura, *História do negro brasileiro* (São Paulo: Editora Ática, 1989).

John Fiola, *Race Relations in Brazil: A Reassessment of the "Racial Democracy" Thesis* (Amherst: Latin-American Studies Program, University of Massachusetts, 1990).

[26] At this point, the reader may ask why I bring politics and ideology into

what purports to be a literary argument. Why link Azevedo's fiction to the beliefs and prejudices of the Brazilian white elite of his time? My position throughout this study has been that, as Terry Eagleton puts it, "there is . . . no need to drag politics into [literature and] literary theory: . . . it has been there from the beginning." See Terry Eagleton, *Literary Theory: An Introduction* (Minneapolis: University of Minnesota Press, 1983) 194. Eagleton further explains his position: "All of our descriptive statements move within an often invisible network of value-categories. . . . The largely concealed structure of values which informs and underlies our factual statements is part of what is meant by 'ideology'. By 'ideology' I mean, roughly, the ways in which what we say and believe connects with the power-structure and power-relations of the society we live in. . . . I do not mean by 'ideology' simply the deeply entrenched, often unconscious beliefs which people hold; I mean more particularly those modes of feeling, valuing, perceiving and believing which have some kind of relation to the maintenance and reproduction of social power" (14-15). According to Eagleton, literature and literary theory have been "indissociably bound up with political beliefs and ideological values. Indeed [they are] less an object of intellectual enquiry in [their] own right than a particular perspective in which to view the history of our times. Nor should this be in the least cause for surprise. For any body of theory [or intellectual endeavor] concerned with human meaning, value, language, feeling and experience will inevitably engage with broader, deeper beliefs about the nature of human individuals and societies, problems of power and sexuality, interpretations of past histories, versions of the present and hopes for the future" (194-195).

See also Eva Paulino Bueno, "Brazilian Naturalism and the Politics of Origin," Modern Language Notes 107 (1992): 363-395. Bueno analyzes the historical circumstances that defined the naturalistic novel of Brazil, focusing on how the genre connected to the social and political power-structure of its time. Specifically, the critic probes the largely undefined structure of aesthetic and political values that informed and shaped the Brazilian *roman expérimental*, and examines how the genre was involved in the maintenance/reproduction or the challenging/transformation of social power in Brazil. Bueno argues that the

Brazilian *roman expérimental* goes beyond merely reflecting the ideology or political agenda of the social groups in power, as was largely the case with the Romantic novel. The critic detects "an oppositional, counter-hegemonic dimension" in the work of Brazilian naturalists, and remarks that they "were the first group of writers to turn a de-centered, or ex-centric, gaze at the totality of the Brazilian society of their time, and to attempt to represent it as a whole composed of contradictory parts, each highly intensified and exacerbated, consisting of blacks, mulattoes, masculinized women and homosexuals or feminized men" (363).

[27] Horton and Edwards, *Backgrounds* 47.

See also Perry Miller, *The New England Mind: From Colony to Province* (Cambridge, Massachusetts: Harvard University Press, 1953).

Perry Miller, *The New England Mind: The Seventeenth Century* (Cambridge, Massachusetts: Harvard University Press, 1954).

Kenneth Murdock, "The Puritan Tradition," in *The Reinterpretation of American Literature: Some Contributions Toward the Understanding of Its Historical Development*, ed. Norman Foerster (New York: Russell and Russell, 1959).

Norman Foerster, *Image of America: Our Literature from Puritanism to the Space Age* (Notre Dame, Indiana: University of Notre Dame Press, 1962).

Kai T. Erikson, *Wayward Puritans: A Study in the Sociology of Deviance* (New York: Wiley, 1966).

Van Wyck Brooks, *The Wine of the Puritans: A Study of Present-Day America* (Folcroft, Pennsylvania: Folcroft Press, 1969).

Sarah Harris, *The Puritan Jungle: America's Sexual Underground* (New York: Putnam, 1969).

Larzer Ziff, *Puritanism in America: New Culture in a New World* (New York: Viking Press, 1973).

Sacvan Bercovitch, *The Puritan Origins of the American Self* (New Haven, Connecticut: Yale University, 1975).

Charles Berryman, *From Wilderness to Wasteland: The Trial of the Puritan God in the American Imagination* (Fort Washington, New York:

Kennikat Press, 1979).

Emory Elliott, ed., *Puritan Influences in American Literature* (Urbana: University of Illinois Press, 1979).

Patricia Caldwell, *The Puritan Conversion Narrative: The Beginnings of American Expression* (New York: Cambridge University Press, 1983).

Richard Forrer, *Theodicies in Conflict: A Dilemma in Puritan Ethics and Nineteenth-Century American Literature* (New York: Greenwood Press, 1986).

Edmund Leites, *The Puritan Conscience and Modern Sexuality* (New Haven, Connecticut: Yale University Press, 1986).

Margaret O. Thickstun, *Fictions of the Feminine: Puritan Doctrine and the Representation of Women* (Ithaca, New York: Cornell University Press, 1988).

Virginia D. Anderson, *New England's Generation: The Great Migration and the Formation of Society and Culture in the Seventeenth Century* (New York: Cambridge University Press, 1991).

Stephen Foster, *The Long Argument: English Puritanism and the Shaping of New England Culture* (Chapel Hill: University of North Carolina Press, 1991).

[28] Horton and Edwards, *Backgrounds* 48.

Chapter 9

Mimetic Desire and the Naturalistic Novel

In *Deceit, Desire, and the Novel*, Girard divides novelists into two groups: those who consciously reveal in their fiction the imitative nature of desire and the pivotal role that mimetic desire plays in literature; and those who only reflect mimetic desire in their work, and either cannot or choose not to disclose its true character. Girard uses the term "novelistic" for the writers who reveal this presence and "romantic" for those who do not. "Novelistic" works, Girard contends, are superior to their "romantic" counterparts because they tell the truth about mimetic desire and about literary fiction itself.

The first "novelistic" writer to be examined in *Deceit, Desire, and the Novel* is Miguel de Cervantes. To Girard, the protagonist in *Don Quijote* is the prototypal hero who has surrendered to the mediator, Amadis of Gaul in don Quijote's case, the individual's fundamental prerogative to choose. The deranged *hidalgo* no longer chooses the objects of his own desire; Amadis does that for him. In Cervantes's novel, the disciple pursues those objects that are determined for him by his mediator.[1] The second "novelistic" writer examined by Girard is Stendhal, whose work Girard compares to Cervantes's in terms of distance between subject and mediator:

In Cervantes the mediator is enthroned in an inaccessible heaven and transmits to his faithful follower a little of his serenity. In Stendhal, this same mediator has come down to earth. The clear distinction between these two types of relationship between mediator and subject indicates the enormous spiritual gap which separates don Quijote from the most despicably vain of Stendhal's characters. The image of the triangle cannot remain valid for us unless it at once allows this distinction and measures this gap for us. To achieve this double objective, we have only to vary the *distance*, in the triangle, separating the mediator from the desiring subject (8).

In Stendhal's novels, the distance between subject and mediator is small enough to allow for the rivalry of conflicting desires to develop. In the works of Cervantes as well as Flaubert, the mediator remains beyond the universe of the subject. If we were to apply these principles to the work of Stephen Crane, *Maggie* would fall into the same category as that of *Madame Bovary* and *Don Quijote*. The forms of mimetic desire examined in *Maggie* are, for the most part, based on external mediation. The protagonist is not physically in contact with the world of refinement that mediates her desire. Maggie does not compete with the mediator for those objects that are desirable to both. The harmony between the two, therefore, is never seriously threatened. Subject and mediator are safely kept apart by distance. Internal mediation, on the other hand, involves doing away with the checks and balances guaranteed by distance (9).

The protagonist in *Maggie* apparently has no qualms about proclaiming aloud the true nature of her desire, and Crane describes her longing for a world of "elegance and soft palms" as something inherently good. In *O cortiço*, the intercourse between the various subjects and mediators develops along very different lines, as exemplified by the relationship between Miranda and João Romão. Here, desire is based on internal mediation. As such, the type of imitation in *O cortiço* on the surface seems more believable. There is less of the conspicuous disparity between the worlds of disciple and model that makes the romantic dreams of a character like don Quijote, Emma Bovary, or Maggie appear at times so unrealistic as to border on the grotesque. Still, the imitation is just as scrupulous in internal mediation (e.g., *O cortiço*) as it is in external mediation (e.g., *Don Quijote, Madame Bovary, Maggie*). If this seems surprising, it is not because the imitation involves a model who is in direct contact with the subject. Rather, it is because the subject of internal mediation, far from boasting about his or her efforts to imitate, actually goes to great lengths to hide them (10). Girard notes:

> The impulse toward the object is ultimately an impulse toward the mediator; in internal mediation this impulse is checked by the mediator himself since he desires, or perhaps possesses, the object. Fascinated by his mode, the disciple inevitable sees, in the mechanical obstacle which he puts in his way, proof of the ill will borne him. Far from declaring himself a faithful vassal, he thinks only of repudiating the bonds of mediation. But these bonds are stronger than ever, for the mediator's apparent hostility does not diminish his prestige but instead augments it. . . . The subject is torn between two opposite feelings toward his model — the most submissive reverence and the most intense malice. This is the passion we call *hatred*. . . . Everything that originates with this mediator is systematically belittled although still secretly desired. Now the mediator is a shrewd and diabolical enemy; he tries to rob the subject of his most prized possessions; he obstinately thwarts his most legitimate ambitions (10-11).

One cannot expect much from the above state of affairs except rivalry, conflict, violence, and perhaps even death. "Novelistic" writers such as Stendhal, Proust, and Azevedo, reveal in their fiction the nature and function of mimetic desire. Some critics have pointed out that the intrigues derived from such complications are essential to literature. Other critics have gone so far as to say that literary fiction as we know it "would not exist without mimetic desire, which explicitly or implicitly can only be a source of rivalry and conflict."[2] Be that as it may, the "novelistic" writers in this second group differ significantly from other writers such as Cervantes, Flaubert, and Crane. This difference exists mainly because Stendhal, Proust, and Azevedo make extensive use in their fiction of perhaps the most harmful form of mimetic desire, namely, the kind based on internal mediation.

The third and last group of "novelistic" authors includes writers such as Dostoyevsky and Gamboa. The rivalry and conflict that make for a potentially tragic atmosphere in Stendhal, Proust, and Azevedo, are brought out in the open and finally resolved the Russian and Mexican authors. However, before this can happen, mimetic desire and internal mediation must be allowed to run their full course, which they do by making explicit and immediate in the text the death and destruction that are their hallmark. In *Santa*, mimetic desire and the havoc that it can wreak are poignantly revealed when the author takes the protagonist from Elvira's brothel down to the lowest and most repulsive levels of the underworld as Santa completes the last stage of her tragic descent. In the case of Dostoyevsky, Girard observes:

> There is no longer any love without jealousy, any friendship without envy, any attraction without repulsion. The characters insult each other, spit in each other's faces, and minutes later they fall at the enemy's feet, they abjectly beg for mercy. . . . The inevitable consequences of desire copied from another desire are "envy, jealousy, and impotent hatred." As one moves from [Cervantes to Flaubert, from Flaubert to Stendhal,] from Stendhal

to Proust and from Proust to Dostoyevsky, and the closer the mediator [gets to the subject], the more bitter . . . the fruits of triangular desire [become].

In Dostoyevsky hatred is so intense it finally "explodes," revealing its double nature, or rather the double role of model and obstacle played by the mediator. This adoring hatred, this admiration that insults and even kills its object, are the paroxysms of the conflict caused by internal mediation. In his words and gestures, Dostoyevsky's hero constantly reveals the truth which remains a secret in the consciousness of previous heroes (41-42).

According to Girard, internal mediation exerts its dissolving power at the heart of the family itself. In *Santa*, internal mediation affects a dimension of existence that remains more or less inviolable in either *O cortiço* or *Maggie*. It is as though each of these three novels had its own specific domain of mimetic desire and mediation. In Crane, the subject and mediator never come together, and desire affects the protagonist strictly in a metaphysical sense. Even if the tragic denouement is very real, Maggie's struggle is never brought out in the open in the physical world like João Romão's or Santa's. It remains largely an abstraction throughout the novel. In Azevedo, not only is the conflict generated by opposing desires brought out in the open, but it also threatens practically all aspects of the public and private lives of those individuals affected by it. The only areas that the evil caused by internal mediation does not contaminate are the cores of the social group and the individual, namely, family and spiritual life. The contamination of family circle and personal faith takes place only in *Santa*. The above division represents an invasion of the vital centers of the individual by mimetic desire. Girard describes this invasion as a malady that gradually infects the most intimate parts of being (42-43), and characterizes it as:

An *alienation* which grows more complete as the distance between model and disciple diminishes. This distance is smallest in familial mediation of father to son, brother to brother, husband to wife, or mother to son, as in Dostoyevsky and many contemporary novelists (43).

The conflict that grows more serious and the disorder that becomes more real as the distance between subject and mediator diminishes erupt precisely where the violence can do the most harm, in the bosom of the family or in the individual's spiritual life. In *Santa*, one is confronted with an apocalypse of sorts, the culmination of the destructive process that is only hinted at in *O cortiço*. In Crane and Azevedo, mimetic desire is revealed but never transcended. In Gamboa, the protagonist is made to suffer a horrible ordeal, but in the end that suffering allows her to overcome the mechanism of internal mediation. However, like don Quijote, Santa is able to free herself from mimetic desire only on her deathbed.

The prototypal novel of mimetic desire is one in which the dissolving power of internal mediation has not yet contaminated either the family or the spiritual life of the individual. Thus, the mimetic configuration of *Maggie*, *O cortiço*, and *Santa* proposed here complements and corroborates the findings presented in Part One and in Chapter 8 of this study. Again, *O cortiço* turns out to be the novel that comes closest to Girard's model, while *Maggie* and *Santa* stand at the opposite ends of this model: the former, because it does not go far enough to reveal the true nature of desire; and the latter, because it goes too far in disclosing and dismantling the mechanism of internal mediation. Through Gamboa's neutralizing of this mechanism, Santa is saved. What was identified earlier as Catholic compassion and forgiveness in *Santa* takes on a more structured form when analyzed in the context of Girard's construct. What we saw before in Gamboa as the negation of the commonly held notion of Naturalism acquires new meaning, and becomes more apparent when viewed as the repudiation and transcendence of mimetic desire, that is, as liberation and salvation.

One could argue that "novelistic" works by writers such as Dostoyevsky or Gamboa should be the models for the prototypal novel of mimetic desire. After all, they are the kind of literature in which one witnesses the last stages of internal mediation, when the mechanism of mimetic desire is at last revealed in its entirety and rendered powerless. Here, desire is finally dissolved from within. Its final stage is both terrifying and cathartic. It works itself out not only in death and destruction but in liberation and epiphany as well. However, the disclosure of mimetic desire in fiction poses a unique problem. On the one hand, it reveals a powerful truth, but on the other, it undermines its own argument. If fiction cannot exist without mimetic desire, as some contemporary critics claim, then it follows that by nullifying this major literary device, one is actually dooming the whole literary enterprise. The problem outlined above is not unlike the one faced by Cervantes in *Don Quijote*. The Spanish author sought to debunk the world of chivalric novels by using the same literary devices that he was criticizing. In an attempt to deride literary fiction, Cervantes creates a character no less fictional, or untrue, than Amadis of Gaul. Because of their fictional nature, Cervantes's characters undermine the very medium that enables them to exist.

As far as New World naturalistic fiction is concerned, a novelist such as Azevedo works better as a model for the prototypal *roman expérimental* of mimetic desire because he is not as extreme or harmful to the literary enterprise as Dostoyevsky or Gamboa. The Brazilian author creates effective literary fiction, but he does not disable the mechanism that allows this fiction to exist in the first place.

In conclusion, we have seen that despite having written their respective novels according to a Zolaesque model of the *roman expéri-*

mental, Crane, Azevedo, and Gamboa differ significantly both from Zola as well as among themselves. These three writers have each shown in his own way that we do a disservice to New World naturalists when we insist on holding on to a derivative and conceptually superficial definition of their art. Donald Pizer's observations on the topic are instructive. Although his study on Naturalism deals only with American writers, his commentary can be extended to include the Mexican and Brazilian authors examined in this study. Like their fellow naturalists in the United States, Crane, Azevedo, and Gamboa express "striking individual and contrasting views of experience, yet [they do] so within a body of shared intellectual and literary assumptions belonging to a common literary moment."[3] Thus, the naturalistic novel of Europe as well as that of the Americas is "no different from any other major literary genre in its complex intermingling of form and theme, in its reflection of an author's individual temperament, . . ."[4] cultural heritage, and — at its best, which I believe to be the case with Crane, Azevedo, and Gamboa — in its skillful treatment of issues fundamental to the modern individual such as desire, conflict, and violence.

Notes

[1] René Girard, *Deceit, Desire, and the Novel: Self and Other in Literary Structure*, trans. Yvonne Freccero (Baltimore, Maryland: Johns Hopkins University Press, 1980) 2. All subsequent quotations from *Deceit, Desire, and the Novel* are from this edition. Citations by page number appear in parentheses in the text.

[2] Cesáreo Bandera, "Conflictive Versus Cooperative Mimesis," *Diacritics* 9 (Fall 1979): 62.

[3] Donald Pizer, "Nineteenth-Century American Naturalism: An Essay in Definition," *Bucknell Review* 13 (December 1965): 18.

[4] Pizer, "Naturalism" 18.

João Sedycias received his Ph.D. in Comparative Literature from the State University of New York at Buffalo. He is currently Assistant Professor of Spanish and Portuguese at California State University, Sacramento, and has presented papers and published articles on foreign language pedagogy, literary theory, the Sephardic diaspora, and Spanish, Spanish-American, and Luso-Brazilian literatures. His current interests include contemporary literary theory, 20th-century Latin-American literature, and Spanish Golden Age drama.